CAMBRIDGE LIBRARY COLLECTION

Books of enduring scholarly value

Medieval History

This series includes pioneering editions of medieval historical accounts by eye-witnesses and contemporaries, collections of source materials such as charters and letters, and works that applied new historiographical methods to the interpretation of the European middle ages. The nineteenth century saw an upsurge of interest in medieval manuscripts, texts and artefacts, and the enthusiastic efforts of scholars and antiquaries made a large body of material available in print for the first time. Although many of the analyses have been superseded, they provide fascinating evidence of the academic practices of their time, while a considerable number of texts have still not been re-edited and are still widely consulted.

Court Rolls of the Manor of Wakefield

The detailed records of the proceedings of the manorial court of Wakefield provide a unique insight into medieval life and commerce, the many legal disputes arising, and the mechanisms for resolving them. The manor court met every three weeks, as well as holding additional courts, or 'tourns', at various locations around the West Riding of Yorkshire. Recognising the historical significance of these exceptionally complete court records for one of the largest manors in England, in 1901 the Yorkshire Archaeological Society began publishing them as part of its Record Series. Up to 1945, five volumes appeared that span the years 1274–1331. Edited with an introduction and notes by John William Walker (1859–1953) and published in 1945, Volume 5 contains the surviving court rolls for the years 1322–31. The texts of the rolls are given in English translation.

T0381846

Cambridge University Press has long been a pioneer in the reissuing of out-of-print titles from its own backlist, producing digital reprints of books that are still sought after by scholars and students but could not be reprinted economically using traditional technology. The Cambridge Library Collection extends this activity to a wider range of books which are still of importance to researchers and professionals, either for the source material they contain, or as landmarks in the history of their academic discipline.

Drawing from the world-renowned collections in the Cambridge University Library and other partner libraries, and guided by the advice of experts in each subject area, Cambridge University Press is using state-of-the-art scanning machines in its own Printing House to capture the content of each book selected for inclusion. The files are processed to give a consistently clear, crisp image, and the books finished to the high quality standard for which the Press is recognised around the world. The latest print-on-demand technology ensures that the books will remain available indefinitely, and that orders for single or multiple copies can quickly be supplied.

The Cambridge Library Collection brings back to life books of enduring scholarly value (including out-of-copyright works originally issued by other publishers) across a wide range of disciplines in the humanities and social sciences and in science and technology.

Court Rolls of the Manor of Wakefield

VOLUME 5: 1322 TO 1331

EDITED BY
JOHN WILLIAM WALKER

CAMBRIDGE UNIVERSITY PRESS

Cambridge, New York, Melbourne, Madrid, Cape Town,
Singapore, São Paolo, Delhi, Mexico City

Published in the United States of America by Cambridge University Press, New York

www.cambridge.org
Information on this title: www.cambridge.org/9781108058650

© in this compilation Cambridge University Press 2013

This edition first published 1945
This digitally printed version 2013

ISBN 978-1-108-05865-0 Paperback

The Anniversary Reissue of Volumes from the Record Series of the Yorkshire Archaeological Society

To celebrate the 150th anniversary of the foundation of the leading society for the study of the archaeology and history of England's largest historic county, Cambridge University Press has reissued a selection of the most notable of the publications in the Record Series of the Yorkshire Archaeological Society. Founded in 1863, the Society soon established itself as the major publisher in its field, and has remained so ever since. The *Yorkshire Archaeological Journal* has been published annually since 1869, and in 1885 the Society launched the Record Series, a succession of volumes containing transcriptions of diverse original records relating to the history of Yorkshire, edited by numerous distinguished scholars. In 1932 a special division of the Record Series was created which, up to 1965, published a considerable number of early medieval charters relating to Yorkshire. The vast majority of these publications have never been superseded, remaining an important primary source for historical scholarship.

Current volumes in the Record Series are published for the Society by Boydell and Brewer. The Society also publishes parish register transcripts; since 1897, over 180 volumes have appeared in print. In 1974, the Society established a programme to publish calendars of over 650 court rolls of the manor of Wakefield, the originals of which, dating from 1274 to 1925, have been in the safekeeping of the Society's archives since 1943; by the end of 2012, fifteen volumes had appeared. In 2011, the importance of the Wakefield court rolls was formally acknowledged by the UK committee of UNESCO, which entered them on its National Register of the Memory of the World.

The Society possesses a library and archives which constitute a major resource for the study of the county; they are housed in its headquarters, a Georgian villa in Leeds. These facilities, initially provided solely for members, are now available to all researchers. Lists of the full range of the Society's scholarly resources and publications can be found on its website, www.yas.org.uk.

Court Rolls of the Manor of Wakefield, 1322–1331
(Record Series volume 109)

The Wakefield manorial court rolls span more than six centuries from 1274 to 1925, making them one of the most comprehensive series now in existence, and the Yorkshire Archaeological Society has been engaged in their publication and preservation for more than a century. The manor of Wakefield was one of the largest in England, covering a huge area of the West Riding of Yorkshire, although it was divided into many sub-manors. The actual area over which the court had jurisdiction during the centuries for which the records survive was approximately 90 square miles. The records of the manor's property transactions, agricultural business and law enforcement are an important source for legal, social and economic historians. In 1898, several members of the Society provided a fund to employ Miss Ethel Stokes, a leading London record agent, to produce translations of the earliest surviving rolls.

This is the last of the five volumes in the Record Series devoted to these early rolls, the others being 29, 36, 57 and 78. It contains translations of the seven surviving rolls from 1322–3 to 1324–5, 1328–9 and 1330–1. By the time this final volume was published, the original rolls had been donated to the Society by the last lord of the manor of Wakefield, the Earl of Yarborough, and were being transferred to the Society's safekeeping. The rolls published in this volume have the references MD225/1/48–52, 54 and 56.

J.W. Walker, the editor of this volume, was president of the Yorkshire Archaeological Society from 1938 to 1948, and an obituary and bibliography appear in the *Yorkshire Archaeological Journal*, 38 (1951–5), 416–18. His many publications included *Abstracts from the Chartularies of the Priory of Monkbretton* for the Records Series (volume 66, 1924, also reissued in the Cambridge Library Collection) and *An Historical and Architectural Description of the Priory of St Mary Magdalene of Monk Bretton*, published by the Society as volume 5 of the Extra Series in 1926.

COURT ROLLS
OF THE MANOR OF WAKEFIELD.
Vol. V.

THE YORKSHIRE
ARCHÆOLOGICAL SOCIETY

Founded 1863   Incorporated 1893

RECORD SERIES

Vol. CIX

FOR THE YEAR 1944

COURT ROLLS

OF THE

MANOR OF WAKEFIELD.

VOL. V

1322-1331

EDITED BY

J. W. WALKER, O.B.E., F.R.C.S., F.S.A.

PRINTED FOR THE SOCIETY

1945

Printed by
THE WEST YORKSHIRE PRINTING CO. LIMITED,
WAKEFIELD

INTRODUCTION.

It is now fifteen years since the fourth volume of these rolls was published by The Yorkshire Archaeological Society.

This fifth volume includes the rolls for the ten years 1322-31. The translation and transcription was made by Miss Ethel Stokes in 1898, and this has been checked with the original rolls by the editor, who is responsible for the indices.

This volume contains some interesting notices of life on a manor in the early part of the fourteenth century.

Under the right of wardship the heir of a tenant became the ward of the lord of the manor, who, as guardian, preserved the right to collect the revenues of the land and to use them for his own profit throughout the heir's minority. These wardships were sometimes bought and sold as commodities.

In 1322 John de Clifton paid three shillings to the king, then in possession of the manor due to the execution of the Earl of Lancaster, for the wardship and right to collect the revenues of William son and heir of William del Bothes.

A similar case occurred when William son of John de Craven, under age at his father's death, was given with his lands, goods and chattels into the custody of William and Richard de Dene, his uncles, who were ordered to honourably maintain him and to render an account when he come of age, and they gave to the lord two shillings for the wardship for six years.

HOMAGE AND FEALTY TO THE LORD.

John de Burgh, succeeded his father Thomas de Burgh at Walton in 1322, and was distrained at a manor court in April 1323, for homage and fealty for the manor of Walton and was fined sixpence for this default.

This delay was probably due to the question of the validity of the marriage of Sir Thomas de Burgh with Lucia de Bellewe, the daughter of John de Bellewe of Bolton-upon-Dearne, having been challenged by Elizabeth, the sister of Sir Thomas de Burgh and wife of Sir Alexander de Mountford, who alleged that her brother Thomas was impotent (*non copulat matrimonii*), and that consequently the two sons of Lucia were not the children of Thomas de Burgh, and were therefore illegitimate. If she could establish this Elizabeth de Mountford could then lay claim to the Yorkshire and Cambridgeshire estates of the Burghs.

To test the matter a suit was entered in the Ecclesiastical Court at York, but prior to the action coming before the Court Sir Thomas de Burgh died early in 1322.[1] The case then came into the Chancery Court at York on 16 February 1322-3, when it was proved that the marriage was a valid one, and that John de Burgh was the lawful son and heir of Sir Thomas de Burgh.

John de Burgh then did homage and fealty, paid two shillings to the lord and gave an ox to the steward, and an order was made to John de Doncaster, the eschaetor to deliver the manors of Cawthorne and Walton to the heir.

At the same Court it was reported that Robert the son of Geoffrey de Stanley was dead, and that Hugh his son and heir, who held two bovates by homage came and did fealty for the same, paying eight shillings and sixpence a year, and to do suit at the Court every three weeks. He also paid seventeen shillings to the king for a relief.

MERCHET AND LECHERWITE.

These were the most odious of all manorial exactions. A villein could not marry his daughter without the lord's consent, and the compulsory payment of *merchet*. It was spoken of as "buying one's blood."

There are several instances in this volume (and in the earlier ones) where a sum was paid for a licence to marry, as in the case of Matilda, the widow of John de Dene, who paid two shillings for a licence, but was also fined sixpence for having married without permission.

Matthew de Totehill in 1324 paid two shillings for permission for his daughter Beatrice to marry. An order of the Court was made that Rosa, the wife of Roger Preest, having married him without licence was to be attached and brought before the Court. Emma, the daughter of John Bunny of Newton paid the lord four shillings for a licence to marry, and the daughter of Adam Hoppe-cogel, a villein, who had married John Cobler without permission was fined forty pence.

If a woman married a man living beyond the manor, the licence cost more, as then the lord lost the rights in the issue of such marriage.

In 1331, Johanna daughter of Richard gave six shillings and eightpence for the licence to marry William Faber, outside the lordship.

The onus of reporting cases of merchet was a communal responsibility, and we find manorial jurors fined for neglecting to prevent offenders.

[1] *Cal. Inq. p.m.*, 10-20, Ed. II, 185.

The tenants of the graveships of Thornes, Stanley and Wakefield were fined for concealment of merchet, and at another time the tenants of the bordland of Wakefield were fined for the concealment of merchet and the lecherwite of several women deflowered.

Akin to merchet was *lecherwite*, the fine levied when the daughter of a villein lost her chastity, for in such cases the lord lost his merchet.

The extent tells us "If any nief shall give his daughter in marriage he shall pay a fine according to the Earl's will, also for lecherwite."

In 1324, Agnes, daughter of William of Neuton was fined four pence for being 'deflowered,' and in 1327 Matilda, daughter of John Munch paid twelve pence, and Alice the daughter of William of Overhall six pence for the same offence.

At a manor court in 1316 the jurors of Alverthorpe said that Juliana, the daughter of John Sibbeson, a nief, was deflowered before she was married, and had not yet paid merchet or lecherwite; that Alice, daughter of the same John Sibbeson was also ordered to be fined, but that her fine was condoned at the instance of the Steward.

On 11 June, 1331 an inquisition held at a Halmote in Brighouse found that John de Holway owed Roger de Clifton three shillings for the lecherwite of a certain daughter of his, then deceased, for whom he was surety. John was ordered to satisfy Roger, but his fine was forgiven by the Steward.

In some cases a flogging instead of a fine was inflicted for these cases, at one Court Thomas of Bradley confessed his misconduct with Agnes, the daughter of Gilbert the Smith. Thomas was flogged, but Agnes was suspended for contumacy and excommunicated by the Dean; this frightened her, she then confessed and was flogged.

Another couple were brought before the Court, when Matilda confessed and was flogged through the market-place of Wakefield; Henry denied it, and was excommunicated.

One Henry Poket was engaged to marry Alice Sourhale, but the fickle Henry jilted the lady, but offered to pay his promised bride the sum of four shillings and eight pence to break the engagement, to which Alice agreed; later he refused to pay, whereupon Alice sued him for its recovery at the Manor Court. Henry was ordered to discharge his debt to the forsaken maid, and was also fined three shillings.

The Court in some cases tried to bring husband and wife together again, for on 11 June, 1331, four sureties were found for Thomas Kenward of Holne that he would be reconciled with Agnes his wife and would treat her well.

If he failed the sureties bound themselves to pay the lord forty shillings. At the next Court Adam Kenward and two others came into Court and acknowledged that they had in their custody sixty shillings worth of goods, belonging to Thomas and Agnes his wife for safe keeping until the said Agnes shall be willing to be duly reconciled to her husband.

Sometimes the Court had to deal with cases of the abduction of a wife. In 1307 the servant of Nicholas the parish chaplain of Wakefield abducted by night Alice the wife of John Hyde of that town on the chaplain's horse and by his command, and with the woman's consent; she was taken to Aylesbury, and with her eleven pence taken from her husband's purse, three gold rings worth eighteen pence, a mazer cup twelve pence, with many other things. Nothing is said as to a trial of the parish chaplain, this may have come before an Ecclesiastical Court. Eventually Alice returned to her husband.

In 1326 Robert Child sued Robert del Cliff for removing Margery his wife from his house, with her goods, and taking her away contrary to her husband's wishes. He laid his damages at twenty shillings.

TITHE.

Tithe seems then to have been the trouble it now is, and cases arising out of non-payment not infrequently came before the Manor Court.

In 1323, John de Burton sued Thomas de Sayvill for certain tithe sheaves of Dewsbury church, which church the said John held to farm.

The debt was acknowledged, and a fine of 6d. imposed.

The church of Dewsbury claimed tithe sheaves from Richard the Chaplain of Hartshead chapel, and in 1324, a claim was made for 39s. 11¾d., being part of 54 marks due to be paid in installments by Richard for the tithe sheaves of his chapel, together with the altarage of the chapel to the Vicar of Dewsbury. The debt was acknowledged, and a fine of 6d. was imposed.

In 1324, the tithe of the mill of Cartworth had been granted to Richard de Thorntlay, who sold one-fourth part of the tithes to Adam le Tailur and Richard Child, without being able to guarantee the same, being prevented by the Rector of Birton, Dom. Robert de Barneby who claimed the same as belonging to his part of Birton church. Richard de Thorntlay claimed that he was in a position to sell the said tithe in the name of Master Thomas de Tynwell, portioner of the said church. The inquisition found that the sale was good, and the plaintiffs were fined 4d. for making a false claim.

MULTURE.

The question of multure—the toll paid to the lord's mills for the grinding of corn, paying one measure in sixteen from August the first to Christmas and one in twenty for the remainder of the year, was constantly cropping up at the Manor Courts. This feudal enaction continued until half-way through the nineteenth century when the various townships bought the soke from the lord.

At Sourby several tenants were fined for withdrawing their corn from the mill there; in 1329, several were ordered to attend at the Sheriff's tourn to answer the lord for multure withdrawn. Michael Sourmilk was arrainged in full court for not paying multure on the twentieth jar of fifteen quartern of oats, which he had ground elsewhere.

At a Halmote held at Halifax on 6 January, 1331, an inquisition found that all tenants who owe suit to the mills at Werlulley and Soland will give multure of their groats of the twentieth vessel, and that they will give no multure of the flour produced from the groats. An order was given the same day to attach six tenants to answer the lord for withdrawing their multure from the lord's mill; they were each fined 18d., and were to satisfy the miller in adddition to the fine.

At a later court William son of Richard was convicted of unlawfully denying multure due to the lord from half a bovate of land which he held of the Graffard fee. He was ordered to satisfy the farmers for the multure, and a fine of 6d. was inflicted.

The use of hand-mills—querns—was not allowed. The Grave of Soureby was ordered to make attachments of all tenants by the rod (copy-holders) who kept hand-mills in their houses to the lord's damage.

In June, 1321 Alice de Benteleyrode was fined 3d. for a pair of hand-mill stones in her possession. In 1335 several men and their wives residing at Holne were fined, some 6d., some 3d. for selling flour mixed with bran and dust.

William Scutard, while he was keeper of the windmill at Ossett, dealt falsely with the stones in order to steal the flour of the customary tenants, as it was found that he was then living out of the manor nothing could be done.

The tenants of the manor had to bake their bread at the lord's bake-houses, though licences were granted at a cost of 6s. 8d. to certain tenants to build ovens to be common to all.

The brewing trade was almost wholly in the hands of women. The wives of the most respectable tradesmen brewed at home, and sold ale to their neighbours. Immediately a brewing was finished it was the duty of the ale-wife to send for the ale-tasters, (officials appointed by the bailiff), whose duty it was to taste the new beer of each brewing before it was supplied to the public. At every Court some of these women were brought up for transgressing the assize, either charging too much or brewing weak beer.

In 1266, a Statute was passed to regulate the assize of bread and ale, by which a graduated scale for the sale of ale was established throughout the whole country. It decreed that when a quartern of wheat was sold for 3s. or 3s. 4d., and a quarter of barley for 20d. or 24d., and a quarter of oats for 15d., brewers could afford to sell 2 gallons of ale for 1d. in cities, and 3 gallons for 1d. out of cities. In order to carry out the assize the lord of every manor was obliged to keep a pillory and a ducking stool.

In 1275 the jurors at a Court said that Juliana Pykard brewed contrary to the assize, and when the ale-tasters came Juliana said that she would sell ale against the will of them and of the bailiff, in despite of the Earl. She was fined 12d.

The wine taverns were furnished with a pole projecting from the gable of the house, bearing a bunch of leaves at the end; hence arose the proverb, "good wine needs no bush."

The oldest sign of all "The Grey Bush," dated from pagan times and the worship of Bacchus. In 1338, Stephen Arkyns' wife and Alice de Wyke were fined 2d. each for not putting out their signs, known as "alepoles" or "alestakes."

FORESTALLING.

Action against forestalling of goods for the market was severely dealt with. In 1322 Richard Stel, a common forestaller of victuals was fined 12d. In 1327 William Salter of Lyngerdes was convicted of being a common forestaller, fine 12d. William Isaud of Almonbury came before the Court as a forestaller and also as a seller of murrain flesh. Henry Drake for selling unsound meat and for forestalling fish and meat was fined 2s., as were also nine other men. William son of Mariota for forestalling hens, eggs and butter, and Robert Litfast for selling unsound meat, 6d. each. At a Sheriff's tourn held 2 July, 1329, a raid was made, and several men were fined for forestalling hens, butter, eggs and fish, and were fined 6d. each.

THE DEATH PENALTY.

The custom of the manor was when sentence of death was passed, at Wakefield by hanging at Agbrigg, but if at Halifax criminals suffered the extreme penalty of the law by the gibbet axe, which is now preserved in the Rolls Office at Wakefield. The last execution at Halifax by the gibbet axe was in the year 1650, when two men were sentenced "to suffer death by having their heads severed from their bodies" for stealing sixteen yards of cloth.

From this extreme punishment arose "The Beggar's Litany—"From Hell, Hull and Halifax, good Lord deliver us."

At Wakefield after the sentence had been pronounced the convicted person's hands were bound, and he or she was taken to the lord's prison, and thence to Agbrigg, and there hanged on the gallows. In 1323 three men were taken out of Wakefield prison, led to Agbrigg and there executed.

Women were hanged, as in the case of Eda de Blakommor, who was convicted of stealing a tunic of blue cloth and a hood of the same material of the value of two shillings. Eda confessed and the verdict of the Court was, "Let her be hanged."

PRICE OF LIVE STOCK.

In the early part of the fourteenth century the price of animals, as shewn in these rolls, was 3 shillings for an ox; a cow 15 shillings; a mare 3 shillings and sixpence, a sheep 2 shillings and sixpence; a pig 3 shillings.

The charge for pannage in the new or old park was 8 pence for an ox, 4 pence for a steer, 2 pence for a calf, 12 pence for a horse, between the Feast of the Invention of the Cross—3 May, and the Feast of St. Oswald—28 February.

In 1327 these grazing fees brought in £15. 0s. 4d. to the lord of the manor.

At this period the wages for a female servant were 3 shillings and sixpence a year.

VILLEINS.

By the custom of the manor a villein was by birth and inheritance bound to the soil, but often aspired to become a freeman. In Whit-week 1275, Robert Ereward of Wakefield was charged at the Court with being a villein. Ereward admitted it, and gave 13s. 4d. for recognition, and agreed to pay 12d. annually. In 1330 William of Sandal, charged with being a bondman, agreed to pay 13s. 4d. on condition of being free for the whole of Earl Warenne's lifetime, and during that time not to be charged or molested for bondage or servile condition.

In 1339 John, Earl of Warenne ordered Sir Simon de Balderston, the steward of his lands in the north, to enquire upon the oath of twelve burgesses as to whether William de Sandal, Maud, Alice and William Tirsi, and thirteen others were bondmen or bondwomen, and to determine this by their inquisition.

The burgesses found that William de Sandal was a freeman and that he should receive his franchise as of right, but determined that the others were in bondage. The matter came up again in 1342, when William and his brother Hugh appealed to the King's Court for final settlement, as the Earl claimed them as his bondmen. They showed a release and quitclaim in French dated 7 November, 1341, by the Steward and by the Rector of Dewsbury, whereby it was shown by the oath of the free tenants of the manor that their grandfather John del Wro was a freeman, and that he begat John their father. The Court pronounced in their favour, and the verdict was recorded in the Patent Rolls of 16 Edward III.

It may be of interest for the history of our publications to add that on 2 May, 1898, Miss Ethel Stokes was engaged to transcribe the earliest series of the Wakefield Manor Court Rolls, permission having been given by Lady Yarborough, the lady of the manor. Five members of the Council of the Society contributed the sum of £131 1s. 0d. for this purpose.

	£	s.	d.
Thomas Brooke, F.S.A. (*President*)	100	0	0
William Brown	1	1	0
S. J. Chadwick, F.S.A.	10	0	0
J. W. Clay, F.S.A.	10	0	0
J. W. Walker, F.S.A.	10	0	0

The first volume was published in 1901, and volumes II to IV in 1906, 1917 and 1930. There is sufficient material prepared by Miss Stokes for a sixth and seventh volume, covering the period down to 1340. In 1943 the Earl of Yarborough made the very welcome gift to the Society of all the Manor Court Rolls in his possession, and they are now available for reference in one of the strong rooms at 10, Park Place.

J. W. WALKER.

TWEMLOW HALL,
    CHESHIRE.

Wakefield Court Rolls.

COURT held at Halifax on Monday after the Invention of the Cross (May 3) 14 Edw. II [1321].

Adam del Bothes surrenders the eighth part of one toft, one bovate and nine acres in Ourom, in the graveship of Hiperum, which were demised to Robert of Werlulley, chaplain, to hold according to custom, etc. And Robert gave 16ᵈ for entry.

PLEAS and PERQUISITES of the Soke of Wakefield from the Vigil of St. Gregory [March 12] 16 Edward II [1322-3] until in the time of John de Doncaster holding the place of Steward.

COURT of the King held at Wakefeld before John de Donecastre, on Friday, the Vigil of St. Gregory (March 12), 16 Edw. II [1322-3].

(1) "Honurs e rewences. Pur ces sir q̃ Roberd de Werlullay chapelayn gest emplede deuaunt vous ad touche recorde des roulles Joħn de Burton q̃ fu senescħ de Wakefeld une piece en temps le Count de Lancastr q̃ demorent en ma garde; vous enuoy tñsescrite de un enroullement du temps le dit John de Birton com vo' verrez de south seel E vous requer au diⁱ Roᵬd voillez eē g̃tiouse e favorable en resone. Sir de Dieu soietz honure.

(2)   "De tempe J. de Burton."

Essoins. John Hode, by Thomas Thorald. Surety—Henry Tasch.

Thomas de Thornton, by Henry Tasch. Surety—William of Castelford.

John de Caylly, by German Filkok. Surety—William del Okes.

Robert le Draper of Stanley, by Robert del More.

Bailiff. Thomas de Totehill and Robert de Lughrigge (4ᵈ) agree by licence; also Thomas and Henry de Totehill (3ᵈ), William, s. of Roger (3ᵈ), and Adam Sparebutter (3ᵈ).

Ellen de Rastrik fined 2ᵈ for pasturing her cattle on the said Thomas's grass; damages, 40ᵈ

Henry de Walda, 3ᵈ, for not prosecuting the said Thomas.

. . . Hugh s. of Hugh de Lighesils, sues Roger de Grenewode for trespass, the judgment to be given by Richard de Birton. Surety—John de Grenegate

. . . John Evotsone does not prosecute suit against John de Bradeforth; his fine forgiven, because he is poor.

. . . John Elyotsone fined 2ᵈ for false claim against John Kaynock.

Bailiff. John le Rede of Pudsey and Ralph de Schefeld, agree. John puts himself in mercy; 6ᵈ

Stanley. Walter Ginne, 3ᵈ for not prosecuting John Tyting.

Bailiff. John del Bothem sues John s. of Robert de Metheley, for detaining a cow worth 20ˢ. Defendant is to make his law. Surety—John Dade.

Sandale. Roger de Bordewricht sues John s. of Thomas de Crigelston, and Robert s. of Hugh, for debt. Surety—German Swerd.

Stanley. Emma Ginne fined 2ᵈ for not prosecuting suit against Walter Ginne.

Hiperom. Simon del Dene, 6ᵈ for the same against Adam Prestman. Roger Clifton was surety for the prosecution.

. . . Adam Prestman, attached to answer Roger Cliffton for seizing his cattle in Hiperom, at a place called Lightcliff, and driving them to Henry de Coldeley's house in that town, is to make his law. Surety—Adam de Middelton.

Robert Johanstepson le Pynder fined . . . for not prosecuting similar suit against Adam le Prestman.

Rastrik. Thomas Taluace and John del Clay of Eland, 6ᵈ for the same against Thomas de Totehill.

Hugh de Totehill sues Robert de Soureby, Adam de Middilton. Thomas of Haytefeld, Roger de Grenewode and Richard de Waddesworth for debt. Surety—John de Gayregrave.

. . . John son and heir of Thomas de Heton, deceased, does fealty for the tenements he holds of the King, and fines 2ˢ for respite of suit till Michaelmas.

Adam de Everingham, 6ᵈ, and John Drak, 3ᵈ for default. Henry de Walda, 3ᵈ for default.

Holne. Henry s. of John del Standbank, surrenders 4¼ acres in Wlvedale, which are granted to John del Grene, who pays 2ˢ for entry.

Hiperom. John s. of Roger de Clifton, pays 3ˢ to the King to take for 12 years all the lands that William del Bothes held in the bounds of Hiperom, with William s. and heir of the said William del Bothes, whom he will maintain honourably, finding him in all necessaries. Surety—Roger de Clifton.

Ossete. Agnes d. of Richard s. of Bate, surrenders ½ bovate of land in Ossete, and it is committed to Thomas, s. of Richard . . . 2ˢ for entry.

Alverthorp. Richard de Colley surrenders a rood in Alverthorp, and John Gerbot another rood, both of which are committed to Julian d. of Robert ad Ulmum, who pays 6ᵈ for entry into each.

Horbiry. Hugh in le Wro fines to the King 18^d as a heriot on ½ bovate and ½ acre in Horbiry, after the death of Robert del Wro, his father.

Alverthorp. Roger le Bordwricht and Alice, his wife, and Christian, sister of Alice, surrender 2 acres in Alverthorp, which are committed to John s. of Hobbe; 12^d for entry.

. . . John Gepsone, 6^d . . . Richard Stele 6^d for dry wood.

Stanley. John Isabell's wife, 6^d; John, s. of Simon Tyting, 2^d; William de Schefeld, 6^d, for coal and vert.

[Here the membrane ends in rags].

Stanley. Walter Gunne sues Robert . . . for trespass. Surety —Philip Gunne.

Rastrik. Thomas Taluace sues Thomas de Totehill. Surety —the bailiff of Rastrick.

Bailiff. John s. of Richard de . . . sues John de Ryley for trespass. Surety—John Clerk of Sandale.

Sandale. Elias de Doncastre sues John del Dene for debt. Surety—Thomas de Holgate.

Bailiff. Henry Nelot sues Emma Fairhegh for debt. Surety —Thomas Tabernator (le Taverner).

Sandale. Richard le Litester of Walton sues William le Parmenter on an agreement. Surety—Adam de Wodessom.

Robert s. of William de Walton, sues Henry s. of Hugh, for debt. Surety—John Clerk.

Stanley. John de Metheley sues John del Bothom for debt. Surety—John Dade.

Bailiff. John de Dyghton sues Thomas de Totehill. Surety —Richard de Birton.

Stanley. Hugh de Stanley sues Emma Gunne for debt. Surety—William de Lokwod.

COURT held at Wakefeld by John de Donescastre on Friday after the Feast of St. Ambrose (April 4), 16 Edw. II [1323].

Essoins. John de Hopton, attorney of Brian de Thornhill, by William Tasch. Surety—William Lokwod.

Richard de Birstall, by Thomas de Birstall.

Bailiff. Thomas de Totehill essoins against Thomas Taluace, by John Patrik. Surety—John Woderoue; also by Richard de Birton. Surety—William de Castelford. Also against Thomas s. of Richard, by William de Totehill.

Stanley. Agnes widow of Hugh le Chapman, fined 2^d for not prosecuting suit against Hugh Forester.

Alverthorp. William Hodelyn and John Gerbot (2^d) agree.

Bailiff. John s. of Robert de Metheley, wages his law against John del Bothem; fine, 2^d

John de Burgh, who holds the manor of Walton in chief from the King, to be distrained for homage and fealty; and fined 6ᵈ for defaults.

Horbiry. John de Hopton sues Adam Hoperborn for 29ˢ 5ᵈ, for which John s. of Hugh was surety. An inquisition is to be taken.

Bailiff. John s. of Richard de Wodesom (fine pardoned) and John de Ryeley agree.

Ossete. Elias de Doncastre sues John del Dene for 5ˢ 4ᵈ, the price of a stone of wool; the debt is acknowledged; fine 3ᵈ

Stanley. John de Metheley sues John del Bothom for 4ˢ in silver, and 2 bushels of corn worth 4ˢ. An inquisition to be held as to 1½ bushels in dispute; the rest acknowledged; fine 2ᵈ

. . . Adam de Everingham, John de Nevill and Ralph de . . . fined . . . for defaults.

Robert s. of Geoffrey de Stanley, is dead . . .

Ivo Faber surrenders 2 acres in a clearing . . .; they are committed to John de Gayrgrave; 6ᵈ for entry.

Robert Hode of Neuton surrenders half a "broddole" in the great meadow of Alverthorp, which is committed to Philip D . . . 6ᵈ for entry.

Hugh s. and heir of Robert s. of Geoffrey de Stanley, who held 2 bovates by homage, came and did fealty for the same, he pays 8ˢ 6ᵈ a year, does suit every three weeks, and will give the King 17ˢ for a relief.

. . . The widow of Walter del Spen, 2ᵈ; the wife of Robert s. of Walter del Spen, 2ᵈ; John Hockespore's wife, 2ᵈ; John Wlmer, 3ᵈ; Beatrice L . . . lynde, 2ᵈ for dry wood, &c.

Wakefeld. John de Skulbrok's wife, 2ᵈ; Margery Junne, 2ᵈ; Ibota Sparwe, 2ᵈ; Robert Prest's handmaid, 1ᵈ for dry wood.

[The end of the membrane torn away].

Agnes widow of Hugh le Chapman, sues Hugh Forester for debt. Surety—William de Castelforth.

. . . s. of . . . s. of Philip de Alverthorp, sues Richard Wythehoundes for debt. Surety—Henry de Wakefeld.

Thomas de Ketelesthorp and Cecilia, his wife, sue Adam Carpenter and Anna his wife, for debt. Surety—William of the Okes. They also sue Matthew Attewell for debt.

Henry Nelot sues Eva, widow of Simon Tyting, for debt.

William de Thirbarwe, chaplain, sues John de St. Swithin, and Alice, his wife, for . . . Surety—German Swerd.

Matilda widow of Adam Broun, sues Hugh del Wro for debt. Surety—Adam Hoperburn.

———

COURT held at Wakefeld by John de Donecastre, on Friday before the Feast of St. George the Martyr (April 23), 16 Edw. II [1323].

Essoins. John de Hopton, attorney of Brian de Thornhill, by William Filch. Surety—William de Castilford.

Thomas de Thornton by William de Castilford. Surety—Richard de Birstall.

Adam Sprigonell by Thomas le Tanner. Surety—Thomas del Bellehous.

Bailiff. Eva widow of Robert le Draper of Stanley, who was seised conjointly with her husband of 2 bovates in Stanley, surrendered her rights therein by charter to Hugh, her son, who did fealty and is received to do suit and other services. An ox to the Steward.

John s. and heir of Thomas de Burgh, does fealty and homage for the manor of Walton, and pays 2ˢ to have respite of suit till Michaelmas. An ox to the Steward.

Sandale. Roger le Bordwricht agrees severally with John s. of Thomas de Crigelston (2ᵈ) and Robert s. of Hugh (3ᵈ).

John de Hopton essoins against John Elyotson of Horbiry by William de Castilford. Surety—John Chicch.

John Elyotson fined 2ᵈ for default at last court.

John de Hopton essoins against John Hudsone, by William de Castilford. Surety—John Bond.

. . . Agnes widow of Hugh le Chapman, and Richard Colley (2ᵈ) agree. Surety—Roger le Bordewricht.

. . . John de Holgate essoins against John Gos by John Paterik. Surety Robert Teller? (*Tell*).

Robert s. of William de Walton, 3ᵈ for not prosecuting suit against Henry s. of Hugh.

John de Metheley, 6ᵈ for the same against John del Bothom.

Agnes widow of Hugh Chapman, and Hugh Forester have a love-day.

John Attebarre sues Richard del Ker for 6ˢ 8ᵈ, which defendant acknowledges, and is fined 6ᵈ

A bovate of land, acquired by Robert de Holand, from John de Ayketon in Crigelston fields, is committed to William s. of Robert de Crigelston, at 3ˢ rent; and he will do to the hermit of Conigsburgh for the time being the service belonging to his hermitship.

John Kyde of Wakefeld surrendered a curtilage and buildings in Thornes, which is committed to John de Gayregrave; and he has entry without fine, because he is in the King's service.

John de Flanshou surrenders 1⅝ acres, which are committed to Thomas Bate; entry, 12ᵈ

Alice Filkock stepdaughter of Thomas More sues William s. of Roger de Snaypthorp, for debt. Surety—William s. of Robert de Crigelston.

John de Nevill, 6ᵈ for default.

Richard Withehounds surrendered ½ rood in Alverthorp,
which is committed to William de Lockewod and Alice his wife;
without fine, because in the King's service.

John Torald surrenders 2⅝ acres, in which Thomas s. of
Laurence has a term for 20 years; they are committed to Matilda
wife of the said Thomas. She pays 6ᵈ for the recognition.

Richard Wythehoundes surrenders 1½ rood in Alverthorp;
committed to John de Grenegate; entry, 6ᵈ

Richard de Colley surrenders 3 acres in Alverthorp; committed to John H . . .leson; entry, 12ᵈ

John de Grenegate gives 6ᵈ to take 1½ rood of meadow in
Alverthorp from John Gerbot, for 12 years.

Ralph s. of Laurence, Elyas Tyrsi, Augustine Skinner and
William Bate, 6ᵈ each, for putting their beasts by night in the
lord's meadows.

Philip de Castelford, 6ᵈ and Thomas le Gardiner, 3ᵈ for the
same.

Thomas de Bellehous sues William Maunsel of Ovendene
for debt. Surety—Roger de Grenewode.

An inquisition finds that Robert s. of Adam de Neubygging,
ousted James Monck from the vesture of a rood of land; to pay
12ᵈ damages, and 6ᵈ fine.

Stanley. Also that John Poket insulted Alice wife of Robert
le Leper. Damages, 12ᵈ; fine, 6ᵈ

Also that Henry Poket slandered the same Alice, by means
of which her husband lost 40ˢ. Fine, 2ˢ

Also that Henry Poket detains 4ˢ 8ᵈ from Alice Sourhale,
which he owes her under an agreement, by which she undertook in
return to withdraw from a matrimonial suit. Fine, 3ᵈ. Sureties
for the fines, and for the payment of 40ˢ damages to Robert le
Leper—Richard Pescy, Richard Poket, Richard del Kerre and
John Poket.

Bailiff. Robert Pelleson and James del Okes (2ᵈ) agree by
licence.

. . . . . . John s. of Elyas, and Hugh in le Wro, acknowledge
themselves bound to John de Hopton, clerk, in 16ˢ 1ᵈ

A jury finds that Henry de Batelay and Robert Sonman
receive from the tithes of Ossete, which they bought from Ger-
manus Filcock, 2 bushels of corn, value 3ˢ 4ᵈ, and 4 quarters of oats,
value 18ˢ besides the depredations (*ultᵃ dep'dacoes*) made in the
said tithes. They are to satisfy him; fine, ? 6ᵈ

[Total of this Court:—] *i.e.* Sandale 8ᵈ, rents 3ˢ Horbiry, 8ᵈ
. . . .
. . . .

COURT held at Halifax on Monday, the Feast of St. Mark the
Evangelist (Apr. 25) 16 Edw. II [1323].

Bailiff. Richard de Holynrakes; Richard s. of Adam; John de Skyrcote; Richard del Bank, and Adam de Sothehagh, 3^d each for not coming.

Sourby. Hugh s. of Hugh de Lichesels, plaintiff (6^d) and Roger de Grenewod, agree on two matters.

New Rent. Robert de Sotehill gives 12^d to take a rood of new land in Warwolfley wood; rent 1½^d

Ellen and Isabel daughters of Robert de Weswode of Warwolfley, surrender an acre in Warwlley; committed to William le Westerne; entry, 6^d

Thomas Eschefeld surrenders ½ acre in Soureby; committed to John s. of Thomas . . . feld; entry, 6^d

3½ acres in Sourby, seised into the lord's hand on the death of Henry Miller; committed to Alice his daughter. Heriot, 12^d

8 acres in Soureby seised as above on the death of Richard del Feld, committed to Adam his son; heriot, 2^s

Adam s. of Henry de Soland, surrenders 14 acres in Soland; committed to Henry s. of Hugh; entry, 4^s

Matilda widow of Elyas, sues Hugh Wade and Julian his wife, for 7^s 4^d for flour bought from her; the debt to be recovered; fine, 3^d

Adam Attetounend surrenders 1½ acre in Soureby; committed to Richard s. of Beatrice; entry, 12^d

William Maunsel of Ovendene fined 2^d for not coming.

Thomas de Waddesworth surrenders 4½ acres in le Mithomrode; committed to John his son; entry, 4^s

Hugh Wade (2^d) and Robert de Saurby agree.

Ivo de Saltonstall sues Richard de Okelsley, Robert de Saurby, Thomas de Saltonstall and William s. of Gilbert de Halifax, for 6^s; the debt is acknowledged; fine, 8^d

Henry del Lone surrenders 2½ acres in Soureby; committed to Adam s. of Hugh de Lichesils and Alice his wife; entry, 12^d

William s. of Hugh de Lichelsils, surrenders a curtilage and 6 acres in Lichesils in exchange with Henry del Lone; Henry pays 3^s for entry.

Henry del Lone surrenders 5 acres in Lichesils in exchange with Adam s. of William de Lichesils; Adam pays 18^d for entry.

John de Soland surrenders 3 acres in Soland; committed to Henry s. of Henry; entry, 12^d

Thomas del Feld and Hobbekin s. of John (3^d) agree.

Robert de Warwolley, chaplain (6^d) agrees with John de Ourum and Isabel his daughter, executors of the will of Adam s. of Ivo. Surety—Henry del Holgate.

Total of this court—24^s 6^d and 1½^d new rent. *i.e.* from Soureby, 23^s 3^d and 1½^d rent. from services xiijd.

TOURN there the same day.

Bailiff. The jury (not enumerated) say that Michael de Routonstall, Adam de Bredensik, living in Langfeld, Robert de Rischelegh, Thomas del Castelstede, Roger Forester, Robert del Bothe, Adam Cappe, William s. of Hugh de Lighchesels, Richard de Windhill, Thomas s. of Eva de Halifax, Roger Spilwode, John Sutor, Henry s. of William de Halifax, John Bridde, Robert Wyldebore and Robert del Skoles, indicted elsewhere at other tourns for divers thefts and felonies, have not yet been delivered as they ought to have been; they are therefore to be taken.

The above Robert de la Bothe and Roger Forester stole cattle from Richard de Byrton's enclosure, belonging to Adam de Holdene and John de Scolfeld's wife; and are notorious thieves; Cecilia wife of Robert de la Bothe, is likewise guilty. Roger s. of Robert del Holme, stole 2 cows at Walleschaghes; Richard del Holme and Malle Colle broke into the house of John s. of Ivo, Christian Wynter sheared five sheep belonging to her mother, and carried off the wool, Thomas s. of John de Haldeworth, stole an old trokettum; value 3ᵈ. To be attached.

William de Sunderland blocked up a path that used to lead to the common pasture; 12ᵈ

The township of Sourby present that Roger de Grenewode stole 2 calves, value 5ˢ from John s. of Roger de Saurby, which are now a calf and an ox in the custody of Michael de Marchdene at Marchdene. He is to be taken.

Roger de Grenwode drew blood from Hugh Wade; 12ᵈ

Isabel wife of Roger Spillewod from Thomas le Tincler, in self-defence.

William s. of German de Grenwod, and Richard his brother, thieved cattle belonging to Michael de Routonstall, William del Estwode, Alice del Clogh and Adam de Claiton. To be taken.

Elias de Waddesworth and Matilda his wife, stole a brass pot worth 5ˢ from William Snayppe. To be taken.

Robert Notyng thieved 40ˢ from the house of Robert Carpenter his father, while the said Robert was on his death-bed; and after his death, William Miller, the executor, threatened the said Robert Notyng, so that he brought the money back. Robert is to be taken for the theft, and William for receiving stolen goods.

John s. of German de Grenwode, and Robert del Bothe, assaulted a strange man at Whitolre, and took from him a horse and cart, etc.

ATTACHMENTS.

Sourby. John del Bothom, 1ᵈ; Robert de Welronwall, 4ᵈ; Adam del Croft, 2ᵈ; William s. of Cecilia, 5ᵈ; William Cissor, ? 6ᵈ; Geoffrey de Cossilegh, 2ᵈ; John del Holgate, 4ᵈ; John de Redyker, 1ᵈ; John Colpen, 2ᵈ; Roger de Grenewode, 2ᵈ; Robert s. of John de Sourby, junior, 4ᵈ; Matilda widow of Henry de Butterworth, 2ᵈ; William le Western, 2ᵈ; Richard de Bayrestow, 2ᵈ; Adam Migg, 2ᵈ; William de Schagh, 1ᵈ, and Henry de Saltonstall, 2ᵈ, for escapes, etc.

Total of this tourn—5ˢ 4ᵈ *i.e.* services. 2ˢ Sourby 3ˢ 4ᵈ

COURT held at Brighous on Wednesday after the Feast of St. Mark the Evangelist (April 25) 16 Edw. II [1323].

Hiperom. Roger de Clifton (3ᵈ) and Adam Prestman of Eland agree.

. . . Robert de Rissheworth (3ᵈ) and said Adam agree, also Simon del Dene (3ᵈ) and said Adam.

. . . An inquisition finds that Thomas de Totehill maliciously detained Henry le Wricht's cattle, fine, 6ᵈ

Henry de la Wald sues Roger de Hasilhirst for 2ˢ 6ᵈ; the debt is acknowledged; fine, 6ᵈ

Hiperom. Robert de Soureby sues John le Pynder, Adam s. of Henry, William del Rokes and Roger de Clifton for 11ˢ for 2 cows bought from him; the debt is acknowledged; fine, 6ᵈ

. . . Thomas de Lynlay proves against Richard de Lethridge, that he is detaining 10ˢ from him, a debt for land bought; fine, 6ᵈ. Surety—Henry le Waynwricht.

Hiperom. An inquisition finds Julian del Whitehill complained without cause against Henry le Waynwricht in a plea of dower, because her husband was not seised of the land in queston after he married her; 2ᵈ for false claim.

Also that Jordan le Pynder is wrongfully withholding 5½ᵈ from Beatrice, widow of Alexander le Waynwricht. Fine, 6ᵈ. Surety—John del Bothe.

Also that Thomas del Rode is withholding 5 quarters of oats from Matilda d. of John del Holway, which he ought to have paid her 10 years ago; he is to pay; fine, 6ᵈ. Matilda fined 2ᵈ for false claim against Thomas. Surety—Simon del Dene.

John de Schepedene, 2ᵈ for not paying Roger de Hesilhirst 3ˢ 6ᵈ for a bacinett bought from him.

John s. of Adam de Hiperom sues Robert de Soureby and John le Pynder for 2 quarters of oats for which they were sureties for Alexander le Waynwricht, now dead; they are to pay; fine, 4ᵈ

Rastrik. Richard s. of Henry de Rastrik, gives 2ˢ as a heriot on 8 acres in Rastrik on the death of his father.

Hiperom. William de Sunderland surrenders a messuage and 8 acres in Schipedene; and afterwards takes them for his life, with remainder to John his son, who pays 3ˢ. The tenement lies between that of Henry Faber and le Raggedbirk, and Frankleysker and Shepedenbirk in the other direction.

Rastrik. Matthew de Totehill surrenders an acre in Rastrik; committed to Henry Moddeson; entry, 6^d

Hiperom. William s. of Henry de Godeleye, gives 12^d as a heriot on 3 acres in Schepedene.

John le Webbester surrenders a messuage and an acre of land in Hyperum; committed to Ivo, his brother; entry, 12^d

William s. of Thomas de Hiperum surrenders an acre there; committed to Ivo le Webbester; fine, 12^d on entry.

John de Ovendene, John Shepherd of Hertesheved, Michael de Helay, Robert s. of Malle de Clifton, Walter de Turnour, and Elias de Skulcote 3^d each for not coming.

Richard s. of Peter de Rastrik, 6^d; Ellen Scot, 6^d; John le Cou . . ., 4^d; John s. of Alexander, 3^d; Thomas s. of Henry, 3^d; Richard de Thorp, 6^d; Richard de Shepedene . . .; Sabina de Haylaye, 2^d, and Julian de Whitehill, 2^d, for vert.

Total of this Court—17^s 10^d *i.e.* services 12^d.   Rastrik, 3^s. Hiperom, 13^s 10^d.

TOURN there the same day.

. . . Hugh Miller drew blood from Cecilia de Bothumley, 12^d

Johanna de Goldale wife of John de Popilwell, stole a calf from Agnes de la Mere; to be taken.

Thomas de Totehill impleaded Alexander de Brighous, the King's villein (*nativus*), in the consistory court, so that he was suspended from entering the Church. To be attached.

William Swayppe, the lord's villein (*nativus*), died intestate; and Robert chaplain, his brother, constituted himself executor, and . . . the goods and chattels of deceased and has received 4^s, 3 horses, etc. etc. from John Drak. The cattle to be taken into the King's hand, and Robert attached.

William brother of Andrew, formerly forester in Hyperom, and John s. of Gilbert Bridd, stole 3 oxen from William de Sundirland, two from Henry de la Rode, and two cows from Robert del Southdene.   To be taken.

Juliana widow of Thomas del Whitehill, drew blood from John Drak, 12^d

Thomas de Totehill, from John de Dighton, 12^d

William Miller's wife and William Peck's wife, 3^d each for brewing, etc.

William s. of Simon Juddeson, stole a cow which he sold to Gilbert, servient of the manor of Schelf, for 8^s. To be taken.

Total of this Tourn—3^s 6^d all from services.

TOURN at Birton the Thursday following.

. . . Thomas de Langeley of Schepeley drew blood from two serving-men of Hanley, 12^d

William s. of Hugh, from John de Brockeholes, 12ᵈ

Richard s. of Henry de Schelley, thieved cattle belonging to Richard Osan, Richard de Langley and Henry de Byngeley. To be taken.

Alverthorp. Hugh s. of Robert de Swalthill received said Richard; to be attached.

William s. of John, narrowed a certain lane (*venella*).

Richard s. of Hugh, was not indicted but slandered. John de Burton took 10ˢ from him.

Robert s. of Thomas, stole beasts from Nicholas s. of Simon, and fled. To be taken when he can be found.

Robert de Beaumond came with several men to Birton church, and assaulted Robert Tyays coming from that church . . . . . . to wit, Adam Shepherd, Nicholas s. of John, Nicholas s. of Simon, Thomas de Billeclif, Thomas s. of Simon.

. . . present that William de Butterley stole 4 oxen in Heppeworth in company with William Bridd.

Total of this tourn—3ˢ. And all from services.

———

COURT held at Birton on Thursday after the Feast of St. Mark the Evangelist (Apr. 25), 16 Edw. II.

Holne. An inquisition finds Adam de Horn is detaining 21ˢ 6ᵈ from Agnes widow of John, being part payment of 43ˢ for 3 oxen bought from her. He is to pay the same; fine, 3ᵈ. Sureties —William Forester and John de Castell.

William Strekeyse, 6ᵈ for false claim against Agnes widow of John.

Thomas Hannekock 3ᵈ for contempt offered to Eva wife of Adam Keneward.

An inquisition finds that Richard Child broke an agreement with Matthew de Ramesdene; to pay damages, and 3ᵈ fine.

Robert Wades sues Richard del Bothe for 5ᵈ for 3 stones of wool, which he had previously recovered against him before Thomas Sayuill. Fine, 3ᵈ

Emma and Cecilia daughters of John s. of Henry de Heppeworth, give 40ᵈ as a heriot on 9 acres in Heppeworth after their father's death.

Matilda widow of John le Dene, 2ˢ for licence to marry; and 6ᵈ for having married without paying a fine.

Adam s. of Elias, surrenders a curtilage containing ½ rood in Wlvedale; committed to John del Bothe; entry, 6ᵈ

John de Anodene, William de Legh, John s. of Julian de Holn, Adam Akirland, John Drabil, Alan de Alstunley and John del Castelle, 4ᵈ each for vert.

Total of this Court—10ˢ 2ᵈ and all from Holne.

TOURN at Wakefield the Friday following. (Apr. 26) 16 Edw. II.

Bailiff. Thomas Gates, 12ᵈ for contempt of the jury.

Richard brother of John de Schelley, stole horses from Gilbert s. of William s. of Henry de Skelmerthorp, and William de Selby, chaplain, servant at Emley. To be taken.

William s. of William, s. of Peter, drew blood from Adam Costnotgh, 12ᵈ

John s. of Alan, impleaded Walter s. of John de Thinglow in the consistory, in contempt of the King, fine, 12ᵈ

Alice wife of Robert Wasshepoke, 6ᵈ for brewing weak ale and contrary to the assize.

Robert Tyays, parson of Tankerisley, John s. of Henry de Schelley, Fraunco de Barneby and Thomas de Baumforth, with other persons unknown, came in the evening to Adam Cosyn's house in Floketon, broke the doors and locks, and stole goods worth 20ˢ, and a horse. To be taken.

John s. of William de Bellomonte, aged 15 years, broke into John Lorimar's house, and stole goods, value 12ᵈ. To be taken.

Adam Trubbe received the said John; to be attached.

Thomas s. of Agnes, indicted for stealing sheaves in the autumn, has not been delivered; he also received William Bellard, a thief, beheaded, and Thomas de Gray a fugitive, who abjured the Kingdom [knowing] them to be thieves. To be taken.

James del Okes is a common thief. To be taken.

Peter le Pynder impleaded Richard de Colley and Roger le Bordwricht in the consistory, and is not a resident. To be attached.

Thomas s. of William le Hayr of Sandale, stole a cow from Emma de Moseley of Westbretton, and is a notorious thief. To be taken.

John Graffard is a notorious horse and cattle thief. To be taken when he can be found.

The township of Sandale, 12ᵈ for concealing theft of above Thomas.

Robert Dypsi cut down trees and thorns round the King's park at Wakefeld; to be attached.

Ralph s. of Laurence Clerk, is accustomed to do the same.

Richard Stel is a common forestaller of victuals coming to the town of Wakefeld; fine, 12ᵈ

Two stalls, to wit, the stall put up by Gregory, and John Broun's stall, are situated in Wakefeld market, so as to obstruct the business of the market, to the injury of the neighbours; the township begs that the rents thereof may be assigned to some other places, and the stalls pulled down. This is ordered to be done.

Alice de Thornhill raised the hue without cause on Idonea Colleson; 6ᵈ

Thomas Chode, and Nicholas his son, are common forestallers; 12ᵈ each.

German Filkock, 12ᵈ for occupying a certain piece of ground in Wakefeud to the injury of the neighbours. The occupation to cease.

Henry le Nautherd drew blood from the wife of William le Badger; 12ᵈ

Robert s. of Robert le Couper is a common thief of pigs, etc.; and is received by his father. Both to be taken.

William de Ludham drew blood from Henry le Nauthird; 12ᵈ

The wife of John le Rased, from William de Sandale's wife, 6ᵈ

John Bullock stole the bar of iron from the door of la Wodehall, and Edusa Crabbe received him. Both to be taken.

William s. of John Paterik broke into Horbiry mill, and carried off corn. To be taken.

William s. of William the Goldsmith, stole a pig in the old park, worth 8ᵈ. To be attached.

Henry s. of Robert s. of Geoffrey de Stanley stole cattle from Philip le Syhour, Robert Ricard, William Attetounend, Robert le Leper, and Robert s. of William s. of Adam. To be taken.

Hugh s. of Robert s. of Geoffrey, stole pigs and cattle from Simon de Monte, Robert s. of Geoffrey, and Thomas Ginne.

Hugh Cort stole a cow from Robert de Wyuerumthorp; Robert Bele, a hoggaster worth 20ᵈ from the same.

Henry Tropinell, the iron bar from the door of La Wodehall, worth 6ˢ 8ᵈ

John serving-man of Richard Forester is a common thief. Hugh de Standene is the same.

Richard Bullock and John his brother, stole cattle, and slaughtered them in le Colepittes. All the above thieves to be taken.

John Castellok impleaded Hugh Forester in the consistory at York; fine, 12ᵈ

Henry s. of Robert le Cartwricht was Henry Cort's associate in his thefts.

ATTACHMENTS.

Wakefeld. Robert Chepp̄, 6ᵈ; John Tenet's wife, 2ᵈ; Thomas de Louche, 2ᵈ; Agnes Hogge, 2ᵈ; Thomas Bate's handmaid, 2ᵈ; Magota le Gardiner, 2ᵈ; John de Grenegate, 4ᵈ; the wife of Robert s. of Ibote, 2ᵈ; German Crakehale's wife, 2ᵈ; William Thrift, 1ᵈ; and Robert Liftfast's handmaid, 2ᵈ for dry wood and breaking palings.

Ossete. John del Dene, 12ᵈ, and Hugh Bulheved, 6ᵈ for breaking and burning palings.

The wife of Richard s. of Bate, 2ᵈ; Henry son of Richard Scut, 2ᵈ; surety, Julian Scut; and Robert Donne, 3ᵈ for wood.

Stanley. Henry Cockeshank, 2ᵈ; Richard Poket, 3ᵈ and Adam le Hewer, 3ᵈ for wood.

Thorns. Ivo Faber and Philip s. of Henry, 2ᵈ each for wood.

Stanley. Richard s. of Robert, Thomas Thore; and Adam le Hewer, 12^d, 6^d and 12^d, for escapes.

Total of this Tourn—20^s 4^d. *i.e.* services, 12^s 6^d. Ossete, 2^s 1^d. Stanley, 3^s 2^d. Thorns, 4^d. Wakefeld, 2^s 3^d.

Sourby. Adam s. of Hugh de Lychesels, sues Hugh Wade and Julian his wife, on an agreement. Surety—William de Castelford.

Bailiff. John Cussing sues John de Heton for trespass. Surety—John Pollard.

. . . John le Mariner sues Henry s. of Robert s. of Geoffrey de Stanley, for trespass. Surety—Thomas Gates.

. . . Henry de Methele, chaplain, sues Dyonisia de Legh for trespass. Surety—John de Fery.

Thomas Bate sues Richard Proudfote, William Malyn, Richard Peger, Richard de Luppesheved, William s. of William Dolfyn, and William de Mora for debt. Surety—William de Castleford.

John s. of Robert de Ourom, sues Beatrice widow of Alexander le Weynwricht, for detaining a cow.

Sandale. James del Okes sues Thomas de Milnethorp and Emma his wife, for trespass. Surety—William del Okes.

Bailiff. Walter Gunne sues Hugh de Stanley for debt. Surety —Thomas Gunne.

John de Horbiri, clerk, sues Richard de Dewesbiry, chaplain, for trespass. Surety—Thomas le Taverner.

. . . Robert de Wa..hes sues Richard del Bothe and Thomas s. of Gilbert, for debt. Surety—Roger de Heselhirst.

Hiperum. Adam del Bothes s. of Thomas de Ourum, sues Robert de Warwlley, chaplain, for seizing cattle. Surety—Roger de Clifton.

Robert de Sourby sues Beatrice widow of Alexander le Waynwricht, for debt. Surety—John le Pynder.

———

COURT held at Wakefeld on Friday before the Feast of Pentecost (13 May) 16 Ed. II [1323].

Essoins. William de Totehill, by Roger de Grenewod. Surety —William de Castelford.

Richard de Birstall, by Thomas de Birstall. Surety— Robert de Gorton.

Thomas de Thornton, by Thomas le Taverner. Surety— Thomas de Sayuill.

Bailiff. Thomas Taluace sues Thomas de Totehill, for taking a horse, worth 13^s 4^d from his house at Fekisby. Defendant says the horse was seized in his own enclosure in le Westfeld, where he was grazing and trampling down the grass; he is ordered to make his law.

Thomas de Totehill sues Thomas Taluace for 30ˢ damage done by his cattle to plaintiff's corn crops; also John de Dyghton, for the like. Both acknowledge slight damage. No order given.

Matilda widow of Richard Forester, 3ᵈ for not prosecuting her suit against Richard de Halifax.

Sabina de Hayeley sues Robert de Warwlley, chaplain, for seizing plaintiff's goods, value 20ˢ, in the town of Northourum damages 30ˢ. Defendant is to make his law. Sureties—John and Adam del Bothe.

Adam del Bothe sues Robert de Warwlley, chaplain, for ⅛ of a bovate of land in Northowrum. Defendant says plaintiff sold the land to William Swayp, defendant's brother, for 20ˢ, and William granted it to Robert, who was to pay the 20ˢ to Adam; and Adam surrendered the land to German Filkock, then bailiff, and German surrendered it to John de Burton, then Steward, who delivered it to Robert, chaplain, to hold to himself and his heirs according to the custom of the manor. He calls the rolls to witness. Robert is ordered to furnish record of the rolls, under a suitable penalty.

Sandale. Richard le Lytester essoins against William Parmenter of Walton, by John Patrik. Surety—Adam de Wodessum.

Agnes widow of Hugh le Chapman, 2ᵈ for not prosecuting suit against Hugh Forester.

Alice d. of Robert s. of Philip de Alverthorp, appoints William de Locwode or Robert de Pikeburne her attorneys against Richard Withehundes.

. . . Henry Nelot, and Eva, widow of Simon . . . (2ᵈ) agree.

William de Schurbarwe, chaplain, (. . ᵈ) and John de St. Swythin and Alice, his wife, agree.

Thorns. Henry de Walda sues Richard Proudfot for receiving the locks of his gates of his manor of la Wodehall. Richard came to the last court and called Henry Bulweys to warranty, whom he does not now produce. He is attainted, and fined 6ᵈ

Thomas Hogge, 3ᵈ for false claim against John Attebarre.

Roger servant of William de Wakefeld, 6ᵈ for false claim against Thomas le Taverner.

Said Roger sues John Attebarre for 8ˢ as surety for John de Stanley; defendant denies he was surety; is to make his law.

Adam s. of Hugh de Lichesels, and Hugh and Julian Wade (4ᵈ) agree.

Robert s. of John Cockespore, gives 12ᵈ as a heriot on 17 acres in Stanley, after his father's death.

John Gos surrenders 2 acres and part of a bovate of meadow in Crigelston; committed to Elias de Donescastre; entry, 12ᵈ

Robert Hode surrenders 3 roods in Alverthorp; committed to Robert de Fetherston; entry, 6ᵈ

Robert Gerbot surrenders 2½ acres in Alverthorp; committed to Ralph Bate; fine for entry, 12ᵈ

Richard s. of Adam, gives 12ᵈ to take 5 acres in Rastrik from William s. of Adam, for 20 years.

Henry de Saltonstall has licence to take an acre in Agneys-hirst in exchange for one he formerly held there; 12ᵈ fine for the exchange.

William son-in-law of John le Webbester, gives 12ᵈ to take an acre of unoccupied land in the same place.

Rastrik. Robert s. of . . . , surrenders 9 acres in le Wodehous; committed to Alexander del Brighous; entry, 2ˢ

Adam de Flanshou surrenders ½ bovate in Flanshou; and he and Christian, his wife, afterwards take it again to themselves and the heirs of their bodies, with remainder, in default, to the right heirs of Adam; paying 12ᵈ for the recognition.

Alice Graffard has licence to take ½ bovate and 8 acres, with buildings, in Snaypethorp, left unoccupied by John s. of Magge, on account of the minority and inability to hold of said John s heir, until the heir is of age.

Richard Withehoundes surrenders ½ acre of meadow called le Brodole in the field of Alverthorp; committed to Henry de Swilington; entry, 6ᵈ

Elena d. of Henry s. of Hugh de Lynley, sues Henry de Totehill for a messuage and 9 acres in Fekisby . . . to one Peter Daldeson . . .

[*At least six lines torn away at the end of the sheet*].

Bailiff. Gilbert de la Lee sues Richard de Burstall for debt. Surety—John de la Lee. Gilbert appoints either William de Lock-wod or Robert de Pikeburne his attorney.

Elias Tyrsi the King's villein (*nativus*) fined 6ˢ 8ᵈ for licence to alienate the tenement he held in free burgage in Wakefeld to Robert Clement, on the condition that after seisin had Robert should re-enfeoff Elias and Milisant, his wife, for the terms of their lives, with remainder to Matilda, d. of said Elias, and her heirs. The charter is enrolled, by which Elias enfeoffs Robert of his tenement in Westgate, between that formerly held by William de Ayketon, and Matilda Rugbagge's tenement, for a certain some of money. No mention is made of re-enfeoffment. Witnesses —John de Donecastre, the King's Steward in Wakefeld; Henry de Wakefeld, bailiff of the liberty; John de Gayregrave; Thomas Aleyn, William . . . le; William de Lockwode; German Kay and others; dated at Wakefeld on Friday before the Feast of SS. Philip and James, 16 Edw. II. [29 April, 1323].

Another deed of the same date effects the sale of all Elias' goods and chattels in the said house, to said Robert.

Alverthorp. Geoffrey de Birkenschagh gives 12^d as a heriot on a toft and 7 acres in Alverthorp, after the death of Alice de Birkenschagh, his mother.

Bailiff. John le Mariner sues Henry s. of Robert s. of Geoffrey de Stanley for debt. Surety—Thomas Gates. Defendant is attached by Hugh, his brother.

Horbiry. John de Horbiri, clerk (2^d) and Richard de Dewesbiry, chaplain, agree by license.

Hiperom. William de Ryley sues Simon del Dene, Roger de Clifton, William le Squier, and John le Pynder, severally, for debt. Surety—Thomas le Taverner.

John de Skircote, 4^d; Thomas s. of Alkock, 3^d; John le Pynder, 2^d; Jordan le Pynder, 2^d; William s. of Thomas, 2^d; Jordan del Brok, 2^d; Roger de Herthill, 2^d, for vert.

Alverthorp. Geoffrey de Birkinschawe, 2^d for vert.

Wakefeld. Robert le Marescall, 2^d and John de Sculbrok, 1^d for vert.

Ossete. Richard s. of John de Ossete, 2^d, and Matilda wife of Hugh Pees, 1^d for vert.

Wakefeld. Ralph s. of Laurence, 2^d for vert.

Stanlay. William Albray, 2^d; Matilda Mous, 1^d for vert.

Wakefeld. John Cussing, 4^d; John s. of Robert, 4^d, and Isabel Sparwe, 2^d for wood.

Sandale. James Carpenter, 4^d; Thomas de Milnethorp, 4^d; John Cokewald, 2^d; Thomas Mounk, 2^d, and Henry s. of Hugh de Holgate, 2^d, for escapes, etc.

Holne. Richard de Erneschagh, 4^d; John Wlf, 6^d, and Julian widow of William, s. of Gilbert, 2^d, for vert.

Bailiff. The persons indicted at the several tourns, are to be attached.

Total of this Court—27^s 2^d *i.e.* services 7^s 10^d. Thornes 3^d. Ossete, 6^d. Saurby, 2^s 4^d. Hiperom, 2^s 2^d. Stanlay, 19^d. Alverthorp, 4^s 5^d. Sandale. 2^s 2^d. Rastrik, 3^s 6^d. Horbiry, 2^d. Wakefeld, 15^d. Holme, 12^d

Bailiff. Thomas de Seyvill sues John de Heton. for debt. Surety—John de Toftclif.

Sandale. John s. of Elias de Horbiry, sues Henry le Quarriour for debt. Surety—Adam Hoperborn.

Bailiff. Thomas del Rode sues Thomas le Taverner and William de Castelforth for seizing animals. Surety—Ivo le W . . .

. . . John Attebarre sues Richard s. of Robert de Bateley, for debt. Surety—Henry Ganton.

Richard s. of Adam de Fekesby, sues Ellen de Wakefeld for land.

[*Parts of 3 lines are torn away at the end of the membrane, all being suits entered, record of which will appear at following courts*].

COURT held at Wakefeud on Friday after the Feast of St. Barnabas the Apostle (June 11), 16 Edw. II. [1323].

Essoin. Thomas de Thorneton essoins by Thomas le Taverner. Surety—John Clerk of Horbiry.

Thomas de Totehill makes his law against Thomas Taluace, who is fined 3ᵈ

Isabel widow of Adam s. of Ivo, 6ᵈ for not prosecuting Robert de Werloulay, chaplain.

Rastrik. Thomas Taluace and John de Dighton, 3ᵈ each, because their cattle damaged Thomas de Totehill's corn.

Stanley. Hugh de Stanley and Emma Gunne (3ᵈ) agree.

Bailiff. John le Mariner and Henry s. of Robert de Stanley (6ᵈ) agree by licence.

John Cussing and John de Heton (6ᵈ) agree.

Henry de Metheley, 3ᵈ for not prosecuting Dionisia de Leghthe.

Sandale. James del Okes and Thomas de Milnethorp and Emma his wife, (2ᵈ) agree. Surety—Robert, bailiff.

Philip del Hill essoins against Peter Spink and Julian his wife, by Hugh de Aberford. John Woderoue, surety.

Recognizance. Adam Sprigonell enters into his own recognizances under a fitting penalty to pay 37ˢ to John de Dyneley.

Stanley. John Attebarre and Richard de Bateley have a love-day.

Sourby. Hugh Wade (4ᵈ) and Adam s. of Roger de Saurby, agree.

Alice le Mercer, whose fine is pardoned because she is poor, agrees with Adam s. of Hugh de Lighesels.

Bailiff. Thomas del Lighrigge essoins against Thomas de Tothill, by Richard de Birton. Surety—James de Eland.

Horbiry. Matilda d. of Jordan Sire, surrenders a toft and two acres in Horbiry; committed to John, Clerk of Horbyry; entry, 12ᵈ

William s. of Alexander, gives 6ᵈ to take 3½ acres in Horbyry from Hugh Modisaule, for two vestures thereof.

Ossete. Richard del Dene surrenders a toft in Erlesheton; committed to John, his son; entry, 6ᵈ

Rastrik. Henry s. of John, bailiff of Rastrik, gives 6ᵈ to take 1¾ acre in Rastrik, left unoccupied by Alexander le Ta . . .

Holne. John Gamell gives 6ᵈ to take ½ acre in Wlvedale, hitherto unoccupied; rent, 2½ᵈ

John del Bothe, 6ᵈ for the same; rent, 2ᵈ

Sourby. Adam s. of Hugh del Lighesels, 6ᵈ to take the dower of Alice le ? Mercer in 2 acres of land . . .

Sandale. John Feldefare surrenders an acre in Crigelston, which is committed to Henry s. of Richard de Crigelston; entry, 6ᵈ

Hiperon. Roger de Clifton surrenders 3 acres in Hiperom, and afterwards takes them again for his life with remainder to Thomas, his son; Thomas pays 12^d for the recognition.

Sandale. Warner de Carleton and Julian his wife, sue Adam de la Grene for land; also John de Wik and Henry Sprigonell. Sureties—Thomas de Holgate, and John, his brother.

Alverthorp. John Attebarre sues John Gerbot, Evol his wife, Henry del Bothom, Roger le Brodewricht, John Swan, and Christian d. of . . . for debt. Surety—Richard Withehundes.

ATTACHMENTS.

Hiperom. John Poyde, 2^d; Richard s. of Jordan, 2^d; Robert s. of Alkoc, 2^d; John his brother, . . . ; John de Birstall; John le Pynder; William s. of Alot; . . . ; . . . 2^d; . . . Monk, 2^d; Robert Aloc, 2^d; Robert Isolde, 3^d; the wife of John le Schapman, 2^d; Robert Ters, 3^d; John Attebarre, 2^d; the handmaids of William le Badger and Henry le Badger, 2^d each; Robert le Couper's wife, 3^d, for vert and dry wood.

Stanley. Richard Ricard's wife; Adam le Hewer, 6^d; Richard s. of Robert de Bateley, 12^d; William Albray [? and] G . . . le Theker, 4^d for wood and escapes.

Horbiry. William, Chaplain of Horbiry, for an escape, 6^d

Thomas de Belehous, for the same, ? 2^d. Surety—Henry de Southwode.

. . . lia de Horbiry . . .

Ossete. Thomas de Southwode, . . . , Thomas le Pynder, 1^d and Robert Scot, 1^d, for dry wood, etc.

Wakefeld. Amice de Swiligton, 1^d; William s. of Isabell, 1^d, and Ralph Bates' handmaid, 1^d for dry wood.

Ossete. Walter Maunsell, 2^d for carrying away palings.

Bailiff. John de Gairgrave, Henry de Wakfeld and William de Lokwod took from the King land and meadow at ? Luppes-heved, Papilionholm for 8 years, paying 37^s a year.

Thomas Aleyn took the Southwode, with its appurtenances, from the King, for 7 years, at . . . rent.

Sourby. Geoffrey de Sladene, 4^d for escapes. Sureties—John de Soland, Thomas de Schambandene and John de Miggeleye.

Adam de Kirkeschagh, 6^d; Richard s. of Cecilia, 8^d; Adam, del Schagh, 4^d; William s. of Cecilia, 6^d; ? John del Reduker, 6^d; Hugh del Hehlee, 1^d; Nigel le Couper, 1^d; Richard Faber, 2^d; Henry del Holgate, 3^d; Adam, s. of Hugh Frere, 4^d; Hugh Wade, 4^d, for escapes.

Holne. Hugh de Alstanley, 12^d; William de Craven, 3^d and John de Brockholes, 2^d, for vert, &c.

. . . The suit brought by Robert de Soureby and John le Pynder, against Beatrice widow of Alexander le Waynewricht, is terminated by defendant's satisfying them for the two quarters of oats for which they were sureties for the said Alexander. She is fined 3^d.

Total of this Court—25^s 5^d. *i.e.* Hiperum, 3^s 3^d

Stanlay, 2^s 3^d	Sandale, 19^d
Wakefeld, 16^d	Sourby, 8^s 4^d
Thornes, 6^d	Services, 18^d
Horberi, 2^s 4^d	Ossete, 11^d
Holme, 2^s 5^d	Rastrik, 12^d

Alverthorp. Cecilia d. of John s. of Philip de Alverthorp sues Roger le Bordwricht, Alice his wife, and Christian d. of Robert s. of Philip de Alverthorp, for land. Surety—Philip del Hill.

Horbiry. Cecilia d. of Thomas de Belhous sues Hugh del Wro for trespass. Surety—William de Castelforth. Hugh is attached by Elias de Horbiry.

Sandale. Nigel de Doncastre sues Henry Sprigonell, John de Wyke and Thomas le Pynder, for debt. Surety—William s. of Robert.

Bailiff. John de Neuson sues Adam Coly of Wodeshom for debt.

Sarah widow of Adam Miller sues Richard Alcock for debt. Surety—John de Rastrick. She also sues Robert Wyvell and William le Swqier, for debt.

Henry Ganton sues Robert Pelleson (*sic*) for debt. Surety—Thomas le Taverner.

Stanlay. Eva widow of Symon Tyting sues Richard del Ker for debt. Surety—Robert Hode of Neuton.

Sourby. William Tournour sues Dom Robert de Werwlley, chaplain, for trespass. Surety—Richard Smyth.

———

COURT held at Wakefeld on Friday after the Quinzaine of the Holy Trinity (16 June), 16 Edw. II [1323].

Essoins. Richard de Birstall, by Thomas de Birstall. Surety—William de Castelforthe.

Thomas de Bellehous, by German Filcok. Surety—John Patrik.

John de Cayly, by William de Castelforth. Surety—Thomas de Thornton.

Brian de Thornill, by Thomas de Thornill. Surety—Thomas s. of Roger.

Bailiff. Thomas del Holgate, 3^d for not prosecuting suit against John Gose.

Thomas de Totehill essoins against John de Dighton, by Robert de Gretton. Surety—John Patrik.

Isabella widow of Adam s. of Ivo, against Robert de Warlulley, chaplain, by William de Castelforth. Surety—Henry Gautrum.

Sabina de Haylay and the said Robert have a love-day.

Stanley. Richard del Ker, bailiff of Stanley, 6^d for not having the inquisition ready, that was ordered for this court.

Bailiff. John Attebarre makes the law he waged against Roger, servant of William de Wakefeld, who is fined 6^d for false claim.

Hugh, surety for his brother Henry, s. of Robert, s. of Geoffrey de Stanley, fined 3^d for not having him in court.

Matilda widow of Adam Broun, (2^d) and Hugh del Wro agree.

Henry de Metheley, chaplain, essoins against Dionisia de Leghthe by Elias de Heton. Surety—William de Birton.

John de Heton, against John Cussing, by John s. of Walter de Heton. Surety—John Patrik.

Adam s. of Thomas de Ourom, fined . . .^d for not prosecuting suit against Robert de Warloley, chaplain.

Sandale. Nicholas Fox del Nubiging surrenders 2 acres in Nubiging; committed to Thomas Munk; entry, 12^d

Alverthorp. Richard Withehoundes surrenders ½ acre in Alverthorp; committed to William de Lokwod, Alice his wife, and William their son and heir. They have entry by the Steward's grace, because William is in the King's service.

Thomas Chode gives 6^d to take 3 roods of meadow in Horbiry, from Henry s. of Adam s. of William, for 3 years.

Robert del Skoles gives 12^d to take an acre in le Skoles, hitherto unoccupied; rent, 4^d

Thomas Attewelle gives 6^d for ½ acre of unoccupied land in Wlvedale; rent, 2^d

Nicholas Keneward surrenders 2 acres in le Skoles; committed to John de la Grene; entry, . . .^d

. . . de la Grene surrenders an acre in Wlvedale; committed to John s. of Nicholas Keneward.

. . . John de Nevill pays . . . for respite of suit till Michaelmas . . . of the lord 3 acres of land in Werlouleye, which Richard de Bairstowe demised without license.

Total of this Court—8^s 2^d and new rent, 6^d. Sandale, 15^d. services, 2^s 2^d. Holne, 2^s 6^d (and new rent, 6^d). Horbiry, 8^d. Stanley, 6^d. Hiperum, 6^d.

. . . (*sic*) and Constance his daughter, sues Thomas s. of Robert Clerk, for land.

Thomas s. of Laurence, sues Richard s. of Swain, for detaining a heifer. Surety—John de Gairgrave.

Hugh Wade sues Adam s. of Roger, for trespass. Surety—John de Miglay.

Thomas del Lich Rigge sues Thomas de Totehill for seizing cattle. Surety—James de Eland.

John Attebarre sues Hugh de Stanley for debt. Surety—Robert Hode.

John s. of Elias, sues John Caynock for land. Surety—Elias de Dalton.

John le Pinder sues de Haselhirst on an agreement. Surety—Jordan le Pynder.

Johanna widow of John Teuet, sues Johanna de Langlay for dower.

COURT held at Wakefeld on Friday after the Feast of the Translation of St. Benedict the Abbot (July 11) in the beginning of the 17th year of Edw. II [1323].

Essoins. Thomas de Thornton essoins by Thomas Taverner. Surety—William de Castelforth.

William de Birton, by Richard his brother.

Bailiff. Henry Nelot and Emma Fairegh (2ᵈ) agree.

Geoffrey de Knochethorp proves a waif beast, value 5ˢ to be his. Surety—John Cussing; he pays 6ᵈ for herbage.

. . . William de Castelforth fined . . . for not having Adam Carpentar of Walton, and his wife, in court.

Hiperum. John s. of Robert de Ourom, 6ᵈ for not prosecuting his suit against Beatrice widow of Alexander le Waynwricht.

. . . Richard Proudfote and others made their law again Thomas Bate. Judgment postponed till next court.

. . . Thomas de Lichrigge fined . . . for not prosecuting suit against Thomas de Totehill.

[The rest of the membrane, as far as preserved, is taken up with orders for summonses, etc. to answer in suits already recorded; judging from the dors of the membrane, there are only 5 or 6 lines gone at the bottom].

Bailiff. John de Burton sues Thomas de Wytwod for debt; likewise Robert de Thorneleyes, John Faber, Thomas Cosyn, Richard Carpenter and Robert s. of Mabille. Surety—Thomas ? Tutche.

Hiperum. John, bailiff of Rastrick, sues Roger de Brighous for debt. Surety—Roger de Olston.

Horbiry. John de Mora sues John s. of Elyot, for debt. Surety—Thomas de Southwod.

Stanlay. Hugh le Barker and Marjory his wife, sue John s. of Philip le Syur, for debt. Surety—William de Castilforth.

In the Court of the town. Richard Withundes sues German Philcock for trespass and debt. Surety—Richard de Collay.

Sandale. Henry Tasse sues Thomas de Holgate for trespass. Surety—William de Castilforth.

Total of this Court—2ˢ 4ᵈ *i.e.* Heperum, 6ᵈ
    Wakefeld, 2ᵈ   Sourby, 6ᵈ
    Services, 12ᵈ   Horberi, 2ᵈ

COURT held at Wakefeld on Friday, the Feast of St. Oswald
(Aug. 5) 17 Edw. II [1323].

Essoins. William de Tothill, by William de Castilford. Surety
—William del Okes.

Richard de Byrstal, by Robert de Grotton, Surety—William
de Lockewod.

John Hode, by John de Sandale.

William de Byrton, by Richard de Byrton.

Hyperum. Sabyna de Haylay, 6^d for not prosecuting her suit
against Robert Chaplain of Warlelay.

The rolls searched shew Adam del Bothe's claim against said
Robert is unfounded. Adam's fine is pardoned, because he is poor.

Bailiff. Thomas de Ketelisthorp and Cecilia his wife, agree
with Adam Carpenter of Walton, and Amice his wife (6^d) by
licence. Likewise with Matthew Attewelle (6^d).

Richard le Lyster appears against William Skinner of Walton,
on an agreement; and as William has nothing on which to distrain,
except 2^s, in the hands of the said Richard, this 2^s is seized as
distraint; and Richard is allowed to withdraw from further
prosecution till William comes.

Peter Spink and Julian his wife, and Philip del Hill have a
love-day.

Thornes. Thomas Bate fined 12^d (?), and Richard Proudfote,
William Malyn, Richard Peger, Richard de Luppesheved, William
s. of William Dolfyn, and William de Mora, acquitted.

Stanlay. Richard de Batelay acknowledges [? he owes]
John Attebarre 14^s; fine, 3^d

Sandale. Constance de Castelford, 3^d for withdrawing from
her suit against Thomas s. of Robert Clerk.

Hyperum. John Pynder fined 3^d for not prosecuting suit
against Roger Haselhirst.

Sandale. Warner de Carleton and Julian, his wife (3^d) and
Adam de la Grene agree. Surety—John del Wyke; to agree with
whom they also pay 3^d

Saurby. William Turnur, 6^d for withdrawing his suit against
Robert de Warloley, chaplain.

[8 *lines follow almost entirely eaten away, or obliterated by
damp; only a word here and there remains*].

Hiperum. William de Ryelay sues Symon del Dene for 38^s
he owes him for tithe sheaves sold by Andrew Forester, his attorney; likewise Roger de Clifton for 30^s for the same. Both defendants deny; an inquisition ordered.

. . . Thomas Pelleson, for an escape, 2^d

James Monck, for vert, 2^d

. . . Elyas Bulnays, for an escape, 2^d

Wakefeld. John de Amyas for an escape, 6^d

Holn. Nicholas s. of John Keneward, 4ᵈ; William s. of William de Heppeworth, 4ᵈ; Philip le Lyster, 2ᵈ; John s. of Roger de Langlay, 3ᵈ; Emma de Langlay, 3ᵈ, for escapes, etc.

Hiperum. Roger de Haselhirst, 3ᵈ; John de Holway, 2ᵈ; Henry Horne, 2ᵈ; Matilda widow of Henry Abraham, 2ᵈ; Robert s. of Christian, 2ᵈ; Symon s. of Jordan, 2ᵈ; Hugh del Wro, 1ᵈ; John de Birton of Kerlinghewe, 2ᵈ; William Graffard, 2ᵈ; and Philip s. of Henry, 2ᵈ for vert, etc.

Wakefeld. Thomas Chode's son, 1ᵈ; Adam le Hewer, 2ᵈ, and Jordan le Mawer, 3ᵈ for escapes, etc.

Alverthorp. John Gerbot, 4ᵈ for escape.

Stanley. Robert de Mickelfeld, 4ᵈ; Richard Picard, 3ᵈ; Hugh le Cartwricht de Methelay, 2ᵈ; surety, Hugh Skayf; John del Bothem, 2ᵈ; Richard s. of John Poket, 3ᵈ; William Cissor of Lofthouses, 3ᵈ for dry wood, etc.

John Isabell for bark, 8ᵈ

Sandale. Adam Sprigonel, 3ᵈ; Henry Sprigonel, 2ᵈ, for vert. Thomas Lewelyn, 4ᵈ for old piles from the new mill.

Hyperum. Peter de Thornioles, 6ᵈ; Thomas s. of Alkok, 2ᵈ; William de Aula, 2ᵈ; Henry de la Rode, 2ᵈ; Richard de Thorp, 2ᵈ; Thomas del Clif, 2ᵈ; Thomas s. of Henry, 3ᵈ; William s. of Richard s. of Walter, 3ᵈ, for dry wood, etc.

Total of this Court—14ˢ 10ᵈ *i.e.*	
Ossete, 3ᵈ	Horbiry, 2ᵈ
Stanlay, 2ˢ 5ᵈ	Services, 18ᵈ
Thornes, 18ᵈ	Alverthorp, 4ᵈ
Sourby, 6ᵈ	Sandale, 22ᵈ
Wakefeld, 12ᵈ	Holne, 16ᵈ
	Hyperum, 4ˢ 2ᵈ

COURT held at Wakefeld on Friday after the Feast of St. Bartholomew the Apostle (Aug. 24), 17 Edw. II [1323].

Essoins. Brian de Thornhill, by Thomas Torald. Surety—William de Castelford.

Hugh de Stanlay, by William de Castelford. Surety—William del Okes.

Thomas de Thorneton, by Thomas le Taverner.

James del Okes, by William de Castelford.

Richard de Byrstal, by John Woderouc. Surety—German Kay, John Hode, by William Filche.

Stanlay. Hugh de Stanley essoins against Walter Gunne, by Hugh de Aberford.

Bailiff. Thomas de Seyuill and John de Heton (6ᵈ) agree.

Sandale. Warener de Carleton, and Julian his wife, 2ᵈ for not prosecuting suit against Henry Sprigonel.

Rastrick. Richard s. of Adam de Fekysby sues Ellen de Wakefeld for 7 acres in Fekysby, of which one Agnes his kins-woman, was seised, from whom the right descended to one Ivo her uncle and heir; from him to Adam, his son, and from Adam to Richard his son, the plaintiff . . .

[*Here great part of several lines is torn away, so that nothing can be read consecutively*].

Thomas le Pynder and John de Wyke, 3ᵈ each for not having one another in court.

Bailiff. Adam Coly of Wodesom essoins against John de Neusom by Robert de Stodelay. Surety—Thomas, s. of Laurence.

Sarah widow of Adam Miller, in the mercy for false claim against Richard Alcock. Fine pardoned because she is poor.

[*Several lines, at least, are torn away at the end of the membrane*].

Alverthorp. William de Byrkynschagh sues Geoffrey de Byrkynschagh his brother, for mowing a meadow belonging to plaintiff, while he was ill, carrying away grass worth 5ˢ. An inquisition is to be taken.

He said Geoffrey sues said William for 6¾ acres in Alverthorp, as his inheritance after his father's death, which land his father acquired from Alice, his mother, before they were married; and Geoffrey is her heir. William says their father had no rights therein, except by marriage with their mother, whose inheritance it was; and that after their father's death, Alice gave the land to defendant. An inquisition to be taken.

John Torald and Edusa his wife, sues the said Geoffrey, for closing up a pathway they are accustomed to have through his courtyard; Geoffrey brings a cross-charge of trampling corn, etc. An inquisition ordered.

Bailiff. John de Burton sues Thomas de Sayuill for 20ˢ as surety for John de Heton, who bought from him certain tithe sheaves (*decimates*) of Dewysbury parish, which church the said John holds to farm. The debt acknowledged; fine, 6ᵈ

Stanlay. John s. of John Pollard, surrenders a rood in Ouchethorp, committed to Henry de Swinlington; entry, 6ᵈ

Alverthorp. Richard Gerbot surrenders 1¾ acre in Alverthorp; committed to John Gerbot, entry, 12ᵈ

Agnes d. of William s. of Walter, gives 12ᵈ as a heriot on a messuage and 7 acres in Alverthorp, after his father's death.

Stanlay. Alice Pollard surrenders 2½ acres in Ouchethorp; committed to Walter Gunne; entry, 12ᵈ

Emma Gunne surrenders 7 acres in Ouchethorp; committed to Walter Gunne; entry, 12ᵈ

Walter Gunne gives 2ˢ to take a messuage and 9 acres in Ouchethorp from Emma Gunne, his mother, for 7 years.

Ossete. John Broun surrenders 6½ acres in Erlesheton; committed to John del Dene; entry, 2ˢ

Sandale. Constance d. of Roger de Castilford, grants to Thomas s. of Robert the Clerk of Sandale, her rights in a messuage and bovate of land in Sandale. Thomas pays 2ˢ for the recognition.

Hyperum. Ivo le Wester ?, for 3 young oaks cut down, 40ᵈ William Cissor, 4ᵈ; William Peck, 8ᵈ; John s. of Roger, junior, 6ˢ 8ᵈ; Symon del Ker, 6ᵈ; Symon del Dene, 2ˢ; Mathew s. of Richard, 12ᵈ; John de Holleway, 12ᵈ; John Attetounend . . .; Adam de Hyperum, . . .; Ivo le Webster . . .; for branches cut, etc. (*Three lines are torn away*).

Total of this Court—34ˢ 10ᵈ *i.e.* Services, 12ᵈ

Sandale, 2ˢ 8ᵈ		Alverthorp, 3ˢ 6ᵈ	
Horbiry, 2ᵈ		Stanley, 7ˢ	
Ossete, 2ˢ		Hyperum, 18ˢ 6ᵈ	

Robert Carpenter sues Robert Clement for land. Surety—William Carpenter.

Bailiff. John s. of Robert de Wittelay, sues John de Mora and Henry le Quarreour, for debt. Surety—William de Castelford.

Wakefeld. William s. of William Jonot, sues Richard s. of Henry, for land.

Peter de Acom sues John Pollard on an agreement.

Alverthorp. Eva, widow of William s. of Walter, and Agnes d. of the said Eva, sue John Pollard, baker, for trespass. Surety—Attebarre. John Pollard brings a cross-suit against said Eva.

COURT held at Wakefeld on Friday after the Exaltation of the Holy Cross (Sept. 14), 17 Edw. II [1323].

Essoins. John de Mora, by Thomas le Taverner. Surety—John Pollard.

William de Byrton, by Richard de Byrton. Surety—William de Castelford.

Adam Sprigonel, by William Grenehod.

Thomas Caylly, by the same.

Stanlay. Hugh le Barker and Margery, his wife, and John, s. of Philip le Syur, have a love-day.

Bailiff. Richard de Byrstall acknowledges he owes Gilbert de la Leye 13ˢ 4ᵈ for a horse; fine, 6ᵈ

Thomas de Tothill essoins against John de Dichton, by John Patrick. Surety—Thomas de Belhous.

Philip del Hull, 3ᵈ for sundry defaults.

Peter Spinck sues Philip del Hill for seizing a sheep belonging to him, worth 3ˢ, in Scnaipthorp. Defendant ordered to make his law. Surety—Elyas de Doncastre.

Walter Gunne sues Hugh de Stanley for 5ˢ, as surety for John Titing in the purchase of a horse; damages, 4ˢ. 4ˢ is acknowledged. Each to make their law. Sureties—John s. of Robert, and Richard Skayf.

Bailiff. Richard de Waddesworth and Roger del Grenwode, 12ᵈ for not having Robert del Bothe in court.

. . . Sarah widow of Adam Miller, fined . . .ᵈ, for not prosecuting suits against Robert Wynell and William Squyer.

. . . John Attebarre and Hugh de Stanlay, agree. Fine . . .

. . . Henry Tasse and Thomas del Holgate agree. Fine . . .

Agnes wife of Lance, and James del Okes, have a love-day.

Ossete. Richard s. of Swayn, 12ᵈ for withdrawing suit against Thomas Laurence.

Thomas de Lichrigge by Richard de Byrton, his attorney, sues Thomas de Tothill for seizing his cattle in the bounds of Fekysby, in le Estrode. Defendant justifies the seizure because one John s. of Henry, holds le Estrode . . . by homage and fealty, and at 4ˢ rent, which is 18ᵈ in arrears . . .; the matter is postponed till next court.

[Ceci]lia d. of Thomas de Bellehous, and Hugh del Wro (. .ᵈ) agree by license.

. . . John de Fery surrenders ½ acre in le Rodes; committed to John Clement; entry, 12ᵈ

Hyperum. Thomas s. of Alexander le Waynwricht, gives 12ᵈ as a heriot on 2 acres in Hyperum, after his father's death. By Roger de Clifton he surrenders the said land, which is committed to John le Pynder; entry, 18ᵈ

Stanlay. William as the head of the town of Stanlay gives 18ᵈ to take ½ bovate, with buildings in Stanleye from John ? Titing . . .

Wakefeld. Roger Priest and Rosa his wife, sue William Cussing for land, which is to be taken into the King's hand for William's failing to answer.

Sandale. William s. of William de Sandale, gives 5ˢ as a heriot on two bovates in Sandale, after his father's death.

Alverthorp. Richard de Collay surrenders 3 roods in Alverthorp fields; committed to Henry de Sw[inlington?]; entry, 6ᵈ

Sourby. John s. of Hugh de Balidene, 2ᵈ; Adam de Notteschaghe, 3ᵈ; William s. of Dobbe del Grenehirst, 3ᵈ; Magola del Wode, 2ᵈ; Richard le Barker de Ourum, 4ᵈ; Adam del Kyrkeschagh, 6ᵈ, and the miller of Miggelay, 6ᵈ for escapes.

Bailiff. An inquisition finds Alexander del Frith and Alan del Heye, have [? obstructed a pathway] in Skambandene, by a ditch. They are attached to answer thereon to the Steward, by . . . John s. of the said Alexander, Hugh del Hill and John de Scambandene.

Ossete. Richard s. of John, 3ᵈ; Adam s. of Ralph, 3ᵈ; Thomas le Pynder, 3ᵈ; Thomas de Bellehous, 2ᵈ; Hugh de Chideshill, 2ᵈ; Jordan Scuet, 2ᵈ, and Emma Peny, 2ᵈ, for escapes.

Alverthorp. John Gerbot, 3ᵈ; Richard s. of Robert, 3ᵈ; Henry del Bothem's widow, 3ᵈ; John le ? Campion's wife, 2ᵈ, for escapes.

Stanlay. The wife of John s. of Hugh, 3ᵈ for an escape.

Wakefeld. Henry Nauthird's wife, 2ᵈ for the same.

Horbiry. Philip Damysell sues Gilbert Day for debt. Surety —Thomas Taverner.

Services. Philip de Castelford sues Robert Schort on an agreement.

Alverthorp. John Erl sues Robert Hode of Neuton for debt. Surety—Henry de Wakefeld.

Nicholas de Bateley sues the said Robert for taking a horse. Surety—Thomas Bille.

Services. Thomas Taluace sues Thomas de Totehill for trespass. Surety—William s. of Roger.

Thomas de Tothill sues John de Dighton for trespass. Surety—Thomas del Wode.

Sandale. Robert Pelleson sues Thomas s. of Hugh de Hollegate, for trespass.

Thornes. Ellen d. of Richard Junne, sues Richard de Luppesheved for land. Surety— . . .

Services. John de Denieton, parson of Sandale church, sues Adam de Wodesom and William . . . for debt. Surety—John de Walton, clerk.

He likewise sues Thomas Pelleson, Henry le Quarre[our], . . . Ketilthorp, carpenter, for debt.

Total of this Court—21ˢ 4ᵈ *i.e.* Horbiry, 6ᵈ

Wakefeld, 14ᵈ	Hyperum, 2ˢ 6ᵈ
Stanley, 2ˢ	Alverthorp, 2ˢ 7ᵈ
Sourby, 2ˢ 2ᵈ	Services, 2ˢ 5ᵈ
Rastrick, 4ᵈ	Sandale, 5ˢ 3ᵈ
Ossete, 2ˢ 5ᵈ	

Grand total—£13 : 8ˢ : 2ᵈ *i.e.* Services, 52ˢ 2ᵈ

Ossete, 12ˢ 3ᵈ	Horbiry, 6ˢ 6ᵈ
Holne, 19ˢ 5ᵈ	Wakefeld, . . .
Rastrik, ? 7ˢ	Stanley, 25ˢ 8ᵈ
Alverthorp, 17ˢ 2ᵈ	Hiperum, 51ˢ 1ᵈ
Thornes, 2ˢ 7ᵈ	Sandale, 15ˢ 5ᵈ
Sourby, 40ˢ 2ᵈ	

COURT held at Wakefeld on Friday after the Feast of St. John before the Latin Gate (May 6), 17 Edw. II [1324].

Essoins. John de Heton, by Nicholas Fleming. Surety— John de Hopton.

Brian de Thornehill, by Thomas de Hopton.
John Hode, by William de Castilford.
John de Mora, by William Cussing.

Horbiry. Nicholas le Fleming and Johanna, his wife; waged and made their law against Hugh in le Wro of Horbiry, who is fined 2ᵈ (*sic*)

Bailiff. James de Eland, 6ᵈ for not prosecuting suit against Thomas de Totehill for seizure of cattle.

The said Thomas, 14ᵈ for withdrawing 7 separate suits against the said James and Adam, his servient, for seizing cattle.

John de Burton sues Roger de Clifton for debt. Surety—William de Castilford.

Thornes. John Bulnais in the mercy (fine not entered), for not prosecuting suit against John s. of Elias de Horbiry.

John de Dinieton, parson of Sandale church, essoins against Adam de Wodesom and William del Okes, by William Cussing.

Holne. Robert s. of Thomas de Frelyston, 6ᵈ for not prosecuting suit against Richard s. of Michael, and Adam de Butterlay, for debt.

Horbiry. Philip s. of Roger de Snaipthorp, sues Alan, servingman of John de Horbiry, for a mare worth 13ˢ 4ᵈ killed in Alan's garden at Horbiry. An inquisition is ordered.

Bailiff. Robert s. of Walter de Stanlay, and Hugh de Stanlay (3ᵈ) agree.

Sourby. William de Scnape, in mercy for not procecuting suit against John de Hirst for trespass.

Rastrik. Thomas Faber of Skamandene surrenders 2 acres in Skamandene; committed to Alexander del Frith; entry, 12ᵈ; also 2 other acres, committed to John del Styhill of Bothomlay; entry, 12ᵈ, and one acre committed to John, s. of William del Frith; entry 6ᵈ

William le Turnour of Scamandene surrenders an acre there; committed to Alan de la Heye; entry, 6ᵈ

Holne. Richard de Carteworth and Ellen, his wife, surrender 2 acres in Alstanley; committed to John del Hole; entry, 12ᵈ

Alverthorp. Richard de Collay surrenders 2 acres in Alverthorp; committed to Thomas Bunny; entry, 12ᵈ

Total of this Court—8ˢ 1ᵈ *i.e.*   Horbiry, 3ᵈ
Services, 23ᵈ   Thornes, 2ᵈ
Holne, 18ᵈ   Sourby, 3ᵈ
Rastrik, 3ˢ   Alverthorp, 12ᵈ

Mabel Waynwright sues William s. of Hugh de Lighaseles, and Margery, his wife, for trespass. Surety—John s. of Robert de Sourby.

William s. of Dobbe de Crigelston, sues Alexander Wodecok for trespass. Surety—Adam Sprigonel.

Thomas s. of Robert de Milnethorp, and Emma, his wife, sue James del Okes and Agnes his wife, for trespass. Surety—Thomas de Katilthorp, James and Agnes bring a cross suit.

William de Birkynschagh sues Geoffrey de Birkynschagh for trespass. Surety—John Attebarre.

Thomas s, of John de Hengeclif, sues John s. of Hugh de Alstanley, for trespass. Surety—Richard s. of Hobbe.

Richard de Cuthworth, chaplain, sues Richard, chaplain of Hertesheved, for debt. Surety—Robert de Grotton.

Agnes Trubbe sues John Nalkeson for debt. Surety—Robert Pelleson.

COURT held at Wakefeld on Friday, the 1st of June, in the year abovesaid. [1324].

Essoins. Richard de Birstal, by Robert de Grotton. Surety—William Filche.

Thomas de Thorneton, by Robert de Mora.

William de Totehill, by Thomas de Totehill. Surety—Henry de Swillington.

Holne. Thomas de Carteworth, 6^d for not prosecuting suit against Hugh de Thornelay and Elias de la Graunge for debt.

Stanneley. Agnes del Bothm, in mercy[1] for the same against Richard Poket.

Bailiff. John de Dinieton, Rector of Sandale church, 12^d to agree with Adam de Wodesom and William del Okes, who acknowledge they owe him 20^s

Horbiry. An inquisition finds that Philip s. of Roger de Snaypthorp, complains without cause against Alan, serving-man of John de Horbiry.

Sandale. William s. of Dobbe de Crigelston, and Alexander Wodecok (4^d) agree.

Thomas s. of Robert de Milnethorp, and Emma, his wife, sue James del Okes and Agnes, his wife, for assault by Agnes on Emma. Jury finds damages, 12^d. Fine, 4^d. James and Agnes sue for assault on Agnes by Thomas and Emma, claiming 100^s damages. Plaintiffs fined 4^d for false claim.

Holne. Thomas s. of John de Hengeclif to recover damages, 6^d against John, s. of Hugh de Alstanlay, for suing him maliciously for blocking up a path in Thwonge. Fine, 6^d

Hiperum. Geoffrey s. of Richard de Schelf, sues William de Castilford on an agreement. Surety—Symon del Dane.

Sourby. Hugh s. of Hugh de Lighasles, 2^d for false claim against Adam, s. of Roger, 2^d for not prosecuting another suit

---

[1] In mercy, *i.e.*, will be amerced, fined.
‘ But I'll *amerce* you with so strong a fine,
That you shall all repent the loss of mine.’
Shakespeare, *Romeo and Juliet*, III, 1.

against him; and Adam, 2^d for detaining 14^d from Hugh; and 2^d for licence to agree.

John le Schephird, 4^d for not doing suit at the mill.

Alice de Bentelayrode, 3^d for a pair of hand mill-stones in her possession.

William le Spener fines 12^d for licence to have an axe and hatchet to cut down . . . and burn ashes of alders, etc. Surety for his good behaviour—Roger de Grenewode.

John Culpoun, 18^d for an escape.

Election of Stock Keepers. Henry de Warlullay and Thomas de Heitfeld are elected stockkeepers for Sourebyschire.

Sandale. James le Lorimer of Ketilthorp surrenders 2 acres in Crigelston, demised to Matilda, his daughter, with remainder, if she died without heirs, to the said John (*sic*) and his heirs; entry, 12^d

Alvirthorp. Agnes widow of Hugh le Chapman surrenders an acre in Neuton; committed to Thomas le Roller; entry, 6^d

Stanneley. John Tyting of Stanley surrenders 2½ roods in Stanley in le Kirkefeild, afterwards demised to Hugh, s. of Geoffrey de Stanley; entry, 6^d

Horbiry. Henry s. of Adam s. of William, surrenders 1¼ bovate in Horbury, demised to Roger del Lane and Alice, his wife; entry, 3^s

Rastrik. Thomas de Staynland surrenders an acre in Scambandene, demised to Adam, s. of William; entry, 8^d

Thomas le Harper surrenders an acre there, demised to the same; entry, 8^d

William le Turnour surrenders 2 acres there; demised to Richard del Frith: entry, 16^d

Hiperum. Matthew de Totehill surrenders 3 acres in Hiperum, demised to William Pek; entry, 20^d

Richard s. of Tibbe, surrenders an acre there to the same; entry, 6^d

Alvirthorp. Robert de Mora surrenders an acre in Alvirthorp, afterwards demised to Henry, s. of Reginald de Swilington; entry, 3^d

Thomas s. of Walter Bille, surrenders 3 roods in Neuton to the same; entry, 3^d

Sourby. Adam s. of Roger de Sourby is elected bailiff, and sworn.

Election of Bailiff. Rastrik. Richard s. of Peter, is elected bailiff of Rastrik.

Holnefrith. John de la Grene, bailiff of Holnefrith.

Sourby. Little John de Cokcroft, 2^d; Henry de Cokcroft, 3^d; John de Cokcroft, 4^d; Henry de Godelay, 4^d; Thomas s. of Robert de Risheword, 4^d; William de Snape, 2^d, and Robert de Walrunwalle, 6^d, for withdrawing from suit of the mill.

Stanneley. John de St. Swithin, 6^d for vert.

Wakefeld. John Dade, 2ᵈ; John de Rideker, 4ᵈ; Henry de Holgate, 2ᵈ; Thomas s. of Elias, 3ᵈ; Adam Culpoun, 2ᵈ; Geoffrey s. of Hill, 6ᵈ, and Matthew de Kirkeschagh, 12ᵈ for escapes.

Thornes. Robert Edmund's widow: Hugh Viroun and Roger Viroun, 2ᵈ each, for dry wood.

Wakefeld. William Damisel's wife; the handmaids of Robert le Mareshal, Philip Fidekyn, and William de la More; Richard s. of Robert; Isabel Sparwe; William Lacer's widow; Robert Liftfast and John Goldsmith, 1ᵈ each for the same.

Hiperum. Thomas s. of Henry del Rode, 3ᵈ; John, s. of Henry Faber, 2ᵈ; Julian de Aderesgate, 3ᵈ; Peter del Barm, 2ᵈ, and William Miller of Brighouse, 2ᵈ for the same, etc.

Total of this Court—22ˢ 6ᵈ *i.e.* Thornes, 6ᵈ

Wakefeld, 11ᵈ	Services, 12ᵈ
Rastrik, 2ˢ 8ᵈ	Holne, 12ᵈ
Stanneley, 15ᵈ	Horbiry, 3ˢ 2ᵈ
Sandale, 2ˢ	Sourby, 5ˢ 10ᵈ
Alvirthorp, 12ᵈ	Hyperum, 3ˢ 2ᵈ

Alverthorp. John Attebarre sues Robert Hood for trespass. Surety—German Kay. He is attached by William de Ouchethorp.

Ossete. Hugh de Disteford sues Richard, s. of John, for debt. Surety—Robert Gunman.

Holne. Richard del Bothem sues John del Hole for trespass.

Adam de Butterlay sues Thomas de Billeclif, Nicholas s. of Simon, and Richard de Elwardhuls for trespass.

Rastrik. Adam de la Lee sues Thomas de Totehill for seizing cattle. Surety—John de Geirgrave.

John, vicar of the church of Rothewell, sues Hugh de Stanneley for trespass; and appoints John Dautrine. Surety— John de Stoke.

Bailiff. Robert Blawer sues Richard, chaplain of Hertesheved for trespass. Surety—Henry de Swylington. Robert appoints Robert de Grotton his attorney.

John de Lynneley sues Thomas de Totehill for seizing an ox.

COURT held at Wakefeld on Friday, the 22nd of June in the year abovesaid.

Essoins. Brian de Thornehill by William Filche, clerk. Surety—Robert de Mora.

John de Cailly, by Adam de Midelton. Surety—Elyas Tyrsy.

Richard de Birstal, by Robert de Grotton. Surety—Henry de Swylington, clerk.

Adam Sprigonel, by Robert de Mora.

Alvirthorp. John s. of Richard de Osset, by William de Castilford, his attorney, sues Roger le Bordwright. The bailiff returns that Roger has nothing on which to distrain, except land; this is therefore to be taken into the lord's hand till he comes.

Hyperum. John de Burton and Roger de Clifton agree.

Bailiff. Roger de Radeclif, 2ᵈ for not prosecuting suit against Thomas Fernoule and Adam de Butterlay.

Hyperum. John, bailiff of Rastrik, and Roger de Clifton (4ᵈ) agree.

Robert de Ligchasles (6ᵈ) and Adam de la Leghth agree. Surety—Roger de Grenewod.

Sourby. Ambilla Waynwright (2ᵈ), and Hugh de Ligchasles and Julian his wife, agree. Surety—John s. of Robert de Sourby.

Services. Robert Blawer and Richard, chaplain of Hertesheved (12ᵈ) agree.

Rastrik. Adam de la Lee essoins against Thomas de Totehill, by John de Geirgrave; surety, William Erl. Thomas says the essoin does not lie, because Adam was seen in court, and this is sworn to by the suiters; wherefore Thomas is acquitted, and Adam fined 3ᵈ

John de Lynneley, 3ᵈ for not prosecuting suit against Thomas de Totehill.

Holne. Adam de Butterlay sues Thomas de Billeclif, Nicholas s. of Simon, and Richard de Elwardhuls, for having indicted him as a thief, which led to his being taken to York gaol and imprisoned there; damages, 5 marks. An inquisition is ordered.

Thornes. John Dade surrenders an acre in Thornes; demised to Matilda d. of Henry Bull; entry, 6ᵈ

Horbiry. John Clerk of Horbiry surrenders a toft and 2 acres in Horbiry; demised to Thomas Betuel (?); entry, 18ᵈ

Alverthorp. John Cussing surrenders an acre in Alverthorp; demised to Robert Gelleson and Constance, his wife; entry, 6ᵈ

Holne. John s. of Nicholas Kenward gives 2ˢ to take 2 acres of unoccupied land in Wulvedale.

Thornes. Agnes and Alice daughters of John s. of Richard, give 16ᵈ as a heriot on a messuage and ½ of two bovates in Thornes, after the death of Elizabeth, their sister, whose heirs they are.

John s. of Richard le Wayte gives 3ˢ 4ᵈ as a heriot on 8 acres in Thornes after his father's death.

Sandale. John s. of Robert Clerk of Sandale, gives 2ˢ as a heriot on 4 acres in Sandale after his father's death.

Thomas s. of John de Littilwod, surrenders a messuage and 14¾ acres in Littilwood, after his father's death; demised to William, s. of the said John; entry, 5ˢ

Recognisance. William de Ouchethorp acknowledges he owes John Sibbeson the crop of a rood of land sown with oats. Surety—Robert Hood.

Ossete. Richard s. of John de Osset, sues Adam s. of Adam de Hoperborn, for debt. Surety—Thomas Hog.

Robert Pelleson sues John s. of Elias, Hugh del Wro, Henry le Prestman, and all their neighbours on an agreement. Surety—William de Ossete.

Ossete. Robert Peny de Chideshill; Jordan Scot; Hugh de Chideshill; Adam le Oxehird; Thomas le Pynder; Richard s. of John Attounende, and Henry de Ourum, 2^d each; William s. of Richard de Osset, 3^d for escapes, etc.

Thornes. Robert s. of Ivo; William Graffard, and John Baret of Snaipethorp, 2^d each for dry wood.

Total of this Court—21^s 3^d *i.e.* Ossete, 17^d

Hyperum, 10^d	Services, 14^d
Sourby, 8^d	Rastrik, 6^d
Thornes, 5^s 8^d	Horbiry, 18^d
Alverthorp, 6^d	Holne, 7^s
Sandale, 2^s	

Bailiff. Thomas de Totehill sues John de Toptklif for debt. Surety—Richard s. of Peter de Rastrik.

Wakefeld. Johanna widow of Robert Estrild, sues Robert s. of Walter, and Amabilla, his wife, for land. Surety—Robert de Gratton.

Sandale. Margery de Coventre sues John de Wik for debt. Surety—John Sibbeson.

Hyperum. Adam de la Lee sues Thomas de Totehill for seizing cattle. Surety—John de Geirgrave.

John de Lynneley sues said Thomas for seizing an ox.

Stanneley. Robert s. of Richard de Stanneley, sues Henry Poket for trespass. Surety—Robert de Leper.

Richard Pescy sues Hugh de Stanneley and Robert s. of Walter, for debt. Surety—John Poket.

Alvirthorp. John s. of Hugh le Chapman, sues Thomas le Roller for land. Surety—John Attebarre, Thomas appoints William Erl his attorney.

COURT held at Wakefeld on Friday, 13th July, 18 Edw. II [1324].

Essoins. Hugh s. of Robert s. of Geoffrey de Stanneley, by Robert de Mora, Surety—William Erl.

Thomas de Thorneton, by Robert de Mora. Surety—Robert de Grotton.

John de Heton, by John de Hopton. Surety—John de Querneby.

Sandale. Agnes Trub in the mercy for not prosecuting suit against John Nalleson.

Alverthorp. John s. of Richard de Ossete, the same, against Roger le Bordwright.

Bailiff. Robert Nodger and Beatrice his wife (6ᵈ) and William Sausemer agree by licence.

Alverthorp. An inquisition finds that Geoffrey de Birkynschagh carried away 2 cartloads of hay belonging to Alice de Birkynschagh, after said Alice's death; to the damage of William de Birkynscagh, her executor, 3ᵈ. Fine, 2ᵈ; and 2ᵈ for detaining 2 cows, value 18ᵈ, from said William.

John Attebarre and Robert Hode of Neuton (4ᵈ) agree.

Osset. Hugh de Disteford and Richard s. of John (4ᵈ) agree.

Holne. John del Hole and Richard del Botham (12ᵈ) agree.

Bailiff. Adam de la Lee sues Thomas de Totehill for seizing 2 oxen in a place called la Lee in the town of Lynneley, and driving them to his manor of Fekesby, etc.; damages, 20ˢ. Thomas says the oxen were seized grazing in an enclosure of his called la Lee, and submits whether this seizure made in his own enclosure can be tried in this court without the King's writ. The Court find that it cannot. The oxen are therefore to be returned to Thomas, and Adam is fined 2ᵈ for false claim.

Judgment in a similar suit by John de Lynnelay against the said Thomas, to be given at the next court.

Ossete. Thomas Hog and John Maunsel (2ᵈ) agree.

Alverthorp. John s. of Hugh le Chapman sues Thomas le Roller for an acre in Alverthorp, which his father took in court in the time of Henry de Walda, Steward; and which, after his father's death Agnes, his wife, sold to the said Thomas, contrary to right and the custom of the manor. Thomas says Agnes joined with Hugh in taking the land; and had the right to sell. The matter postponed till next court.

Bailiff. William de la Lee sues Thomas de Totehill for trespass. Surety—John de Geirgrave.

Osset. 12 acres in Erlesheton, which were lying unoccupied, for want of a tenant, committed to William, s. of Richard Baycok of Dewesbiry; entry, 40ᵈ

Alverthorp. Matilda and Johanna daughter and heirs of John de Flansowe give 2ˢ for licence to heriot on a messuage and a bovate of land in Alverthorp, after their father's death.

Sourby. A messuage and an acre of land in Warlullay, lying unoccupied, committed to Roger de Hertlotrode and Alice, his wife; entry, 6ᵈ

Hyperum. Henry de la Rode of Hiperum surrenders 3 acres there; demised to Thomas s. of Henry de la Rode, junior; entry, 2ˢ

Thomas Fernoule of Fouleston surrenders 3¼ acres in Fouleston; committed to Thomas, his son, entry, 18ᵈ

Stanneley. Richard de Bateley, Adam le Hewer, John Isabel, Richard de Collay, John Flachard, Hugh Cort and Robert de Wyronthorp, 2ᵈ each for escapes.

Total of this Court—13ˢ 10ᵈ *i.e.* Stanneley, 13ᵈ
       Osset, 3ˢ 10ᵈ   Sandale, 3ᵈ
       Alverthorp, 3ˢ   Services, 8ᵈ
       Holne, 2ˢ 6ᵈ   Sourby, 6ᵈ
       Sourby, 6ᵈ   Hyperum, 2ˢ

Bailiff. Henry Nelot sues Robert s. of Ivo, for treapass. Surety—Robert de Mora.

Rastrik. Adam de la Lee sues Thomas de Totehill, for seizing cattle. John s. of Philip de Lynley sues the said Thomas.

Stanneley. Walter Gunne sues John Campyon for trespass. Surety—John Attebarre.

Sandale. Alina widow of Robert s. of Adam, sues Henry s. of Hugh, for dower. Surety—John Monk.

———

COURT at Wakefeld on Friday after the Feast of St. Peter and Vincula (Aug. 1) in the year abovesaid [1324].

Essoins. Thomas de Thorneton, by Robert de Mora. Surety —Thomas de Totehill.

William de Birton, by German Kay. Surety—William le Wright.

Richard de Birstal by Thomas de Birstall. Surety—William del Okes.

Alverthorp. Roger le Bardwright to be distrained to answer for sundry defaults.

John Dautrine, chaplain, attorney of John, vicar of Rothewell, essoins against Hugh de Stanley by John Woderoue. Surety— Henry Clerk.

Hugh de Stanley, against the said vicar by Hugh Pikard. Surety—Henry Clerk.

Stanley. Robert s. of Richard de Stanley, and Henry Poket (6ᵈ) agree.

Wakefeld. Rosa, widow of Roger Preest, sues William Cussing for land. Surety—Robert le Wriht.

An inquisition finds that the ½ acre of land claimed by Johanna widow of Robert Estrild, and Thomas her son, against Robert s. of Walter, and Amabilla his wife, belongs to Amabilla after the death of her father, John Chaffar. Plaintiffs fined 2ᵈ

Sandale. John Nalkson makes his law against Adam Sprigonel and Thomas Clerk, regarding a cart worth 3ˢ; they are fined, 4ᵈ

Osset. Thomas de Seyuill and Hugh de Disteford (6ᵈ) agree.

Wakefeld. Robert s. of Walter, and Amabilla his wife, and Julian sister of Amabilla, give 6ᵈ for licence to heriot on 1¼ acres in Wakefeld after the death of John Schaffar father of the sisters, whose heirs they are.

Sandale. Thomas s. and heir of Robert Beausir, 18^d for the same on 3$\frac{3}{4}$ acres in Sandale after the death of his father; which he surrenders; they are committed to Thomas s. of Roger, for 8 years; entry, 12^d

John le Shepehird surrenders a rood in Sandale, to William de Osset of Sandale; entry, 6^d

Rastrik. Thomas de Lihtrigge sues Thomas de Totehill for trespass. Surety—Richard, his son.

Total of this Court—5^s *i.e.*   Stanneley, 6^d
     Wakefeld, 8^d Sandale, 3^s 4^d
     Ossete, 6^d

Alvirthorp. Henry Nelot sues Robert Hood of Neuton for trespass. Surety—John Attebarre.

Stanneley. Robert Wayte sues William Isbel for trespass. Surety—William, servient of Thomas Nundy. He also sues Henry de Twyford.

———

COURT held at Halifax on Tuesday after the Feast of St. John the Baptist (June 24) 17 Edw. II [1324].

Sourby. Ellen del Feld sues John s. of William del Bothom, because his dog throttled one of her sheep, value 3^s; damages taxed at 2^s. Fine, 6^d

Roger de Stanbiry, 2^d for false claim for debt against William del Ridding.

William del Ridding sues said Roger for having him arrested without cause by the bailiff of Thomas, late Earl of Lancaster, and causing his corn, growing on land at Saltonstall to be put in defence in the autumn three years ago; damages, 10^s. Roger says the land in question was his land. An inquisition is ordered. They afterwards agree, William paying 4^d

William le Couhird sues John s. of Magge, for default in keeping up his fences, etc.; damages, 20^s. A jury taxes damages at 6^s 8^d; fine, 6^d

John s. of Robert de Sourby, and William s. of Hugh de Lihchasles (3^d) agree.

Robert Warloley, chaplain, executor of the will of William de Warloley, sues Richard Faber for 8^d. They afterwards agree, Richard paying 3^d, and 3^d for an agreement in another matter.

William s. and heir of Hugh de Lihchasles sues Hugh Wade for 18 acres in Lihchasles, as his right after his father's death. Defendant says the father of plaintiff surrendered the land in a court held at Halifax by John de Donecaster, and that it was committed to Robert, his son; Robert afterwards committing the land to his father for his life. And after his father's death Robert entered; whereupon plaintiff sued him, and an agreement was made by which William was to have 5 acres of the said land,

and Robert the remaining 13, which defendant bought of Robert in Court. An inquisition confirms defendant. William fined 2^d

Robert de Warloley, chaplain, and Henry s. of Ley, 2^d agree.

Ellota de Castro, 6^d; John Maynard, 3^d, surety, John de Miggeley; John de Hadirshelf, 2^d; Roger de Grenewode, 4^d, and John Culpoun, 2^d for escapes.

John del Rediker, 1^d; Robert de Wolrunwall, 2^d; William del Smalleye, for the same.

Total of this Court—4^s 6^d. All from Sourby.

TOURN there the same day.

Sourby. Hugh Wade drew blood from William, his brother, 12^d; Julian Wade, 6^d for the same.

John s. of Matthew del Wade, from John de Wales, 4^d

Sarah wife of Bate, 2^d; and Matilda wife of John de Kipas of Heptonstall, 3^d for brewing, etc.

John le Harper, 3^d; Matthew de Shipeden, 6^d; Richard del Sikes, 12^d for not coming.

Total of this Tourn—5^s, and all from Sourby.

COURT held at Rastrik the Wednesday following.

Hiperum. Cecilia and Margery daughters of William del Bothes, by Richard del Shagh, their attorney, sue Thomas de la Rode of Hiperum, Roger de Clifton and John le Pinder, for withholding from them 60^s for which they were sureties for Andrew Forester; damages, 20^s. The debt is acknowledged, fine, 18^d

Avice widow of William de Hiperum surrenders 2 acres in Hiperum ; committed to Jordan le Pinder; entry, 12^d

An inquisition finds that John le Pinder owes John s. of Richard de Rastrik, 10^s, for which he was surety for Richard Forester, because he had nothing on which to distrain; fine, 3^d

Roger de Clifton sues Thomas del Wodeheved for 12^d for a fine for breaking the lord's fold in the time of Thomas Deyvill, Steward; the fine is proved by an entry on the roll, and an order made for payment; fine, 3^d

An inquisition finds that John s. of Stephen, and Matilda his wife, wrongfully withhold 14^d from Matilda d. of Roger del Brighouse; damages, 2^d; fine, 2^d

John de Burton sues Thomas Baude for 16^s, which he acknowledges; fine, 2^d

William Pek fined 3^d and to pay damages to Thomas de Totehill, for carrying off his grass, value 2^d

Robert de Rissheworth recovers 2^s against John . . . for two sheep sold him; fine, 2^d; also two quarters of corn against Roger de Hasilhirst; fine, 3^d; and 3^s 1^d against said Roger; fine, 2^d

Robert de Warloley, chaplain, executor of the will of William de Warloley, and the said Roger (4^d) agree.

Roger de Hasilhurst recovers 4^s 2^d against Robert de Risshe-worth; fine, 4^d

Thomas de Totehill recovers 2^s against Henry Horn, being the rent of a house for 4 years; fine, 2^d

The imparlance between John de Burton and William de Mirfeld, terminated because John de Burton is dead.

William Yonghare, 1^d; and John Pinder of Ourum, 1^d, for dry wood . . .

John Pinder of Hiperum, 1^d; Richard de Shippeden, 1^d; John de Bucsc . . . , 1^d; Beatrice Lyly, 2^d, for dry wood and vert.

Total of this Court, 6^s 10^d all from Hyperum.

TOURN there the same day.

John de Holway, 3^d; John le Seyuill, 12^d, for not coming.

John de Lihtrigge, 12^d, and William del Hole, 6^d for raising the hue without cause.

William le Milner, 12^d; Hugh le Milner, 2^s 6^d, and Richard Grotton, 12^d for drawing blood.

COURT held at Holne the same day.

Holne. William de Mada . . ., forester of Holne, charged by the Steward with making false charges in his bailiwick, finds sureties—Thomas de Billeclif and Henry de Birton.

Bailiff. 21^s 8^d to be levied on Adam de Butterley, Adam de Horne, Thomas Fernoule and Richard de Staneley to the use of Roger de Radeclif, to whom they were sureties for William Fernoule.

Holne. Adam le Tailur and Richard Child sue Richard de Thorntlay, who sold them a fourth part of the tithe of mill-toll of Carteworth, without being able to guarantee the same, being prevented by Dom. Robert de Barneby, rector of Birton church, who claims the same as belonging to his part of Birton church. And Richard de Thorntlay, proctor for Master Thomas de Tynwell, portioner of the said church, says he was in a position to sell the said tithe of toll in the name of said Thomas, his master. An inquisition finds the sale was good; plaintiffs fined 4^d for false claim.

Robert del Wades sues Richard del Bothe for 10^s; 6^s 8^d is acknowledged; a jury find the remaining 3^s 4^d is not owing; Robert fined 6^d

Adam le Bagger and Robert Clerk, both of Birton, come before the Steward at Birton and find sureties for their mutually keeping the peace; for Adam—John de Riley and Gilbert s. of Julian de Birton; for Robert—Robert le Milner and John Kithusband.

John s. of John de Thwong, surrenders 14 acres in Thwong; committed to Adam Strekeyse; entry, 6ˢ 8ᵈ

Total of this Court—8ˢ 4ᵈ, and all from Holne.

TOURN there the same day.

Holne. Gilbert del Mersh, 12ᵈ for drawing blood from John Robinman.

Adam Bate's wife, 3ᵈ; Johanna d. of Christian, 3ᵈ; William de Whitteley's wife, 1ᵈ for brewing, etc.

John Kithusband, Henry s. of Henry, and Henry le Taylur, 6ᵈ each for breaking the assize of bread.

John Aliceson; Henry le Smithson; John del Birches; John le Dauber; John de Shellay, senior, and Henry le Smith, 6ᵈ each for not coming.

Total of this Tourn—6ˢ 7ᵈ all from Holne.

COURT at Wakefeld on Friday after the Feast of St. John the Baptist (June 24) in the year abovesaid [1324].

Ossete.   Thomas de Ceyuill sues Hugh de Disteford for setting his dog on to worry plaintiff's sheep; damages, 20ˢ. An inquisition is to be taken.

Alvirthorp.   Thomas s. of John le Taylur of Alvirthorp, pays 6ᵈ for licence to heriot on 2 acres in Alvirthorp, on the death of his father.

Sandale.   Adam Sprigonel and Thomas Clerk of Crigelston, and the whole of the community of that town who were indicted for the death of John Patrik, William and John, his sons, and who lost thereby altogether £8, came before the Steward and begged that the townships of Sandale, Bretton and Horbiry might bear their share of the said £8, because they were at the taking, imprisonment and death of the said John, William and John, together with the applicants and others of the township of Crigleston, which was the fourth town involved. The communities of the said three townships say they were present at the taking of John, etc., with the township of Crigleston, and took them to Wakefeld prison, and there left them in prison in the custody of the bailiffs of the town of Wakefeld, and afterwards went away. And after they had left, and without their assent, the prisoners were taken out of the prison, and led to Agbrigg, and there killed. An inquisition finds the said townships joined in taking the men from the prison. Afterwards the townships of Sandale and Horbiry say they are not and never have been answerable with the township of Crigleston before the itinerant Justices, and that therefore they ought not to be obliged to share in the said £8. An inquisition is to be taken.

Rastrik. John de Eland by John s. of Richard, bailiff of Rastrik, surrenders two acres of new land in Fekesby; committed to John de Totehill; entry, 2ˢ

Total of this court—2ˢ 6ᵈ Alvirthorp, 6ᵈ
Rastrik, 2ˢ

TOURN there the same day.

Bailiff. The township of Stanneley, 6ᵈ, Ossete, 4ᵈ, and Erdeslouwe, 4ᵈ for contempt.

Richard de Collay, 2ᵈ; John Swan, 2ᵈ; William Alayn, 3ᵈ; Richard de Eccleshill, 3ᵈ, and William le Grayne, 3ᵈ for not coming.

Elias de Dalton and Robert Dipsy, 6ᵈ each, for drawing blood from Richard de Whitteley.

Peter de Whitteley, from Robert Dipsy, 12ᵈ

James de la Halle, 3ᵈ for not coming.

Henry le Hyme drew blood from William Beaufuere, 12ᵈ

Ralph Ryendecunt, from John de Deneby, 6ᵈ

Margery, wife of William de la More, from John Malyn, 12ᵈ

Richard s. of Richard de Bouderode, from Robert Shurting, 6ᵈ

William de Ouchethorp from John Thorn, 6ᵈ

Robert le Webster from Gilbert, serving-man of Robert Fichir, 6ᵈ

Agnes, wife of James del Okes, from Emma de Milnthorpe, 12ᵈ

John Hobbeson and Thomas Bunny, for blocking up a road, 12ᵈ

Agnes, d. of William de Neuton, 4ᵈ for being deflowered.

Robert de Chikkinley, 3ᵈ for concealing a waif, which is taken to the use of the lord.

The wife of John de Holgate, 6ᵈ, of William Dobbeson, 6ᵈ, of Adam de la Grene, 6ᵈ; of John de Wyk, 3ᵈ; of John Payn, 3ᵈ; Agnes Jonkynwif, 3ᵈ; Paulinus de Emmelay, 6ᵈ; William le Hyne, 6ᵈ, and Margery le Carter, 6ᵈ, for brewing, etc.

Alice Scot, 6ᵈ; Margery Trubbe, 3ᵈ; the wives of Adam del Wodehouse, 2ᵈ; John Hudson, 3ᵈ, and Henry le Prestman, 3ᵈ, for the same.

John Malle, Hugh Besse, John de Wyk, John le Harpour, Henry le Quarreour, and John Payn, 3ᵈ each for perjuring their oaths.

Henry Tasche, 12ᵈ; William Pollard, 3ᵈ, and Agnes, d. of Walter Hog, 2ᵈ for raising the hue without cause.

Henry Tassche drew blood from Adam s. of Philip de Castilford, 12^d

William s. of Robert de Castilford, 6^d for the same.

John Mous from Matilda, d. of John Joise, 6^d

Johanna Laundere from Julian Gurdon, 6^d; fine forgiven.

Adam Grenehod 6^d for raising the hue without cause.

COURT held at Wakefeld on Friday, the Feast of St. Bartholomew the Apostle (Aug. 24) 18 Edw. II [1324].

Essoins. William de Tothill, by Thomas de Tothill. Surety— Robert de Grotton.

John de Heton, by John de Hopton. Surety—Nicholas Flemyng.

Bailiff. William de Castelford essoins against Geoffrey s. of Richard de Schelf, by German Swerd. Surety—Robert de Mora.

Margery de Coventre, in mercy for not prosecuting suit against John de Wyk; pardoned, because she is poor.

Hugh de Stanneley essoins against John, vicar of Rothwell, by John Gledeholt. Surety—Henry Clerk.

Alvirthorp. An inquisition finds that Hugh le Chapman and Agnes his wife, conjointly took an acre in Alvirthorp, before Henry de Walda, then Steward. Agnes therefore had the right to sell it after her husband's death to Thomas le Roller. John s. of of the said Hugh, fined 4^d for false claim.

Wakefeld. Rosa widow of Roger le Prest, 3^d for not prosecuting suit against William Cussing.

Sandale. An inquisition, taken by the oath of Robert de Wyronthorp, Thomas de Ceyuill, Thomas del Belhous, German Filcok, William Erl, Thomas Alayn, Richard de Birstall, William de Birton, Henry de Cheuet, Thomas Gates, John Cailly and Hugh de Stanneley, find that the townships of Walton and Wakefeld are answerable with Sandale and Crigeleston in the case touching the Crown at Agbrigg; and that the township of Horbiry is not answerable. Also that Robert Pelleson of Sandale, who sued Hugh del Wro, Henry le Presteman, and other inhabitants of Horbiry, in the said matter, made a false claim; fine, 6^d

Alvia widow of Robert s. of Adam, recovers against Henry s. of Hugh, her dower in a messuage and 12 acres in Sandale; fine 6^d

Bailiff. Robert le Wayte sues William Isabell for assault in the town of Wakefeld. Defendant is to make his law. Surety— Robert de Mora. Robert also sues Henry de Twyford for the same, and an inquisition is ordered.

Wakefeld. Rosa widow of Roger le Preest, sues William Cussing for land. Surety—Robert Carpenter.

Rastrik. Thomas de Stainland surrenders 12 acres in Scambandene, granted to William del Hole; entry, 5^s

Thornes. Johanna Dade surrenders ⅝ acre in Thornes; committed to Thomas de Lepton; entry, 6ᵈ

Wakefeld. William s. of William Jonot, surrenders 6 acres in Wakefeld; committed to William s. of Robert Carpenter; entry, 2ˢ

Sandale. John de Sandale, clerk, surrenders a messuage and 4 acres in Sandale; committed to Matilda, his sister; entry, 2ˢ

Matilda d. of Robert Clerk of Sandale, surrenders a messuage and 7¼ acres in Sandale; committed to Robert de Sandale, chaplain, for 5 years; entry, 3ˢ 4ᵈ

John s. of Nalk, surrenders a cottage in Crigeleston; committed to Agnes Trub, entry, 6ᵈ

Thornes. Robert de Luppesheved surrenders 3 acres in Thornes; committed to Henry de Swynlington, clerk, for 12 years. The Steward grants him licence to take the land gratis.

Thomas s. of John de Sandale, sues John de St. Swythin and Alice his wife, for 2 tofts and a bovate of land in Sandale. Defendants made default, and the land in question was therefore taken into the King's hand by William Whitbelt, . . . Carpenter, William del Okes and James del Okes; and they were summoned by John s. of Geoffrey de Sandale. Alice says John has no rights in the land, except as her husband; and is to make her defence.

Wakefeld. John Wlmer, 4ᵈ; Thomas le Carter, 1ᵈ; Ralph Bate, 1ᵈ; Henry de Welda, 3ᵈ; Robert Rodde, 1ᵈ; John Cussing, 2ᵈ; William Lacer's wife, 2ᵈ; Ibota Sparou, 2ᵈ; Matilda Tropinel, 2ᵈ; Robert Capon, 2ᵈ; Philip Pikescull, 2ᵈ; Walter Ape's son, 2ᵈ; Margery, his sister, 2ᵈ, and Walter Stedeman, 3ᵈ for dry wood, etc., etc.

Ossete. Moke de Ossete, 1ᵈ; John del Dane, 2ᵈ, for dry wood.

Sandale. William s. of Thomas Fissher, 3ᵈ; John Cokewald, 2ᵈ; Henry de Holgate, 2ᵈ; for escapes.

Hiperum. Symon le Stedeman, 6ᵈ; William s. of Richard s. of Walter, 2ᵈ; John s. of Thomas Poyd, 2ᵈ; Richard de Thorp, 2ᵈ; John le Pynder, 2ᵈ, and Thomas del Rokes, 2ᵈ, for escapes, etc.

Alvirthorp. John Swayn, 2ᵈ for an escape.

Stanneley. Johanna de Wodehall, 2ᵈ; Agnes d. of William s. of Walter, 2ᵈ; Richard s. of Robert, 2ᵈ; ?Henry Cort, 2ᵈ; John s. of Hugh Forster, 2ᵈ; Walter Gunne, 4ᵈ, for dry wood, etc.

Robert Ricard, 3ᵈ; Thomas Odam, 2ᵈ; Alice, handmaid of Thomas Gunne, 2ᵈ; Agnes sister of Thomas Hyam, 3ᵈ; William Hardy, 2ᵈ; John servant of Walter, 3ᵈ, for breaking palings, etc.

Sourby. Thomas de Waddesworth, 4ᵈ; John de Hadirschelf, 3ᵈ; Roger de Grenewode, 8ᵈ; Adam Culpon, 4ᵈ; John de Rediker, 4ᵈ; Geoffrey de Cressilegh, 2ᵈ; for escapes, etc.

Total of this Court—24ˢ 11ᵈ

Bailiff. Thomas s. of German Filcok, sues John de St. Swithin for seizing cattle . . . He is attached by Thomas Gunne. He also sues Richard, servant of Matilda de Miggeley . . .

Stanneley. John Attebarre sues Richard s. of Robert for trespass, etc. . . .

Holne. Hugh del Hole sues Thomas Fernoule, and Thomas and Richard his sons

Robert Nalleson sues Thomas Thore, Thomas le Taverner,

COURT held at Wakefeld on Friday, the Feast of the Exaltation of the Cross (Sept. 14), 18 Edw. II [1324].

Essoins. William de Birton, by Richard de Birton . . .

Thomas de Ceyuill, by Thomas de Belhous. Surety—Robert de Mora.

William de Tothill, by German Kay. Surety—Henry de Gouton.

Thomas de Thorneton, by Robert de Mora. Surety—William Cussing.

John de Heton, by John de Hopton. Surety—John de Gledeholt.

Bailiff. Henry de Stanneley fined 8ᵈ for not having his brother Hugh in court.

William de la Lee essoins against Thomas de Tothill, by John s. of John de Gairgrave. Surety—German Kay.

Thomas s. of German Filcok, against John de St. Swithin, by John Pollard . . .

Thornes. Henry Nelot, and Robert s. of Ivo, (6ᵈ) agree. Surety—William Graffard.

Alvirthorp. The said Henry and Robert Rodd (3ᵈ) agree.

Bailiff. Roger le Perci, distrained by a cow to answer John de Burton, fined 3ᵈ for not coming.

William Isabel made his law against Robert le Wayte; fine, 4ᵈ

Rosa widow of Roger le Preest, sues William Cussing for 5½ acres of land in Wakefeld, after the death of Gerard Cussing, her uncle, whose heir she is. Defendant says Gerard Cussing surrendered the land through William le Taillur, then bailiff, and it was committed to John Cussing in the time of John de Donecastre, Steward. An inquisition is to be taken.

Stanneley. John Attebarre sues Richard s. of Robert, for 6ˢ; 5ˢ is acknowledged; fine 3ᵈ. The defendant to make his law as to the odd 1ˢ.

Holne. Hugh del Hole, 3ᵈ for not prosecuting suit against Thomas Fernoule and his sons.

Bailiff. John s. of Nalk, sues German Philcok, executor of Henry de Wakefeld, for a cow worth 30ˢ, which Henry took from John, whilst he was bailiff of the free court of Wakefeld. The cow is taken into the King's hand.

Stanneley. An inquisition finds that Richard s. of Robert, depastured animals on John Attebarre's land; damages, 4ˢ; fine 3ᵈ

The said Richard sues the said John for not keeping up his fences; an inquisition to be taken.

Bailiff. Thomas s. of John de Walton, sues John de St. Swithin and Alice his wife, for land. The land to be taken into the King's hand, by reason of fresh default of Alice; order given to that effect to the bailiff of the free Court.

Wakefeld. Thomas s. of Laurence, for an escape in Lyndon, 2ᵈ

Alvirthorp. Henry del Weld, 2ᵈ, and Adam le Hewer, 4ᵈ for the same. Robert Hood of Neuton, 2ᵈ, and Richard del Ker, 6ᵈ for vert, etc.

John Cussing surrenders 3½ acres in Alvirthorp; committed to Thomas Kay and Alice his wife, after the death of John Cussing; entry, 12ᵈ

Total of this Court—5ˢ 1ᵈ	Holne, 3ᵈ
Bailiff, 15ᵈ	Alvirthorp, 2ˢ 5ᵈ
Wakefeld, 2ᵈ	Thornes, 6ᵈ
Stanneley, 6ᵈ	

Bailiff. John de St. Swithin sues German Filcok and Thomas his son, for seizing cattle. Surety—Robert de Lyedes.

Beatrice d. of Thomas de Fekesby, sues Thomas de Tothill, for trespass. Surety—John s. of Henry de Rastrik.

Rastrik. Thomas de Lighterigge sues Thomas de Tothill for land.

Bailiff. Thomas Gunne sues German Filcok and Thomas his son, for seizing a cow. Surety—John de St. Swithin.

———

COURT held at Wakefeld on Friday next after Michaelmas, 18 Edw. II [1324].

Essoins. Ralph de Sheffeld by William Alayn. Surety—William Attekirk.

William de Nevill, by Hugh le Nodder. Surety—Henry de Swilington.

Matthew de Bosco, by Henry Tasshe. Surety—German Kay.

William de Totehill, by Robert de Mora. Surety—Thomas de Totehill.

John de Burgh, by John de Sandale.

Richard de Birstall, by William Cussing. Surety—Thomas de Birstall.

Attorney. William de Nevill appointed Hugh le Nodder his attorney to do suit of court.

Bailiff. Thomas de Totehill essoins against Thomas de Lihtrigge by German Filcok. Surety—William Filche, clerk.

John s. of Richard de Shelf, and William de Castilford 3ᵈ agree.

John, vicar of Rothewell, 4ᵈ for not prosecuting suit against Hugh de Stanley.

Stanneley. Richard Pesci, 3ᵈ for the same.

John Campion, 4ᵈ, and 18ᵈ damages, at the suit of Walter Gunne, for removing a bridge by which plaintiff had the right of carrying his corn.

Bailiff. John de Lynneley, 5ᵈ for not prosecuting suit against Thomas de Totehill.

Adam de la Lee sues Thomas de Totehill, for coming to Adam's house in the town of Lynneley, and driving two oxen thence to his own house in the same town, keeping them from Monday till Saturday; damages, 100ˢ; they were delivered by the sworn bailiff, known by the name of Robert. Defendant says he found the cattle in his enclosure called la Lee, feeding on his grass, and chased them to Adam's house, and there took them. Adam denies this, and wages his law. Thomas says he ought not to be admitted to make his law, because it is a real action, and law can be made only in a personal action; and on this they both seek judgement.

Henry de Twyford essoins against Robert le Wayte by William Cussing. Surety—Laurence de Castley.

Bailiff. Thomas de Whitewod 2ᵈ for not coming to answer John de Burton.

John de Burton and Roger de Percy (4ᵈ) agree.

Thomas Cosin, 2ᵈ; Richard le Couhird, 3ᵈ; John s. of Oliver, 2ᵈ; Richard s. of Cecilia, 2ᵈ; Walter le Turnour, 3ᵈ, and John le Hunter, 2ᵈ, for not coming to answer John de Burton.

Stanley. Richard s. of Robert, failed to make his law against John Attebarre for 12ᵈ debt; fine, 3ᵈ; and 2ᵈ for another false claim.

Wakefeld. Rosa widow of Roger le Preest, 6ᵈ for not prosecuting her suit against William Cussing.

Alverthorp. Thomas s. of John, surrenders 2 acres in Alvirthorp; committed to Agnes wife of Richard Withoundes; entry, 12ᵈ

Sourby. Thomas le Crouther surrenders a messuage and 7¼ acres in Sourby; committed to Thomas s. of John del Hole; entry, 40ᵈ

Hyperum. William Pek surrenders a toft containing one rood in Hyperum, committed to John s. of Stephen; entry, 12ᵈ

Alvirthorp. John Gerbod surrenders ½ acre in Alvirthorp; committed to Robert de Swylington; entry, 6ᵈ; and another 6ᵈ for ½ acre surrendered by Richard de Collay.

Thornes. Richard s. of John Pymme, a minor, and William de Abirford and Isabella his wife, Richard's guardians, surrender ½ bovate in Thornes; committed to Thomas Bate for 12 years; entry, 2ˢ 6ᵈ

Sandale. Robert Faber of Sandale gives 12^d to take 3 acres in Sandale of the land formerly belonging to Thomas Cocus, at 5^d an acre.

Thornes. Richard s. of John Pymme, and his guardians, surrender ½ bovate in Thornes; committed to Henry de Swilington for 12 years; entry only 12^d, because the land is poor and of hardly any value.

Bailiff. The land for which Thomas s. of John de Walton, sued John de St. Swithin and Alice his wife (taken into the lord's hand by default of Alice, admitted defendant, by William Whitbelt, John s. of Thomas Carpenter, William and James del Okes) is awarded to plaintiff owing to continual default of defendant, who is fined 3^d for ousting him wrongfully.

Sir John le Flemeng, knight, 12^d, and William de Langefeld, 6^d for not coming. Both these fines forgiven.

Sir John de Eland, knight, 12^d for the same.

Alvirthorp. Henry de Swilington, clerk, has licence to take a piece of land and meadow in Alvirthorp, called Coushotedole, given into the lord's hand by John Gerbod; for 12 years.

Stanley. Robert Tropinel sues Hugh s. of Hugh Scaif, for debt, etc. Surety—Robert de Mora.

Total of this Court—16^s 10^d, and new rent, 15^d per annum.

Sourbi, 3^s 4^d	Bailiff, 4^s
Thornes, 3^s 6^d	Stanley, 12^d
Hyperum, ? 12^d	Wakefeld, 6^d
Holne . . .	Alvirthorp . . .

Sandale, 12^d and new rent, 15^d per annum.

Bailiff. Thomas de Livirsege sues Richard de Selby, chaplain of Hertesheved for trespass, etc.; and Richard de Lihtrige for the same. Surety—Robert de Grotton.

———

COURT held at Wakefeld on Friday after the Feast of SS. Simon and Jude (Oct. 28) 18 Edw. II [1324].

Essoins. John de Eland, by John Sibbeson. Surety—Robert de Grotton.

Brian de Thornhill, by John de Hopton. Surety—Thomas de Livirsege.

Thomas de Bellehous, by Robert de Mora. Surety—Robert de Whiteley.

John de Shipdene, by Roger de Clifton. Surety—Robert de Mora.

Hugh le Nodder, attorney of William de Nevill, by German Kay. Surety—Henry Clerk.

William de Birton, by John de Grenegate.

Bailiff. John de Toftclif, against Thomas de Totehill, by Walter de Thinglowe.

William de la Lee, against the same, by German Filcok. Surety—John de Geirgrave.

Thomas de Lihtrige, 4ᵈ, for not prosecuting suit against Thomas de Totehill.

Essoins. Thomas de Thornton essoins by Adam de Coplay. Surety—William Cussing.

Thomas s. of German Filcok, against John de St. Swithin, by Henry Tasshe. Surety—German Liverd. Also against Thomas Gunne, by William Tirsy.

The inquisition pending between Robert le Wayte and Henry de Tuiford respited until the next Burgess Court of the town of Wakefeld, because Robert is a burgess of the said town, and the offence was committed there.

Bailiff. John de Burton sues Thomas de Whitewade for 39ˢ 11¾ᵈ, being part of 54 marks to be paid in instalments by Richard chaplain of Hertesheved, for the tithe sheaves of the church of Dewesbiry of the chapel of Hertesheved, together with the altarage of the said chapel of Hertesheved, for payment of which defendant was surety. The debt is acknowledged; fine, 6ᵈ

Thomas Cosyn, Richard le Couhird, John s. of Oliver, and Walter le Turnur acknowledge they owe said John 39ˢ 11¾ᵈ each, as part sureties for the above sum; each fined 6ᵈ

Adam de la Lee, 4ᵈ, for not prosecuting his suit against Thomas de Totehill; the two beasts to be returned to Thomas.

Holne. Hugh del Hole, plaintiff, and Thomas Fernoule, and Thomas and Richard, his sons (6ᵈ) agree.

Richard de Lihtrige and his surety, Richard Cordwaner, 2ᵈ for the former's not coming to answer Thomas de Totehill.

Essoins. Hugh de Stanneley essoins from suit by Thomas s. of Laurence.

Matthew de Bosco, by Adam s. of Roger. Surety—Robert de Mora.

Holne. William de Legh surrenders 9¼ acres in Holne, committed to Alice d. of Richard Child; entry, 2ˢ 6ᵈ

Stanneley. John de Heton surrenders a messuage and 1¼ acre in Stanneley; committed to Henry Poket, entry, 6ᵈ

Henry Poket acknowledges he owes Thomas Broun 27ˢ

Sandale. Thomas s. of Roger de Crigleston surrenders 2⅜ acres in Crigleston; committed to John le Harper; entry, 12ᵈ

Wakefeld. John s. of William, 2ᵈ for escape of beasts in Thurstanhagh

Philip Damysell, 2ᵈ for an escape in Stocklay coppice.

John s. of Hugh Chapman, 2ᵈ; Henry Bagger, 1ᵈ; William de Sandale's wife, 1ᵈ; William le Lacer's daughter, 1ᵈ, for dry wood.

Ossete. Robert Sonman; Adam de Goukthorp, and Hugh de Disteford, 2ᵈ each for dry wood.

Robert Ricard, 6ᵈ for dry wood.

Henry de Walda, 6ᵈ for a horse caught and taken from the new park without license.

Alvirthorp. Richard de Collay surrenders 1⅞ acres in Alvirthorp; committed to John Swerd; entry, 6ᵈ; and 6ᵈ for entry into one rood surrendered by Richard Withoundes.

William le Parker surrenders 3½ acres there; committed to Henry de Swilington, clerk; entry, 6ᵈ

Stanneley. Henry de Swilington surrenders a rood in Stanneley; committed to William le Parker, entry, 6ᵈ

Total of this Court—12ˢ 1ᵈ	Bailiff, 3ˢ 4ᵈ
Holne, 3ˢ	Stanley, 2ˢ
Sandale, 14ᵈ	Wakefeld, 7ᵈ
Alvirthorp, 18ᵈ	Osset, 6ᵈ

John Attebarre sues Richard de Collay and William de Birkinschagh for debt. Surety—Robert de Mora.

Richard del Bothe sues John Gerbod for debt.

COURT held at Wakefeld on Friday, the Feast of St. Edmund, Bishop and Confessor (Nov. 16), 18 Edw. II [1324].

Essoins. Hugh le Nodder, attorney of William de Nevill, by Robert de Mora. Surety—Thomas de Wakefeld.

John de Heton, by John de Hopton. Surety—William de Heton.

John de Shipdene, by Thomas de Wakefeld. Surety—Robert de Mora.

Brian de Thornhill, by German Kay.

Bailiff. William de la Lee, against Thomas de Totehill, by Thomas Torald.

Thomas s. of German Filcok, sues John de St. Swithin, for taking 2 of his horses from a place called Colyhall in the town of Stanneley, to John de Geirgrave's house in Wakefeld; they were delivered by the sworn bailiff, German Kay; damages, 20ˢ. Defendant says he took the horses as bailiff of Matilda de Miggeley, and asks her assistance in the defence, which is granted.

The said Thomas sues Richard, servant of Matilda de Miggeley, in a similar matter; a similar permission is given.

John de St. Swithin sues German Filcok for taking 2 cows from his croft in Stanneley, and driving them to his own house in Wakefeld; damages, 20ˢ. German says he seized the cows in the croft, as in his enclosure, feeding on his grass, and submits to the court whether he is bound to answer concering his own enclosure, except under the King's writ, and applies to have the cows returned; which is granted.

Thomas Gunne sues German Filcok on a like charge; a similar defence and order made.

Robert Nalleson sues Henry Tasshe, Thomas Thore and Thomas le Taverner, if he is present, for carrying off his cow, worth 20ˢ, from Stanneley, and driving her to Wakefeld, 1 Nov. 1324; they still keep her; damages, 100ˢ. Henry Tasshe denies the charge, and is to make his law; sureties, German Filcok and German Swerd. Thomas Thore says the cow was eating the plants in his garden, and that he gave her over to Thomas le Taverner, under-bailiff of Henry de Wakefeld, then bailiff of the free-court of Wakefeld. Robert seeks judgment on the acknowledgment of the seizure &c. of the cow. The suitors of court find for the recovery of the cow by Robert, with damages; he is fined 3ᵈ. The cow and damages taxed at 5ˢ

Bailiff. John de Toftclif, 3ᵈ for not coming to answer Thomas de Totehill.

Robert Tropinel (6ᵈ) and Hugh Skaif agree.

John de Burton, 3ᵈ for not prosecuting suit against John le Hunter; and 3ᵈ for the same against Adam s. of the widow, and Elias Faber.

William de Mirfeld to be attached to answer John de Burton; he is dead.

Beatrice d. of Thomas de Fekesby, 3ᵈ for not prosecuting suit against Thomas de Totehill.

Rastrik. Matthew de Totehill, 2ˢ for licence to marry Beatrice his daughter.

Osset. John Maunsel, 12ᵈ to marry Eva his daughter.

Sandale. Elias Goldhor surrenders 3½ acres in Sandale; committed to Robert s. of John de Crigleston, for 18 years; entry, 18ᵈ

Stanneley. Johanna d. of Thomas de Milnethorp, gives 4ᵈ for licence to heriot on a messuage and 13 acres in Stanneley after the death of Richard del Ker, whose heir she is.

Holne. Peter s. of Ralph de Cartworth, surrenders a messuage and 20½ acres in Cartworth; committed to Nicholas Wade; entry, 6ˢ 8ᵈ

Hyperum. John del Bothe, 3ᵈ; Hugh s. of Richard de Mixendene, 2ᵈ; Adam del Bothes, 3ᵈ; Adam Poydeson, 2ᵈ; John Dobson of Haldeworth, 3ᵈ; John s. of Matilda de Haldeworth, 1ᵈ; Thomas s. of Julian de Ovendene, 3ᵈ; Elias de Sculcote, 3ᵈ; William del Hyngandrode, 2ᵈ; Adam de Stainclif, 1ᵈ; Henry le Hucher, 2ᵈ; William s. of Richard de Shipdene, 2ᵈ; John de Holway, 3ᵈ; Simon del Dene, 3ᵈ, for escapes.

Sourby. Adam del Kirkshagh, 12ᵈ for an escape in le Withnes.

Geoffrey del Crossilee, 12ᵈ; Amoria de Stadeley, 2ᵈ; Ellota del Castilstede, 4ᵈ; William Clerk, 4ᵈ; John del Rediker, 6ᵈ; John Culpoun, 12ᵈ; Hugh de Totehill, 12ᵈ; Thomas del Dene, 6ᵈ; William Miller, 2ᵈ; John Miller, 2ᵈ; Alcok de Ovendene, 6ᵈ, and Roger de Grenewode, 8ᵈ for escapes.

Wakefeld. The handmaids of Henry Poyde and Richard de Mora, 6^d each, of Robert Willeson, Richard Steel, Robert Rose, Robert Goldsmith and Robert Capoun, 2^d each; Magota Rahgenyld, 2^d; the handmaids of John Clement and Thomas le Taverner, 2^d each, of Robert Couper, 1^d; Ibbota Chapman, 2^d and Adam le Hewer, 2^d, for escapes.

Stanneley. Henry Prepter, and John le Saghor's daughter, 3^d each for dry wood.

Thornes. William Dolfyn, 6^d for breaking a paling.

Alvirthorp. Richard Withoundes, 2^d for an escape.

Total of this Court, 34ˢ		Bailiff, 21ᵈ
Wakefeld, 2ˢ 10ᵈ		Stanley, 4ˢ·6ᵈ
Alvirthorp, 2ᵈ		Osset, 2ˢ
Thornes, 6ᵈ		Sandale, 18ᵈ
Hyperum, 3ˢ 4ᵈ		Rastrik, 2ˢ
Rastrik, 2ˢ		Holne, 6ˢ 8ᵈ
Sourby, 8ˢ 9ᵈ		

Horbiry. Thomas de Bellehous sues Henry le Prestknave for trespass. Surety—John s. of Hugh.

Bailiff. Thomas de Ceyuill, sues John s. of Thomas de Heton for debt. Surety—William de Castilford.

Thornes. Henry Nelot sues Robert s. of Ivo for debt. Surety—John Tyde.

Holne. Thomas s. of Hancok, sues Henry Wade for debt. Surety—John de la Grene.

Alvirthorp. John Bulneis sues John Gerbod for trespass. Surety—William Dolfyn.

William de Castilford sues Richard Collay for debt. Surety—John Attebarre.

John de Rastrik sues Richard Withoundes for debt. Surety—Richard, bailiff of Rastrik.

Thornes. Henry Nelot sues William Graffard for debt. Surety—Robert de Mora.

William servant of Thomas, sues Elias Bulneis. Surety—William s. of Philip.

Alice Goure sues Ivo Faber for detaining cattle. Surety—Richard de Lupsete.

COURT held there on Friday after the Feast of St. Nicholas, Bishop and Confessor (Dec. 6), in the year abovesaid [1324].

Essoins. Adam de Stainclif, by Roger de Clifton Surety—Robert de Mora.

William de Birton, by Richard de Birton. Surety—John de Gledeholt.

Thomas de Thornton, by Robert de Mora. Surety—Thomas Launce.

Richard de Birstall, by Thomas de Birstal.

Brian de Thornhill, by John de Hopton, whom he appoints his attorney for suit of court.

Bailiff. William de la Lee sues Thomas de Totehill for assaulting him in the town of Wakefeld, in a certain place called le Markethstede; damages, 40ˢ Thomas denies it, and says William appointed John de Geirgrave his attorney in court, and essoined at the last court without mentioning his said attorney; and both seek judgment thereon; which is postponed till next court. And Thomas appoints Richard de Birton his attorney.

Rastrik. Thomas de Lihtrigge, 6ᵈ for false claim against Thomas de Totehill.

Bailiff. John de Birton agrees with Richard s. of Cecilia (2ᵈ) and Adam s. of the widow (2ᵈ).

Thomas de Totehill sues John de Toftclive for 6ˢ 6ᵈ, which is acknowledged; fine, 3ᵈ

Alvirthorp. Richard del Bothe sues John Gerbod for 4ˢ 3ᵈ; an inquisition finds for the plaintiff; fine, 2ᵈ

Rastrik. Thomas de Totehill and Richard de Lihtrige (6ᵈ) agree.

Sourby. Elias s. of Peter de Sourby, sues Hugh Wade and John de Migeley for debt; and appoints Hugh de Coplay his attorney.

Alvirthorp. John Bulneis sues John Gerbod for 5ˢ, which is acknowledged; fine, 2ᵈ

John Attebarre sues Richard de Collay and William de Birkinshagh for 14ˢ 4ᵈ, which is acknowledged; fine, 2ᵈ

William de Castilford and Richard de Collay 2ᵈ agree.

Sandale. Robert s. of Adam, s. of Adam, gives 3ˢ 4ᵈ for licence to heriot on a messuage and a bovate of land in Sandale, after the death of his father, whose heir he is.

John Nalkson surrenders an acre in Sandale; committed to Robert Pelleson; entry, 6ᵈ. The said land lies at le Fleches.

Total of this Court—6ˢ 1ᵈ   Rastrik, 12ᵈ
    Bailiff, 7ᵈ   Alvirthorp, 8ᵈ
    Sandale, 3ˢ 10ᵈ

TOURN held at Halifax on Monday after the Feast of St. Nicholas (Dec. 6), 18 Edw. II [1324].

John de Shipedene, 4ᵈ for not prosecuting suit against John le Taillour.

Gilbert de la Legh, 6ᵈ for false claim for debt against John del Russilegh.

The said John acknowledges he owes said Gilbert 10ˢ for the maintenance of Agnes de Langefeld; fine, 4ᵈ

Richard de Backale and Adam de Notteschagh (9ᵈ) agree.

William de Counale sues Adam s. of Adam Mygge for killing an ox worth 20^s; Adam denies, and makes his law; fine 4^d

Alice widow of Henry de Godelegh sues Nigel de Russheworth for killing a cow worth 15^s; he makes his law. Alice fined 4^d

William de Middelmor sues John de la Russhelegh for 76^s 8^d; which is acknowledged; fine, 10^d

Peter de Crosselegh drew blood from William de Estwode; 3^s 4^d

John Culpon, 3^d; Richard del Whitelegh, 3^d; Thomas le Taillourson, 6^d; Peter del Crosselegh, 3^d; William de Hiperom, 3^d; Ameria Ibbotdoghter, 2^d; Richard del Sykis, 3^d; Alice del Lone, 4^d; Constance le Taillour, 6^d; John Kypes' wife, 6^d; the wife of Alexander del Hyngandrode, 4^d; Roger Spilwode's wife, 4^d, and Margery Juddoghter, 6^d, for not coming.

Robert le Tynker surrenders an acre in Sourby; committed to Hugh Oteson; entry, 6^d

Adam s. of William de Soland, surrenders a messuage and 3 acres in Sourby; committed to William s. of Nigel le Mouner; entry, 2^s

Three acres in Sourby, formerly held by William le Smyth, committed to John le Smythson; entry, 12^d

Total of this Tourn—15^s 4^d all on Sourby.

TOURN at Brighous, held the Wednesday before the feast of St. Lucy the Virgin (Dec. 13) in the above-said year [1324].

John de Holleway sues Roger de Illingworth for assaulting him at Northouram. An inquisition finds him guilty. Damages, 12^d; fine, 6^d

William de Sunderland sues Alice widow of Matthew de Shipeden for 11 acres in Shipedene. Defendant says plaintiff sold the land to her husband. It is found by an inquisition that Matthew ousted William, who is to recover; Alice fined 6^d

Adam s. of Elias, sues Thomas, perpetual vicar of Halifax, for a messuage and bovate of land in le Bothes, of which he says Elias his father, died seised. Defendant says Elias demised the land to Robert de Warlullay, chaplain, for 20 years; an inquisition finds for defendant; fine, 3^d for false claim.

An inquisition finds Richard de Thorp owes Julian de Quytehill 16^d; fine, 3^d

Robert del West, Robert Gibson and Richard Seliheved, 3^d each for not coming.

Philip le Mouner, John Pepil and Robert de Rissheworth, the same.

William de la Legh, for rescue of beasts, 6^d

Adam Bate drew blood from Emma de Stanlay, 6^d

William de Godelegh, from Simon del Ker, 12^d

John le Mouner, from Adam s. of Thomas, 6^d
John Robynson, from John Blakmantel, 12^d
John del Dene, from Thomas Alcokson, 6^d
Jordan le Pynder, from John le Pynder, 12^d
The wives of William Peck, William le Mouner and Thomas Bande; and Henry s. of Henry, 6^d each, for brewing, etc.

Matilda widow of John Warde surrenders 3 acres in Northourom; committed to John le Pynder; entry, 18^d

Julian de Quythill surrenders 2$\frac{1}{4}$ acres in Hyperum; committed to Simon del Dene, for 13 years, with remainder after that term to Julian; entry, 12^d

Adam Bythebrok surrenders a messuage and 13 acres in Rastrik; committed to Henry his son; entry, 3^s 4^d

William le Mouner surrenders 1$\frac{1}{2}$ acres in Hyperum; committed to William Peck; entry, 9^d

Robert Willeson del Wodehous surrenders 6 acres in Rastrik; committed to Henry s. of Henry de Rastrik, for 8 years, with remainder to Robert; entry, 12^d

John le Mouner, 3^d for escape of cattle in Hyperumwood.

John Judson, 2^d; John Willeson, 2^d; Richard Judson, 2^d; John Alotson, 3^d; John de Birstal, 3^d; William s. of Richard Watson, 2^d; Robert Cristianson, ? 2^d; Richard del Hole, 2^d; Richard del Wro, 4^d; Thomas de Wolfker, 3^d; William del Rode, 2^d; Peter de Southclyf, 3^d; Richard de Thorp, 3^d; Jordan le Pynder, 2^d; Henry del Rode, 1^d for the same.

Total of this Tourn—23^s. 7^d Rastrick, 8^s 8^d
                                         Hyperum, 14^s 11^d

TOURN at Byrton held on Thursday before the Feast of St. Nicholas (Dec. 6), 18 Edw. II [1324].

Thomas s. of William, sues John de la Castel . . .

Elias de Cartworth sues Hugh de Hole for 12^d . . . both are fined, ?6^d and 2^d

Hugh del Hole sues said Elias for trespass; Elias fined . . .

John de Brodholes sues Thomas s. of Thomas Fernoule, and Richard his brother, for debt, which they acknowledge, and are fined 4^d

Thomas s. of Henry, sues Henry Wade and Robert s. of John, for 22^s; they are fined 4^d

John del Hole surrenders 1$\frac{1}{2}$ acre in Alstanley; committed to Mariota de Wildborlegh; entry, 8^d. Also a messuage and a rood of land there, committed to William Gibbeson.

Nicholas le Pertricour surrenders a rood in Wolvedale; committed to Alice d. of Henry; entry, 6^d

Adam Denias surrenders an acre in Fogheleston; committed to Robert Molleson entry, 6^d

Adam s. of Thomas Wodmen, surrenders 1¼ acre in Fogh-eleston; committed to Robert Molleson; entry, 6ᵈ

Alice de Slaghthwayt surrenders an acre in Heppeworth; committed to Edmund s. of Robert.

New rents.   William Hick took ½ acre in Cartworth; he gives 12ᵈ and pays 2ᵈ per annum.

John de Stanelegh took an acre in Cartworth; 12ᵈ; rent, 4ᵈ

William del Mersh, an acre in Wolvedale; 16ᵈ; rent, 4ᵈ

Thomas de Billeclyf an acre in Hepworth, in exchange for another acre there; he pays 8ᵈ

Thomas de Holme drew blood from William s. of Amabilla; 12ᵈ

Adam le Badger's wife, 6ᵈ; William de Quytteley's wife, 3ᵈ; John del Legh's wife, 6ᵈ; John Kythuseband, 3ᵈ, and John le Forester's wife, ? 3ᵈ for brewing, etc.

Total of this Tourn—13ˢ 2ᵈ all from Holn.

TOURN at Wakefeld, held on Friday after the Feast of St. Lucy the Virgin (Dec. 13), 18 Edw. II [1324].

Bailiff.   Henry le Hyne drew blood from Robert de Bretton, 12ᵈ

The wife of William le Hyne of Emmelay, 6ᵈ; Magot le Carter, 3ᵈ; Robert le Mouner's wife, 3ᵈ; Diota de Bretton, 6ᵈ; Magota d. of Thomas de Bretton, 6ᵈ and the wife of Jokyn de Crigleston, 3ᵈ for brewing, etc. Also the wife of Pauline de Em-melay, 6ᵈ

John Iveson de Sothill, for not coming, 3ᵈ

Alvirthorp.   Henry Campion of Neuton blocked up a path at Wyrunthorp, fine, 12ᵈ

Bailiff.   Henry le Dyker, 6ᵈ for fishing in the lord's water at Keldre without licence.

Wakefeld.   Thomas le Taverner drew blood from Robert s. of German, 12ᵈ

Bailiff.   Henry Bullok from a certain woman, 12ᵈ

Wakefeld.   Thomas le Taverner, 12ᵈ for sueing Peter de Stanneley in the Consistory, for a debt resulting neither from a will nor a marriage.

Robert Ters, 12ᵈ for the same against John Haget.

Bailiff.   Robert Monk for the same against John de Holgate, 12ᵈ

Philip Damysell, for the same against Ralph Launce, 12ᵈ

Total of this Tourn—13ˢ 9ᵈ   Wakefeld, 3ˢ
        Bailiff, 9ˢ 9ᵈ   Alverthorp, 12ᵈ

COURT there on Friday, the Feast of St. Thomas the Apostle (Dec. 21) 18 Edw. II [1324].

John de Schippedene essoins by Robert de Mora. Surety—Roger de Clifton.

John de Newyle, by Thomas, s. of Laurence.

William de Tothill, by Robert de Mora. Surety—Thomas de Tothill.

Thomas de Thorneton, by Robert de Mora.

Henry Tasse essoins against Robert Nalleson, by John de Gledeholt. Surety—German Swerd.

Wakefeld. Henry Nelot, 2ᵈ for not prosecuting Robert s. of Ivo.

Horbiry. Henry Prestnave (3ᵈ) and Thomas de Bellehouse agree.

Thornes. William Nundy sues Elias Bulnays for 3ˢ, a surety for Agnes Wlf. An inquisition is to be taken.

Bailiff. The inquisition between John de Querneby and John Godcheyr, acquit the latter; plaintiff fined 3ᵈ for false claim.

Sourby. An inquisition finds that John de Querneby lost cattle to the value of 16ˢ 6ᵈ from default of John de Risselay; he is to recover the amount; fine, 4ᵈ

Henry s. of Richard de Skambandene, sues Henry s. of Cristian de Risseworth on an agreement. Defendant wages his law. Surety—Adam s. of Roger.

Holne. Richard Willeson sues Thomas Fernhoule for 5ˢ for a cow sold him; which is acknowledged. Fine, 4ᵈ

Stanneley. The inquisition to which Johanna d. of Thomas de Milnthorp, and Richard Pesci referred their claims to 22 acres of land in Stanneley, which Johanna claims after the death of Robert Pescy whose heir she is, finds that Robert surrendered the said land in court, and it was committed to Richard; she is therefore fined 3ᵈ for false claim.

Bailiff. German Philcock sues Richard Withundes for trespass. Surety—John Pollard.

Cissota d. of Philip de Castelford, sues Henry s. of Robert s. of Geoffrey de Stanley, for trespass. Surety—Philip de Castilford.

Thomas Philcock sues Richard, servant of Matilda formerly wife of William de Miggelay, for seizing cattle.

Sourby. Adam s. of Nelle de Sourby, sues John Miller del Bothes for land. Surety—Thomas de Heitfeld.

Stanley. Gilbert le Theker of Stanlay and Eva his wife, sue Johanna d. of Thomas de Millynthorp for land. Surety—Henry Dyker.

Henry Dyker and Isolda his wife, sue said Johanna for land.

John Erl sues Adam Sprigonel for debt. Surety—John Pollard.

James del Okes sues William Erl on an agreement. Surety—William del Okes.

John Dade sues William de Estwod on an agreement. Surety —Robert de Mora.

Gilbert del Legh sues John Ceyuill for debt.

Holne. William del Scoles 2^d; Robert del Scoles, 2^d; John s. of Matilda, 2^d; Hugh del Scoles, 2^d; Nicholas del Scoles, 2^d; Robert le Riche, 1^d; Henry de Langeley, 1^d; John Wlf, 3^d; Cecilia Pye, 1^d; Adam de Hoglay, 2^d; Hugh Dobyn, 2^d; William Godefelagh, 2^d; William Gibson, 2^d; Alan de Alstanley, 6^d; Mariota de Wildborlegh, 3^d; Matthew Gibson, 1^d; Adam de Holn, 2^d; Julian de Holne, 2^d; John de Loukes, 2^d; John Michel, 2^d; John Drabil, 2^d; Adam Akirland, 1^d; and Ralph Pye, 4^d, for green earth and vert.

Sandale. John Cokewald; Thomas Monk; John Monk and Henry de Holgate, 2^d each, for escapes.

Stanneley. Hugh de Stanneley, 4^d; Richard Poket, 1^d; Richard Pesci's handmaid, 1^d, for dry wood, etc.

Wakefeld. John Cussing 4^d for vert.

Robert Couper, 4^d; pardoned because in the King's service.

Robert Couper's handmaid, 1^d; Ibbota Sparow, 2^d; Ibbota Chapman, 2^d; William Bul's handmaid, 2^d; Ralph Bate's handmaid, 2^d, for dry wood.

The servant of Adam le Hewer, 4^d for breaking or paling.

Osset. William Hirning, 2^d; Jordan Eliot, 2^d; John s. of William, 1^d; Richard s. of Swayn, 2^d; Thomas le Pinder, 5^d; Robert Scote, 1^d; Robert Sonman, 3^d; John del Dene, 2^d, and Richard Snart's handmaid, 4^d, for escapes, etc.

Total of this Court—10^s 5^d	Sandale, 10^d
Sourby, 4^d	Horbiry, 3^d
Wakefield, 9^d	Bailiff, 3^d
Holne, 4^s 7^d	Osset, 22^d
Stanneley, 9^d	

COURT held at Wakefeld on Friday after the Feast of St. Hilary, (Jan. 13), 18 Edw. II [1324-5].

Essoins. Hugh le Nodder, attorney of William de Nevill, by Henry Tasshe. Surety—Robert de Mora.

John de Hopton, attorney of Brian de Thornhill, by Richard de Birstall. Surety—William Cussing.

Hugh de Stanneley, by William Filche, clerk. Surety—Thomas Launce.

William de Totehill, by Thomas de Totehill.

Robert de Mora, surety for the essoin of Thomas le Taverner at the last court, fined 2^d, because Thomas does not come.

Rastrik. Henry de Walda fined 3^d for defaults.

Bailiff. John s. of Thomas de Heton, distrained to answer John de Burton by 4 oxen, broke the lord's fold, and took them out. Fine, 12^d

John s. of Thomas de Hertesheved, 2^d for not appearing to answer John de Burton.

Sourbi. Hugh Wade and John de Migelay, and Robert s. of John, their surety, 6^d for their not coming to answer Elias s. of Peter de Sourby.

Bailiff. German Filcok, surety for William Graffard, 3^d, because said William does not come.

Bailiff. Edmund le Boteler sues John le Flemeng for debt, and appoints Thomas Alayn his attorney.

Alvirthorp. Richard Withoundes, 3^d for not coming to answer John de Rastrik.

Thornes. William Nundi and Elias Bulneis 2^d agree.

Rastrik. Henry s. of Richard de Skammandene, 6^d for not prosecuting suit against Henry s. of Christian de Rissheworth.

Thornes. Robert s. of Ivo de Snaipthorp, taken and imprisoned at the instance of Emma Brounsmith for stealing beasts from her, in company with William Graffard, comes into court, and pleads not guilty, and submits himself thereupon to the Court, reserving his clergy. An inquisition is taken by the oath of Thomas de Ceyuill, Thomas de Bellehous, Thomas de Southwode, John Hood, William del Okes, James del Okes, Nicholas de Bateley, Thomas s. of Henry, William de Castelford, Elias de Dalton, John de Mora and Hugh Viroun, who acquit Robert. Emma is sent to prison.

William del Estwode essoins against John Dade by Robert de Stodeley. Surety—Matthew de Bosco.

Sourby. Adam s. of Nelle de Sourby, sues John Miller for $\frac{1}{4}$ of $\frac{1}{2}$ bovate of land in le Bothes. John says that he and Matilda his wife, acquired the land conjointly, and that he cannot answer without her. Adam denies this, and they both seek judgment thereon.

Alvirthorp. William de Ouchethorp surrenders $\frac{1}{2}$ acre in Alvirthorp; committed to William de Burdeus; entry, 6^d

Thornes. Agnes Hog surrenders 7$\frac{1}{2}$ acres in Thornes; committed to William Cussing; entry only 12^d, because the land is poor.

Ralph Bate surrenders 3 acres in Thornes; committed to Thomas Basset; entry, 2^s

Bailiff of Stanneley. Walter Gunne is elected bailiff of Stanneley by the whole graveship; he is received and sworn.

Thornes. Elias s. of Peter, gives 12^d not to be bailiff this year.

Bailiff of Thornes. William Malyn is elected bailiff, etc.

Hiperum. John s. of Walter de Adrithegate, gives 2ˢ as a heriot on a messuage and 7 acres in the graveship of Hyperum, after his father's death, whose heir he is, to hold after the death of Julian his mother.

Rastrik. Henry de Totehill, 12ᵈ; Thomas Taluace, 12ᵈ; William s. of Roger, 2ᵈ; William Molox, 12ᵈ; Henry Wynter, 6ᵈ and Robert de Lihtriche, 2ᵈ, for wood cut in Fekesby wood.

Wakefeld. John Wolmer, 2ᵈ; William Cussing, 1ᵈ; Robert de Feri, 1ᵈ; Richard Hannebrothir, 2ᵈ; Ibbota Sparowe, 6ᵈ; Ibbota d. of Hugh Capman, 2ᵈ; Magota Spink, 4ᵈ; Lacer, 2ᵈ; Robert Couper's handmaid, 1ᵈ; Thomas s. of Laurence, 6ᵈ; and Adam le Hewer, 2ᵈ, for vert, etc.

Osset. Richard Snart, 2ᵈ, and John Maunsel, 1ᵈ for escapes.

Alvirthorp. Richard Withoundes, 4ᵈ; John Swan, 2ᵈ, and Henry del Bothem's wife, 1ᵈ for escapes.

Stanneley. Richard de Bately, 4ᵈ; Elizota de Bateley, 2ᵈ; John Isabell, 3ᵈ; Robert Pesci, 2ᵈ; Richard Poket, 1ᵈ; Henry Poket, 1ᵈ; John Flachard, 1ᵈ; Hugh Cort, 1ᵈ; Thomas Thore, 1ᵈ; William Arkel, 3ᵈ, for dry wood, etc.

Total of this Court—18ˢ 6ᵈ   Rastrik, 4ˢ 7ᵈ
   Bailiff, 19ᵈ   Alvirthorp, 16ᵈ
   Wakefeld, 2ˢ 6ᵈ   Sourby, 6ᵈ
   Stanneley, 19ᵈ   Osset, 3ᵈ
   Thornes, 4ˢ 2ᵈ   Hyperum, 2ˢ

COURT held at Wakefeld on Friday after the Feast of the Purification of the B.V.M. (Feb. 2) 18 Edw. II [1324-5].

Essoins. Thomas de Thorneton, by Robert de Mora. Surety—William Cussing.

Hugh de Stanneley, by Thomas Launce.

Richard de Birstall, by Thomas de Birstall.

Bailiff. Robert Nalleson (3ᵈ) and Henry Tasshe agree.

Robert Nalleson sues Thomas le Taverner for taking a cow belonging to him from Thomas Thore's house, in the town of Stanneley, and driving it to Wakefeld, where he still keeps it; damages, 20ˢ. Defendant is to make his law. Surety—William de Castilford.

John de Burton and John s. of Thomas de Heretesheved (2ᵈ) agree. Surety—Thomas de Livirsege.

Sourby. Elias s. of Peter de Sourby, 2ᵈ for not prosecuting Hugh Wade and John de Migeley.

Thornes. Ivo Faber, 2ᵈ for not appearing to answer Alice Goure.

Alvirthorp. Richard Withoundes essoins against German Filcok by William Cussing. Surety—John de Mora.

John de Rastrik and Richard Withoundes (3ᵈ) agree.

Thornes. Henry Nelot and Robert s. of Ivo (2ᵈ) agree.

Sourby. Adam s. of Nelle de Sourby, 6ᵈ for not prosecuting John Miller.

Rastrik. John de Dihton, 18ᵈ for wood cut in Fekesby.

Stanneley. Gilbert le Theker of Stanneley and Eva his wife, 3ᵈ for false claim against Johanna d. of Thomas de Milnthorp.

Henry le Dyker and Isolda his wife, 2ᵈ for the same.

William Filche, clerk, sues William Albray for 6ˢ 8ᵈ as surety for Richard del Ker. Defendant says he was surety for only half the amount, concerning which he is to make his law. Surety— German Filcok. Fine, 3ᵈ

Hiperum. Adam s. of Thomas de Hyperum, 3ᵈ for not prosecuting suit against William de Copplay.

Roger de Hasilhirst 4ᵈ for the same against Richard s. of Christian.

Election of the bailiff of Alvirthorp. Richard Withoundes is elected bailiff of Alvirthorp.

Bailiff. Adam Sprigonell owes suit of court; 6ᵈ for not coming.

Holne. An inquisition finds that Adam s. of William de Buttirley and Richard s. of Michael, are ousting Robert s. of Thomas, from a messuage and 18 acres in Holne, which he is to recover. Fine, 6ᵈ

Stanneley. Johanna d. of Thomas de Milnthorp surrenders a messuage and 13 acres in Stanley; committed to Adam de Nauthird, for 20 years; he keeping up the houses in as good repair as he finds them; entry, 3ˢ 4ᵈ

Thomas s. of Robert Estrild sues Agnes d. of William de Neuton, for ½ acre in Neuton, saying his father, whose heir he is, died seised thereof, and after his death plaintiff was seised, in the time of the present king Edward, until Agnes wrongfully dispossessed him. Agnes says her father demised the land to said Robert, for a term now expired. An inquisition finds William gave the land to Robert and his heirs, in court. Thomas is therefore to recover. Fine, 2ᵈ

Total of this Court—8ˢ 11ᵈ	Holne, 6ᵈ
Sourby, 8ᵈ	Rastrik, 18ᵈ
Thornes, 4ᵈ	Bailiff, 11ᵈ
Hyperum, 7ᵈ	Alvirthorp, 3ᵈ
	Stanneley, 7ˢ 2ᵈ

COURT held at Wakefeld on Friday after the Feast of St. Matthias the Apostle (Feb. 24) 18 Edw. II [1324-5].

Essoin. James del Okes, by William de Castilford. Surety— Robert de Grotton.

Bailiff. Richard de Cotheworth, chaplain, 2ᵈ for not prosecuting suit against Richard, chaplain of Hertesheved.

Thomas de Ceyuill essoins agqinst John s. of Thomas de Heton, by German Kay. Surety—William Filche. John afterwards acknowledges he owes Thomas 20^s; fine, 6^d

Thornes. Henry Nelot, 2^d for not prosecuting William Graffard. Alice Goure and Ivo Faber (2^d) agree.

German Filcok sues Richard Withoundes for taking a horse of German's, worth 20^s, from the house of John s. of Hugh, in Horbiry; damages, 14^s 4^d. Richard wages his law. Surety— John Attebarre.

Stanley. William Filche sues Thomas s. of Hugh Skaif, for ½ quarter of corn, which is acknowledged; fine, 3^d.

Robert le Roller sues Philip le Sagher, for corn worth 8^s 9^d, which is acknowledged, fine, 2^d

Thornes. William s. of Robert de Castilford, 2^d for not prosecuting suit against William Cussing.

Sandale. Thomas de Milnthorp, 4^d for the same against Thomas s. of Robert the Clerk of Sandale.

Rastrik. Henry s. of Henry de Fekesby, 3^d for the same against Thomas le Tailur.

Stanley. Johanna d. of Thomas de Milnthorp, 3^d for not coming, when summoned, to answer Margaret, Eva and Isolda daughters of Thomas Nallison.

Holne. Richard del Bothes and John del Brounhill, plaintiffs, and Adam Strekeyse (4^d) and Henry Wade, agree.

Bailiff. John de Burton and Henry del Weld (3^d) agree.

Sourby. Amicia formerly wife of John de Migeley, surrenders 9 acres in Sourby; committed to John s. of William de Eland, and Julian his wife; entry, 2^s

Roger de Stanbiry surrenders 6 acres in Saltonstall; committed to Hugh s. of John de Migeley; entry, 2^s 6^d

Holne. Thomas s. of William, surrenders 7½ acres in Hepworth; committed to Richard s. of John; entry, 2^s

Bailiff. Adam Sprigonel, for default, 6^d

Wakefeld. Alice Heselay, 4^d; Magota Margery, 2^d; Robert Liftfast's handmaid, 1^d; John Wlmer, 2^d; Adam Brus, 4^d; Philip de Castilford's handmaid, 3^d, for dry wood, etc.

Osset. Adam de Goukthorp, 2^d; Robert Sonman, 1^d; Hugh de Disteford, 2^d, and Richard s. of Swayn, 2^d, for escapes.

Stanneley. Robert Ricard's handmaid, 1^d; John le Sagher, 1^d for dry wood.

Hyperum. Roger del Brighous, 3^d; John Podeson, 2^d; William Miller, 1^d; for dry wood and escapes.

Holne. John del Mersh, 2^d; Agnes de Hyengeclif, 3^d; Matthew de Rammesdene, 2^d; John de Bromhill, 2^d, and Henry de Langeley, 3^d for escapes and vert.

Total of this Court—14ˢ 5ᵈ   Sourby, 4ˢ 6ᵈ
      Hyperum, 12ᵈ   Sandale, 4ᵈ
      Holne, 3ˢ 8ᵈ   Wakefeld, 16ᵈ
      Bailiff, 17ᵈ   Osset, 7ᵈ
      Thornes, 6ᵈ   Stanneley, 10ᵈ
      Rastrik, 3ᵈ

Bailiff. Henry Tasshe sues Robert Alot, Thomas de Holgate and Henry le Quarreour for debt. Surety—William de Castilford.

Henry s. of Richard de Heton, sues John s. of Thomas de Heton, for seizing cattle. Sureties—Hugh de Disteford and Ralph de Karlgrave

Adam Badger of Birton sues John de Shellay, senior and Adam de Helay for debt. Surety—William de Whitteley.

Stanneley. Philip le Sagher sues Margaret del Ker for debt.

———

COURT held at Wakefeld on Friday after the Feast of St. Gregory (March 12), 18 Edw. II [1324-5].

Essoins. Richard de Birstall, by Thomas de Birstall. Surety —Thomas de Livirsege.

Hugh le Nodder, attorney of William de Nevill, by William de Castilford. Surety—William Cussing.

Brian de Thornhill, by William Filche.

Bailiff. Robert Nalleson and Thomas le Taverner (2ᵈ) agree.

John Erl and Adam Sprigonel, 4ᵈ agree.

The bailiffs present that nothing can be found to attach belonging to Henry s. of Robert de Stanneley, because he has no goods, and is fled. Philip de Castilford therefore has licence to withdraw his suit.

John Dade and William de Estwode (. . .ᵈ) agree.

John de Cayuill fined . . .ᵈ for not appearing to answer Gilbert de la Lee.

Stanley. Emma Gunne surrenders a messuage and ½ bovate of land in Stanley; committed to Walter . . .; entry, 2ˢ

Osset. Adam s. of Richard de Goukthorp, gives 3ˢ 4ᵈ for licence to heriot on a messuage and eleven acres in Osset, after the death of . . . s. of . . . de Stanley, whose heir he is.

Alan del Hey, arrested for cutting vert in Scambandene, has respite till next court to acquit himself.

Bailiff. John Cailly owes suit; 6ᵈ for not coming.

Wakefeld. John Dade, 1ᵈ; German Filcok, 2ᵈ; Alice del Lyli, 2ᵈ; John Tailur's daughter, 2ᵈ; Walter Ape's wife, 2ᵈ; the handmaids of Robert Capon and Robert le Walker, 2ᵈ each; Johanna de Sandale, 2ᵈ; Magota Spink, 2ᵈ; William Badger's maid, 1ᵈ; Thomas de York's maid, 3ᵈ; the handmaids of John Wlmer and Anabilla Lacer, 1ᵈ each; Cecilia de Sandale, 1ᵈ; Hugh Bille's handmaid, 1ᵈ; Twentipair's wife, 2ᵈ; Thomas Cussing, 1ᵈ; Hugh Chapman's handmaid, 1ᵈ; for dry wood.

Adam le Hewer, 2ᵈ for escape in Lindhou.

Thomas Bate's handmaid, 1ᵈ; the wife of John s. of Walter Pollard, 1ᵈ; Robert Marshal, 1ᵈ; and Philip de Castilford's handmaid, 1ᵈ, for dry wood.

Sourby. Robert de Wolronwall, 2ᵈ; John de Legherode, 2ᵈ; Hugh Wade, 2ᵈ, and William de Lihthasles, 1ᵈ

Stanneley. Richard Poket, 1ᵈ; Robert Ricard, 1ᵈ; John Poket, 2ᵈ; Henry Poket, 1ᵈ for dry wood.

Henry de Walda, 12ᵈ for a paling struck down in Lindhou.

Thornes. Alice Goure, for an escape in the new park, 2ᵈ

Rastrik. William del Hill, 12ᵈ; Thomas Gilleson, 4ᵈ and John Faber, for escapes in Scambandene.

Hyperum. Robert Faber of Bairstau, 12ᵈ; Henry Horne, 2ᵈ; William Pek, 2ᵈ; for dry wood, etc.

Sourby. Thomas del Dene, 4ᵈ; Richard de Bairstawe, 2ᵈ; Roger de Herteleirode, 4ᵈ; Adam de Kirkshagh, 4ᵈ; William Miller, 1ᵈ; William de Raupighel, 1ᵈ; John Nelleson, 2ᵈ; William de Ovendene, 6ᵈ and Henry del Bank, 3ᵈ, for wood, etc.

Total of this Court—21ˢ 11ᵈ	Bailiff, 2ˢ 4ᵈ
Sandale, 11ᵈ	Alvirthorp, 6ᵈ
Horbiry, 12ᵈ	Stanneley, 4ˢ 5ᵈ
Ossete, 3ˢ 4ᵈ	Wakefeld, 3ˢ
Sourby, 2ˢ 11ᵈ	Thornes, 2ᵈ
Rastrik, 22ᵈ	Hyperum, 18ᵈ

Thornes. Hugh le Neucomen sues William Dolfyn, junior, and John Bulneys for trespass. Surety—William de Castilford.

Alvirthorp. William de Loncastre and Agnes his wife, sue John Gerbod for debt. Surety—Richard Withoundes.

Rastrik. Henry del Weld sues John del Okes and Roger Fox for trespass.

Sandale. John Payn sues William de Collay for debt. Surety—Thomas Pelle.

COURT held at Wakefeld on Friday, the 12th of April, 18 Edw II [1325].

Essoins. William de Totehill, by Thomas de Totehill. Surety—William Cussing.

Thomas de Thornton, by William de Castilford. Surety—John de Mora.

William de Birton, by Richard de Birton.

John Cailly, by Thomas de Wakefeld. Surety—Richard Withoundes.

John Hood, by William Cussing. Surety—John Attebarre.

Thornes. Hugh le Neucomen, William Dolfin, junior, and John Bulnais (4ᵈ) agree.

Bailiff.   John Flemang, defendant, in the king's service, essoins against Edmund le Boteler, by John de Everingham.

Stanneley.   Margaret, Eva and Isolda daughters of Thomas Nalleson, 6^d for false claim against Johanna d. of Thomas de Milnethorp.

Philip le Sagher and Margaret del Ker (2^d) agree.

Alvirthorp.   John s. of Hugh Chapman, and Agnes his mother, surrender an acre in Alvirthorp; committed to Thomas le Roller, entry, 12^d

William de la Lee, 12^d for not prosecuting suit against Thomas de Totehill.

Bailiff.   Henry Launel sues John Erl for debt.   Surety— Hugh de Nodder.

Holne.   Richard Fernoule surrenders a messuage and 20½ acres in Fouleston; committed to Henry le Waynwriht; entry, 40^d

Sandale.   Thomas de Ketilthorp surrenders 5 acres in Crigleston; committed to James Monk; entry, 2^s

Thornes.   Robert s. of Ivo, gives 12^d to take a messuage and ½ bovate of land in Snaipthorp, in the graveship of Thornes, which fell into the King's hands by forfeiture of William Graffard; to hold for 10 years, which was the term William Graffard had therein.

Osset.   John Scot gives 2^s for licence to heriot on a messuage and 2 bovates in Osset, after the death of John s. of Robert le Couper, whose heir he is.

Stanneley.   Agnes d. of Robert Daneys, surrenders a messuage and bovate of land in Wodehall; committed to Robert Danays; entry, 2^s

Wakefeld.   John Wolmer, 2^d; the handmaids of William Bul, Robert Liftfast, and Cecilia de Sandale, 1^d; each; Magota Spink, 1^d; Henry Badger, 1^d; German Filcok, John Taylur and Walter Lacer, 1^d each; Megge Preest, 4^d; John Botcher and Agnes de Ripon, 3^d; Johanna Estrild, 2^d; for dry wood, etc.

Sandale.   William de Collay, 2^d; John Monk, 1^d; Henry de Holgate, 1^d; Thomas Monk, 1^d; and Robert del Grene, ?j^d, for dry wood, etc.

Stanneley.   Richard Pescy, 1^d; Richard Poket, 2^d; Robert Ricard, 1^d; William Albray, 1^d; John Poket, 1^d; Gilbert le Theker, 1^d; Richard de Bateley, 6^d; Elizabeth de Bateley, 2^d; William Isabell, 1^d; John Flachard, 2^d; Hugh Cort, 1^d; and Henry de Walda, 6^d, for wood, etc.

Alvirthorp.   Avicia de Horbiry, 2^d, for ivy and wood.

Osset.   John Maunsel, 1^d and Richard Snart, 1^d for dry wood.

Total of this Court—22^s 2^d

Wakefeld, 20^d	Alvirthorp, 16^d	
Thornes, 16^d	Holne, 6^s 8^d	
Osset, 2^s 7^d	Rastrik, 12^d	
Grave of Stanneley, 4^s 10^d	Bailiff, 2^d	
	Sandale, 2^s 7^d	

William s. of Hugh, sues Hugh Wade for trespass. Surety—
Adam s. of Hugh.

William Nundy sues William s. of Thomas, for debt . . .

Matilda formerly wife of Adam Broun, sues Roger de Furton
for detaining a horse. Surety—John s. of Ibbote.

———

COURT held at Wakefeld on Friday, the Feast of the Invention
of the Holy Cross (May 3) 18 Edw. II [1325]

Essoins. Thomas de Thornton by William de Castilford.
Surety—John de Mora.

Hugh le Nodder, attorney of William de Nevill, by Thomas
de Wakefeld. Surety—German Kay.

John de Heton, by John de Hopton. Surety—Robert de
Mora.

Bailiff. Thomas de Livirsege, 8^d for not prosecuting suit
against Richard de Selby, chaplain of Hertesheved.

Adam le Badger, 6^d for the same against John de Shellay,
senior, and Adam de Helay.

Gilbert de la Lee and John de Ceyuill (6^d) agree.

Bailiff. Edmund le Boteler sues John le Flemyng for 43^s 4^d,
which is acknowledged; fine, 6^d

Ralf de Sheffeld essoins against John Hobson, by John
Alayn. Surety—German Filcok.

Thomas le Roller 6^d, Adam del Hill and William Alayn
agree.

Thornes. William s. of Thomas, 6^d, for not appearing, when
summoned to answer William Nundy.

Sandale. Adam Wylmot surrenders an acre in Sandale;
committed to John s. of William de Osset; entry, 8^d

Horbiry. John s. of Elias de Dalton, gives 12^d to take $\frac{1}{2}$
bovate of land formerly held by Hugh le Lambhird, and now
unoccupied; rent, 4^s

Wakefeld. Ibbota Sparou, 4^d; Ibbota Chapman, 2^d; William
Badger's wife 2^d; the wives of William Twentipair and Thomas
Cussing, 1^d each; Ellen Gurdon, 2^d; Anabilla Lacer, 1^d; Magota
Spink, 1^d; Johanna de Sandle, 1^d; John Badger's wife, 2^d; Alice
Badger, 1^d; Henry Badger, 1^d; Robert Liftfast's maid, 1^d; Robert
Clement's maid, 2^d; the maids of Robert Walker and Robert
Byghilbayn, 1^d each, for dry wood.

Stanneley. Nicholas de Bateley, 3^d; William Isabell, John
Flachard, Hugh Cort, Robert Bele, Johanna Poket, Richard
Poket, John Filcok, Robert de Mikilfeld, Robert Ricard, Richard
Pescy, Henry Poket and William Albray, 1^d each; John Isabele,
2^d; for ivy and dry wood.

TOURN there the same day.

Bailiff. Margery d. of Thomas Erkinson; Diota formerly wife of Richard de Bretton; William le Hyne's wife, and Alice Scot, 3ᵈ each; the wife of Pauline de Emmeley, 6ᵈ, for brewing, etc.

Osset. Richard Pasmer's wife, 6ᵈ for the same.

Sandale. Robert, chaplain of Sandale, 12ᵈ; John s. of Hugh, 6ᵈ, for not coming.

John servant of Adam de Wodeson, 12ᵈ for drawing blood.

Robert s. of William de Wolvedale for the same 6ᵈ

Hugh de Stanneley, for drawing blood, 12ᵈ

John s. of John Damyias for herbage detained from the common of the town of Wakefeld, 40ᵈ

Alvirthorp. Robert Danays, for a coal pit in the king's highway at Neuton, 40ᵈ

The township of Alvirthorp, for concealing the same 12ᵈ

John Attebarre for obstructing a path, 12ᵈ, and the township of Alvirthorp, 6ᵈ for concealing the same.

Stanneley. John s. of Robert Geppeson, 12ᵈ; Robert le Leper, 12ᵈ; German Filcok, 6ᵈ.

Joint Total of the Court and Tourn—29ˢ 10ᵈ

TOURN held at Halifax on Monday, the Feast of St. John before the Latin Gate (May 6), 18 Edw. II [1325]

William del Estwode sues John de Holgate for 17ˢ, which is acknowledged; damages, 6ᵈ; fine, 4ᵈ

Hugh Wade and William de Lighthasles (2ᵈ) agree.

Hugh Wade and William de Leghtrige (2ᵈ) agree.

John s. of Elias, 6ᵈ for not prosecuting suit against Adam de Kirkeschagh, for killing his pig.

Alice d. of Robert de Stansfeld, and John s. of Thomas del Halle, (6ᵈ) agree.

John le Mouner and John s. of Matthew (2ᵈ) agree.

John le Smithsone sues Robert de Sourby for 21ᵈ which he owes him for service; Robert wages his law. Surety—Adam s. of Roger. He afterwards makes his law, and John is fined 1ᵈ for false claim.

Elias s. of Peter, sues Hugh Wade and Julian his wife, for 6ˢ 8ᵈ in payment of land bought by the said Julian for Thomas her son. An inquisition finds they owe 5ˢ. Plaintiff fined 2ᵈ for false claim, and defendants 2ᵈ for detention.

Thomas de Halifax, 6ᵈ for false claim against the community of the town of Skircote.

John del Hole and Henry Attbanc (4ᵈ) agree.

John de la Legh and William de la Lowe (6ᵈ) agree.

Adam de Russilegh and Adam de Stainlegh drew blood from Adam s. of Thomas Louerd; 12ᵈ each.

Hugh Wade, 12^d for the same.

John Culpoun surrenders 1½ acre of meadow in Sourby; committed to John s. of John Culpoun; entry, 6^d

Henry de Saltonstal surrenders 6¾ acres in Werlullay; demised to Thomas de Northclif; entry, 2^s

Matilda widow of Elias s. of Ivo, surrenders all the dower accruing to her in her late husband's free tenement in Sourby, which is committed to Adam, s. of Elias; entry, 3^d

Adam s. of Elias, surrenders all his right, with its appurtenances in Werlullay, except Luddingdene; committed to Matilda widow of Elias s. of Ivo, for life, with remainder to said Adam; entry, 3^d

Thomas de Heitfeld surrenders an acre in Sourby; committed to Adam s. of Hugh de Lighthasles; entry, 6^d

Half an acre of unoccupied land in Sourby, demised to John, s. of John Culpoun, rent, 3^d; entry, 6^d

Three acres of land recently proved unoccupied demised to Adam s. of Roger; rent, 18^d; entry, 18^d

Adam Hancokson sues Adam s. of Hugh, for killing his cow; damages, 6^s. An inquisition finds him not guilty. Plaintiff fined 6^d for false claim.

William s. of Cecilia, 12^d; Geoffrey de Stodeley, 12^d; John Maggeson, 6^d; John del Rydiker, 6^d; John Culpoun, 4^d; Hugh de Totehill, 4^d; Roger de Grenewode, 6^d; William Evoteson, 4^d; Hugh de Totehill, 2^d; John de Haderschelf, 6^d; William del Lone, 6^d; Hugh del Helilegh, 4^d; Adam de Covintre, 6^d; Hugh Wade, 4^d; Roger de Benteleyrode, 4^d; Henry del Wode, 3^d; Henry de Ludyndene, 2^d; Adam s. of Roger the bailiff, 6^d; Jordan del Brigge, 2^d; Robert de Wolrunwalle, 2^d; William the bailiff, 2^d; Thomas del Bothem, 2^d; William de Paupeghill, Ivo Sourmilk, William le Sponer, Henry de Saltonstal, Richard de Bairstowe, Thomas del Dene, Henry Clerk, William West, Roger de Hertlayrode, Richard Faber, John de Illingword, Thomas le Mercer, William del Smalleghes, 2^d each; Roger le Schephierd, 6^d; William de Soland, 4^d and Jordan le Schepherd, 4^d, for escapes.

Total of this Tourn—26^s 9^d and 21^d new rent—all from Sourby.

TOURN at Briggehous, held on Friday after the Feast of St. John of Beverley (May 7) in the year abovesaid [1325].

Hyperum. Roger de Clifton sues John Speght for 4^s 6^d for corn sold him; an inquisition finds the debt is owed; fine, 2^d

Rastrik. Adam del Waterhous, defendant, makes his law against John de la Legh; fine, 3^d

Simon del Dene, 6^d for false claim against Richard del Scagh. John le Pynder, 3^d for the same.

Adam del Bothes, 3^d and Adam s. of Henry, 6^d, against William de Sunderland.

Adam s. of Henry, 6^d and Hugh de Ovendene, 3^d, against the same.

Rastrik. Hugh le Schephird recovered 16^d against John de la Legh. Fine, 3^d

Thomas le Harper surrenders a messuage and 10 acres in Scambandene; committed to Thomas s. of John de Steynland; entry, 2^s 6^d

Hyperum. Adam s. of Elias, gives 6^d as a heriot for a tenement in Northourum, on the death of William Iveson, his uncle, whose heir he is.

A rood of land in Northourum, committed to said Adam; entry, 4^d

The said Adam surrenders a messuage and $\frac{3}{4}$ bovate of land in Northourum; committed to Richard s. of Adam de Hyperum; entry, 18^d

Rastrik. Henry s. of Hugh de Bothmley, surrenders 5 acres in Scambandene; committed to John his brother; entry, 12^d

Hugh de Bothomley surrenders 6$\frac{1}{2}$ acres in Scambandene; committed to Henry his son; entry, 18^d

Hyperum. Peter de Southclif surrenders a messuage and 11 acres in Hyperum; committed to Adam his son, entry, 2^s

New rents. Half an acre of unoccupied land in Hyperum demised to Thomas Bande; rent, 3^d; entry, 6^d

Adam s. of Elias, surrenders 8 acres in les Bothes; committed to John s. of John le Mouner; entry, 12^d

An acre and half a rood of unoccupied land in Northourum, demised to John Attenorthend; rent, 6$\frac{1}{4}$^{d}; entry, 12^d

Three roods of unoccupied land in Hyperum demised to John le Pynder; rent, 4^d; entry, 6^d

Three roods in Northourum, to Symon del Kerheved; rent, 4^d; entry, 12^d

One rood there, to John de Schipden; rent, 1^d; entry, 6^d

Peter de Southclif surrenders a messuage and 5 acres in Hyperum; committed to . . . ; entry 18^d

John del Wotherode, 12^d; John le Couhird, 12^d; John del Okes, 6^d; Richard, bailiff, 6^d; Thomas le Smith, 6^d for vert.

Henry le Waynwrigght, for obstructing a path, 6^d

The township of Rastrik for concealment, 6^d

Laurence de Casteley, 12^d; Elias de Scolcote, 2^d; John le Mouner, 2^d; Symon del Dene, 2^d; John le Pynder, 2^d; Alan de Bothomlay, 2^d; Jordan le Pynder, 2^d; Ivo le Webbester, 3^d Henry del Rode, 2^d; Richard de Thorp, 2^d; William del Rode, 2^d; Richard del Hole, 2^d; Thomas le Walker, 2^d; Thomas Chapman, 2^d for rent, etc.

William Peck's wife, for brewing, etc., 3^d

Thomas Bande's wife, 3^d, for not coming.

Total of this Tourn—31ˢ—and 20¼ᵈ per ann. new rent.
        Rastrik, 5ˢ 6ᵈ   Hyperum, 25ˢ 6ᵈ

———

TOURN at Birton, held on Saturday after the Feast of St. John of Beverley (May 7) in the year abovesaid [1325].

Richard s. of Michael, and Robert le Rich 3ᵈ agree.

John del Grene, defendant against Nicholas Kenward, 6ᵈ

Alan de Merston sues Richard Gris for seizing his cattle. They are to come to the next court at Wakefeld without essoining.

Margery d. of Roger de Langelegh sues John Attegrene, for detaining a cow, worth 14ˢ. An inquisition finds him guilty; damages, 18ᵈ; fine, 6ᵈ

John del Grene sues Nicholas Kenward for damage done to his meadow by defendant's pigs. An inquisition gives damages, 12ᵈ; fine 6ᵈ

John del Hole sues Matthew s. of Gilbert, for trespass; Matthew is convicted; damages, 12ᵈ; fine, 2ᵈ and in a second suit, damages, 2ᵈ; fine, 2ᵈ

Richard s. of Michael, surrenders 4½ acres in Foghliston; committed to Richard Hebbeson; entry, 12ᵈ

Mariota de Wildeborlegh surrenders 2 acres in Alstanley; committed to William s. of Gilbert; entry, 6ᵈ

John de Langeley surrenders an acre and two parts of a rood in Wolvedale; committed to John del Grene; entry, 6ᵈ

New rent. An acre of unoccupied land in Foghleston demised to Richard Hebbeson; rent, 4ᵈ; entry, 6ᵈ

Margaret d. of Robert le Syneman, sues Robert le Mouner and Matilda his wife, for violently assaulting her at Birton; an inquisition finds Matilda guilty and Robert innocent; damages, 20ˢ fine 2ˢ

Nicholas Kenward is elected to the office of bailiff at Holne.

Margery Bridde surrenders 5 acres in Wolvedale; committed to John le Couper and William Wether; entry, 6ᵈ. To be held for 9 years.

New rent. Half an acre of unoccupied land in Holne, demised to Adam de Holne; rent, 2ᵈ; entry, 6ᵈ

Mariota de Wildborlegh, 6ᵈ; Robert Chopard, 2ᵈ; Adam del Grene, 2ᵈ; John de Avendene, 2ᵈ, for vert.

The wives of Adam le Wagger and John de Kesseburgh, 6ᵈ each, of William de Whitelay, 4ᵈ, for brewing, etc.

Anabilla d. of Emma le Bagger, 4ᵈ for the same.

Malina wife of Robert Miller, 2ˢ for blood.

John de Harope, 2ᵈ; Adam Strekays, 6ᵈ; John del **Hole,** 12ᵈ; Adam de Akirland, 3ᵈ; Agnes de Hengeklif, 6ᵈ, for vert.

John Weaver, for blood, 12ᵈ

John del Merse and Gilbert his brother, for blood from one another, 4ˢ

Richard s. of Hugh, for blocking up a path, 12ᵈ

Total of this Tourn—22ˢ 11ᵈ—all from Holne.

COURT held at Wakefeld on Friday, the 7th of June, 18 Edw. II. [1325].

Essoins. Richard de Birstal, by Thomas de Birstal. Surety—William de Castilford.

Thomas de Thorneton, by William de Castilford.

John de Mora, by Robert de Mora. Surety—William Cussing.

Sandale. Thomas Pelleson who attached William de Colley to answer John Payn, fined 2ᵈ for not having him in court.

Bailiff. Henry s. of Richard de Heton, 4ᵈ for not prosecuting suit against John s. of Thomas de Heton.

William de Lancaster and Agnes his wife, and Jon Gerbot, agree. Surety—Richard Withoundes. Fine not entered.

Henry de Welda, by his attorney, sues John del Okes, for cutting wood belonging to him in a place called Calfcroft; damages, 6ˢ 8ᵈ. Defendant wages his law. Surety—John de Botherode.

A love-day is given to John de Burton and William de Rilay.

Hyperum. John Pynder, 4ᵈ for not prosecuting suit against Thomas de Totehill.

William de Lockewod essoins against John de Mora, by William de Stansfeld. Surety—William Filche.

John de Mora, against William de Lockewood by Thomas del Belhous.

John de Lynne, against William s. of Richard Baycok, by Ralph de Kerlinghowe; and William, against John by Richard de Dewesbiry, chaplain. Surety—Richard Baycok.

Sandale. Robert Pelleson and James del Okes (4ᵈ) agree.

Holne. Alan de Mersheton and Richard Gris (—ᵈ) agree.

Edmund Gates, arrested by the king's bailiff on a charge of seizing the goods of Richard de Selby, is found innocent by an inquisition, and discharged acquitted.

Thomas de Totehill sues William de la Lee, for hindering his servants from making distraint on defendant for arrears on land, which he holds of plaintiff, in Oldelynley. William wages his law. Surety—John de Geirgrave.

Alvirthorp. Thomas Broun sues Richard Withoundes, John Atbarre and William de Birkynschagh for 13ˢ for a horse sold to Richard de Colley, for whom they were surety; they acknowledge the debt; fine, 6ᵈ

Sandale. Nigel de Doncaster and William de Colley have a love-day.

John Shepherd, 3ᵈ for not prosecuting Thomas de Ketil-thorp.

Stanley. An inquisition finds that Robert Lepar did not interfere with Richard Pescy, by destroying a fence in Stanley. Richard fined 6^d for false claim.

Holne. Richard s. of Adam Shepherd, surrenders in Heppeword; committed to William s. of Nicholas; entry, 40^d

New rent. Thomas de Holne gives 3^d to take a rood of unoccupied land in Fouleston; rent, 1^d

Horbiry. William s. of Alexander de Wakefeld, gives 6^d to take a bovate of land in Horbiry, formerly held by Robert de Look, at 9^s per ann., which Roger left unoccupied; he paying 6^d per ann. until a fitting time when the old rent can be levied on the said bovate.

Wakefeld. John Pollard surrenders an acre in the graveship of Wakefeld; committed to German Kay and Alice his wife; entry, 6^d

Alvirthorp. German Kay surrenders two acres in Alvirthorp, in a place called les Leghes; committed to Henry s. of Reginald de Swilyngton. Entry, 6^d

Thomas Broun surrenders a messuage and 30 acres in Alvirthorp, committed to the said Henry; entry, 18^d

Henry Nelot and John Gerbod (2^d) agree.

Wakefeld. Hugh Chapman's daughter, Isabella Sparoghe, William de Mora, Twentipair, and Anabilla Lacer, 2^d each, for dry wood.

The handmaids of Philip de Castilford and Robert de Fery, 2^d each; Mariota Spink, 2^d, and the maid of Cecilia de Sandale ?. . . .^{d} for dry wood.

Alverthorp. Richard Withoundes and John Attebarre . . .^{d} for vert.

Total of this Court—

Alverthorp, 3^s
Hyperum. 7^d
Wakefeld 2^s

Christian widow of Adam de Flanshou, sues Henry Tashe for trespass. Surety—Geoffrey de Birkynscagh. Henry brings a cross suit.

Richard s. of Roger de Hyperum, sues Peter de Heton for debt. Surety—Roger de Clifton.

Cecilia widow of Adam le Schephird sues Robert de Bernedside for land.

Adam de Buterley sues Robert s. of Sarah for trespass. Surety—Thomas de Billif.

Robert s. of Walter de Stanley, sues Robert Lepar on an agreement.

COURT held at Wakefeld on Friday, the 5th of July, 18 Edw. II.
[1325].

Essoins. Thomas de Sayuill, by William de Sayuill

John de Hopton, attorney of Brian de Thornehill, by John
de Gledeholt. Surety—Robert de Mora.

Hugh le Nodder, attorney of William de Nevill, by William
de Castilford. Surety—German Swerd.

Thomas de Thorneton, by Robert de Mora. Surety—John
de Mora.

Bailiff. Thomas de Holgate, Henry le Quarreour and Robert
Alot, 3ᵈ for sundry defaults.

William Erl makes his law against James del Okes, who is
fined 4ᵈ for false claim.

Sourby. William del Hyngandrode sues Robert de Werlulley,
chaplain, who is fined 6ᵈ for defaults.

Rastrik. John del Okes fails to make his law against Henry
de Weld; they pay 2ᵈ to agree.

Bailiff. A day is given Adam le Bagger, Adam de Helay and
John de Schelay till next court.

William de Lockewode, who is in the King's service, essoins
against John de Mora, by German Kay.

John de Lynne, 2ᵈ, for not prosecuting his suit against
William s. of Richard Baycok; and 2ᵈ to agree with him in another
matter.

Rastrik. William de la Lee makes the law he waged against
Thomas de Totehill, who is fined 2ᵈ for false claim.

Henry s. of Robert s. of Geoffrey essoins against John
Watknave by German Kay.

William de Castilford and Robert Hode of Neuton have a
love day.

Sandale. Nigel de Doncaster and William de Colley, 6ᵈ for
license to agree.

Christian widow of Adam de Flanshou sues Henry Ateshe
and the bailiff of the Court of Wakefeld, and requests it may be
removed to the burgesses' Court, because Henry is a burgess of the
said town; this is therefore void; but it is respited till the Steward
comes.

Henry Atesshe essoins against Christian, by German Kay.

Stanneley. An inquisition is taken by the oaths of twelve
jurors of the graveships of Horbiry, Alvirthorp, Thornes, Stanley
and Osset, to wit, Elias de Dalton, John s. of Hugh, John Isabelle,
John Attebarre, John Gerbot, Geoffrey de Birkynscagh, William
Malyn, Robert de Lupsete, William s. of Philip, Hugh Forester,
Richard Ricard and William Hirnyng, to Richard Pescy and
Robert Lepar submit themselves with regard to a seizure of cattle,
they say Robert took Richard's cattle in a place called Thornesryding, as though in his own enclosure, because the said land is

"rodeland," and all lands of this kind of tenure have, from time immemorial all the year and at all seasons of the year, been enclosures. Richard is therefore fined 4ᵈ for false claim.

An inquisition between Robert s. of Walter de Stanley and Robert Lepar, on an agreement, awards 6ᵈ damages to Robert Lepar, fine, 3ᵈ

Stanneley. John Tyding surrenders a messuage and 1½ rood of land in Stanley; committed to Robert de Mora; entry, 4ᵈ

Holne. Cecilia widow of Adam Shepherd, 6ᵈ for not prosecuting her suit against Robert de Berneside.

Adam de Buterley, 3ᵈ, for the same against Robert s. of Sarah.

Alice de la Bothe surrenders 3½ acres in Wolvedale, committed to Robert Broun.

Total of this Court—4ˢ 11ᵈ	Sandale, 13ᵈ
Sourby, 6ᵈ	Bailiff, 4ᵈ
Rastrik, 4ᵈ	Stanley, 11ᵈ
	Holne, 21ᵈ

COURT held at Wakefeld on Friday, the 26th of July, 19 Edw II [1325].

Essoins. John de Hopton, attorney of Brian de Thornhill, by Richard de Birstal. Surety—Robert de Mora.

John Hode of Wakefeld, by John Hode, clerk.

John de Mora, by German Swerd.

William de Totehill, by Thomas de Totehill. Surety—William de Castelford.

Sandale. William de Colley, and John Payn (3ᵈ) agree.

Robert Alot, fined 3ᵈ for not coming to answer Henry Tashe.

Alvirthorp. Roger le Bordewright, 6ᵈ for sundry defaults.

Servient. John de Birton and William de Rilay; John de Metheley and John de Heton, have a love-day.

Adam le Bagger, 3ᵈ for not prosecuting Adam de Helay and John de Schelley.

Stanley. Henry s. of Robert s. of Geoffrey, because he is in the King's service, essoins against John Walknave, by Thomas Thorald.

Sandale. Thomas de Ketilthorp and John Shepherd of Walton (6ᵈ) agree.

Stanley. Nicholas de Bateley, 4ᵈ; Thomas Odam, 2ᵈ; Hugh Forester, 2ᵈ; Henry Forester, 2ᵈ; for absenting themselves from the verdict of the inquisition between Hugh de Stanley and Richard Poket; they are to be distrained to come to next court.

Thornes. Philip Damisel and Robert Peger have a love-day.

Osset. Thomas de Schelley sues Henry le Walker for trespass.

Robert Sunman, 2ᵈ for false claim against William Hirning.

Sandale. Thomas Lewlyn, by Robert de Grotton, his attorney, sues Adam s. of Elias de Crigleston, for trespass.

Thornes. Elias Bulneys sues Agnes Wlf for debt; and as Agnes is a burgess of the town of Wakefeld, the burgesses petition for their court, which is granted them.

John Tashe and William s. of Elias Bulneys have a love-day; also John Bulneys and Emma d. of Robert Gelleson.

Alvirthorp. William de Ouchethorp surrenders a rood in Neuton field in Alvirthorp, committed to William de Bordeaus; entry, 6^d

Sourby. Henry de Migeley surrenders 12 acres in Sourby; committed to Robert s. of John de Sourby; entry, 3^s 4^d

Richard del Wodeheved surrenders 2 acres in Scamandene; committed to Adam s. of William de Scambandene; entry, 12^d

Hemry de Werlulley gives 6^d for license to take an acre left unoccupied by John de Haldeworth.

Holne. John de Staneley surrenders an acre in Holne; committed to Robert del Bothe; entry, 6^d

Thomas s. of John, surrenders 2 acres in Carteword; committed to John s. of John de Carteword; entry, 12^d

Stanneley. Hugh de Stanley surrenders $\frac{1}{2}$ acre in Stanley in le Kirkefield; committed to Robert s. of Ralph; entry, 6^d

Wakefeld. Thomas le Hidebyer, for vert, 2^d. Surety— William Aubray. John Goldsmith, 1^d; John Wilcok, 2^d; William le Bagger, 2^d; Anabilla Lacer, 1^d; John Tyde, 2^d; William le Wright, bailiff, 2^d, for dry wood.

Thomas le Hidebier for vert in Lyndowe, 6^d Surety—John Cussing.

Holne. Robert de Walton and his partners, for license to cut turves, 10^d

Ralph de Thurleston, 8^d; Peter de Birkes, 4^d; John Whither, 4^d; John del Stokke, 4^d; Thomas s. of Thomas Shepherd, 4^d; and William Beman, 3^d for escapes.

Total of this Court—15^s 3^d	Sandale, 12^d
Sourby, 4^s 10^d	Alverthorp, 12^d
Bailiff, 3^d	Osset, 2^d
Stanley, 16^d	Holne, 5^s 2^d
Wakefeld, 18^d	

COURT held at Wakefeld, Friday, the 16th of August, 19 Edw II [1325].

Essoins. Thomas de Thorneton, by William de Castilford. Surety—Thomas de Sayuill.

Hugh le Nodder, attorney of William de Nevill, by Richard de Wadesword. Surety—John de Mora.

Adam Sprigonel, by Thomas Thorald.

Richard de Birstal, by Thomas de Birstal.

William de Totehill, by Thomas de Totehill.

John de Mora, by Robert de Mora.   Surety—Robert de Wyrnthorp.

James del Okes, by Robert, s. of Laurence.   Surety—William del Okes.

Sandale. Henry Tashe, and Thomas de Holgate, Henry le Quarreour and Robert Alot, have a love-day.

Servient. John s. of Thomas de Heton essoins against John de Metheley of Thornehill, by Robert Tilly

Alvirthorp. Henry Nelot and John Gerbot (2^d) agree.

Bailiff. The bailiff testifies that nothing can be found to distrain upon Richard de Selby, chaplain of Hertesheved; the suit of John de Birton is therefore annulled at his request.

Stanley. John Walknave, 1^d for not prosecuting suit against Henry s. of Robert s. of Geoffrey.

Alvirthorp. William de Castilford sues Robert Hode of Neuton for debt for 6^s, which is acknowledged; Robert fined 4^d

Christian widow of Adam de Flanshou, and Henry Tashe (4^d) agree in two matters.

Thornes. Philip Damisell and Robert Peger (2^d) agree.

Osset. Thomas de Schelley appears against Henry le Walker; William Hirning, bailiff, who was to have attached the said Henry, fined 2^d for not having yet done so.

Thornes. Thomas Tashe and William s. of Elias Bulneys (2^d) agree. Also John Bulneys and Emma d. of Robert Gelleson (2^d).

Bailiff. John Godefrai appears against William de Ledes, Laurence de Casteley, surety for the said William's appearance, fined 2^d for not having him in court.

Sourby. Adam s. of Roger and Hugh Wade (6^d) agree.

Alvirthorp. John Attebarre sues John Gerbot, because, after he had taken a piece of meadow in Alvirthorp from Gerbot, he came and mowed the vesture thereof; damages, 5^s. An inquisition taxes damages at 18^d; fine, 2^d

John Attebarre surrenders ½ acre of arable land in Alverthorp; committed to William s. of William Grenehod of Wakefeld; entry, 4^d

Bailiff. John de Keresford sues John Wolmer for debt, and appoints William de Castilford, his attorney.

John de Heton is attached by William de Heton, to answer Laurence de Casteley, on the part of the king, for trespass committed in the soke of Wakefeld.

Holne. Richard, bailiff of Meltham, 2^d; Thomas le Schephird, 4^d; John del Stokkes, 6^d; Peter del Birch, 4^d, for escapes.

Wakefeld. Idonea Colleson, 1^d for vert.

Total of this Court— Alvirthorp, 18ᵈ
                      Thornes, 6ᵈ
                      Bailiff, 3ᵈ
                      Wakefeld, 1ᵈ
                      Osset, 2ᵈ

Horbiry. Hugh de Disteford sues John s. of Elias de Horbiry for debt. Surety—William Hirnyng. He also sues Adam Godali for debt. Surety—Robert Sunman.

Stanneley. Margery Mote sues Richard Poket for trespass. Surety—Walter Gunne.

Walter Gunne, executor of the will of Robert Gunne, sues Robert Lepar for trespass.

Bailiff. Robert Clement sues James del Okes for trespass. Surety—John Clement.

COURT held at Wakefeld on Friday, the 6th of September, 19 Edw. II [1325].

Essoins. Hugh le Nodder, attorney of William de Nevill, by William de Castilford.

Thomas de Seyuill, by John de Hopton.

Thomas de Thornton, by Robert de Mora.

Richard de Birstall, by Thomas de Birstall. Surety—German Kay.

Thomas le Forster, by John de Mora. Surety—William de Birton.

Robert de Wyneronthorp, by German Filcok.

Hugh de Stanneley, by German Kay.

William del Okes, by Robert de Grotton.

Bailiff. William de Lockewode sues John de Mora for carrying away 3 horses from a place called Luppesheved in Thornes; value 20ˢ; and he afterwards suffered them to stray; and also seized wood in the same place; value, 5ˢ. John says he found two horses in Luppesheved, in a place called Dykbankes, eating his grass; and he kept them till they were delivered by the sworn bailiff, Robert de Mora. He is to wage his law with regard to the third horse.

Sandale. Henry Tasshe, and Thomas de Holgate, Henry le Quarreur and Robert Alot (6ᵈ) agree.

Bailiff. John de Metheley and John s. of Thomas de Heton have a love-day.

Hyperum. William del Hingandrode, 4ᵈ for not prosecuting Robert de Werlulley, chaplain.

Bailiff. John de Burton, and William de Rylay and John s. of Thornes de Heton have a love-day.

John de Shelley essoins against Robert Tyeis by John de Gledeholt. Surety—John Woderoue.

Thomas Gates to be resummoned to answer William **de** Cresacre, rector of the church of Mirfeld.

Sandale. John del Dene, attacher of Henry le Walker to answer Thomas de Shelley, in the mercy.

COURT held at Wakefeld, the Friday after the Feast of St. Dunstan (7 Sep.) 19 Edw. II. [1325].

Essoins. Richard de Birstall, by Thomas de Birstall. Surety —William Cussing.

John Hood, by Thomas Torald. Surety—William del Okes.

Hugh le Nodder, attorney of William de Nevill, by William Cussing. Surety—Robert de Mora.

Bailiff. James del Okes sues William Erl for breaking an agreement, made between them at Wakefeld in 17 Edw. II, by which William was to acquit James and keep him unharmed from the king's bailiffs' and servants; and afterwards, Henry Russell, the king's sub-escheator in these parts, entered James's land, and carried off the vesture thereof, value 30ˢ. Defendant wages his law. Surety—German Kay.

John s. of Robert (3ᵈ) and Ralph de Sheffeld agree.

Rastrik. Alan del Hey, 40ᵈ for vert cut in Scambandene.

Henry del Weld and Roger Fox (4ᵈ) agree.

Imparlance removed into the Burgesses' Court. The imparlance between Henry Launel and John Erl for debt is removed into the Burgesses' Court of the town of Wakefeld, at the suit of the burgesses of the said town, because the said John is a burgess. And as the said John, summoned a second time to the Court Baron of Wakefeld, does not come, an order is given for him to be distrained for the first time in the Burgesses' Court there.

Thornes. William Nundy sues William s. of Thomas, for 3ˢ 6ᵈ for a quarter of oats, which is acknowledged. Defendant's fine pardoned, because he is poor.

Horbiry. Matilda formerly wife of Adam Broun 2ᵈ for not prosecuting Roger de Friston.

Hyperum. John de Hyperumhirst, 6ᵈ for withdrawing suit from Shipdene mill.

Holne. John de Castro surrenders a messuage and 21½ acres in Wolvedale in the graveship of Holne; committed to William, s. of Henry Wade; entry, 6ˢ 8ᵈ

New rent. Adam de Holne gives 2ᵈ for licence to take ½ acre of new rent in Holne; rent, 2ᵈ

Alvirthorp. Robert s. of Adam de Flansou gives 12ᵈ as a heriot on ½ bovate and 2 acres of land and meadow in Flansou, in the graveship of Alvirthorp, on the death of his father, whose heir he is.

Stanneley. Edusa Preste surrenders ½ acre in Stanneley; committed to Margaret formerly wife of John Kay; entry, 4ᵈ

Thornes. Thomas Tutche surrenders ½ bovate in Thornes; committed to John s. of Elias Bulneys; entry, 3ˢ 4ᵈ

Holne. John del Grene surrenders an acre in Holne; committed to Robert s. of Sarah; entry, 6ᵈ

Thomas de Hyengeclif surrenders 8 acres in Holne; committed to William de Hyengeclif; entry, 2ˢ

Osset. Richard s. of Henry le Grayne, surrenders 6 acres in Goukthorp, in the graveship of Osset; committed to Hugh de Disteford; entry, 18ᵈ

Robert Sonman surrenders ½ acre in Osset; committed to Adam de Goukethorp; entry, 6ᵈ

Walter Maunsel surrenders ⅓ of a rood in Osset; committed to Gilbert le Smith and Eva, his wife; entry, 3ᵈ

Stanneley. Edusa Preste surrenders 2 acres in Stanneley; committed to Robert le Lepar and Alice his wife; entry, 12ᵈ

Holne. Amabilla le Badger, 6ᵈ; Thomas Folp, 6ᵈ; John le Ficheler, 3ᵈ; Alan le Mercer's wife, 6ᵈ; John Abraham, 6ᵈ; Henry s. of Henry de Birton, 3ᵈ; John le Mathon's wife, 2ᵈ; the wife of William s. of Tille, 3ᵈ; Robert le Fissher, 3ᵈ and Elias his partner, 3ᵈ, for selling flour mixed with bran and dust.

Stanneley. Richard de Bateley, for cutting down two saplings, 12ᵈ

Thomas Beel, 1ᵈ; Elizota de Bateley, 12ᵈ; John Isabel, 4ᵈ; John Flachard, 1ᵈ; Hugh Cort, 4ᵈ; Robert Beel, 1ᵈ, for dry wood.

Walter Gunne, for cutting alder, 2ᵈ; and 12ᵈ for not doing his share of the maintenance of ditches.

John Bateman, 4ᵈ; and John s. of Thomas de Lofthous, 6ᵈ, for escapes.

Hyperum. John de Holway of Hyperum sues Roger de Hasilhirst for debt.

Four acres of land in Hyperum, left unoccupied for the last 12 years, formerly held by Mogota Maure, committed to John del Clif; rent 3ᵈ and acre, as it formerly paid; entry, 6ᵈ

Alvirthorp. Half a rood left unoccupied by Richard Roddok, for the last 4 years, which used to pay 3ᵈ a year, committed to Richard Withoundes; entry, 2ᵈ. Void, because claimed by Richard Ruddok's heir.

Wakefeld. Ibbota Sparow, 2ᵈ; Ibbota Chapman, 2ᵈ; Johanna de Sandale, 2ᵈ; Magota Spink, 4ᵈ; Twentipair's wife, 1ᵈ; Thomas Cussing, 1ᵈ; Liftfast's handmaid, 1ᵈ; William Bul, 2ᵈ; Alice d. of Peter de Acom, 3ᵈ; Richard Kay's handmaid, 1ᵈ; John Haget, 1ᵈ; and Henry Badger, 1ᵈ for dry wood.

Sandale. Henry s. of William de Plegwyk, 12ᵈ; William de Collay, 12ᵈ; and William s. of John, 6ᵈ, for saplings.

Adam del Grene and Adam le Dey, 12ᵈ each for three small saplings.

Osset. Robert Peny, 2ᵈ; Hugh de Chideshill, 2ᵈ; Jordan Scot, 2ᵈ Adam le Oxhird, 2ᵈ, and Thomas le Pinder, 2ᵈ, for dry wood.

Wakefeld. Agnes Hog; John Hood; Richard de Waterton, 2ᵈ each for dry wood.

John Pollard, Jordan le Mauwer, 2ᵈ each; Dom. John Wolmer and Richard Man, 6ᵈ each, for dry wood and timber, etc.

Total of this Court, 40ˢ
      Bailiff, 9ᵈ and 12ᵈ rent.   Rastrik, 3ˢ 4ᵈ
      Horbiry . . .   Hyperum, 12ᵈ and rent, 6ᵈ
      Alvirthorp 14ᵈ (rent. 6ᵈ)   . . .

COURT held at Wakefeld on Friday, the tenth of October, 20 Edw. II [1326].

Essoins. William de Totehill, by Thomas de Totehill. Surety—John, s. of Robert.

Robert de Wyrunthorp, by William de Stansfeld. Surety—Robert de Mora.

Thomas de Thorntone, by Robert de Mora. Surety—William Alayn.

Dom. Ralph de Sheffeld, by William Alayn. Surety—Thomas Alayn.

Ellen de Rastrik, by William Cussing.

Hugh le Nodder, attorney of William de Nevill, by Henry Tasshe.

Adam de Stayncliffe, by John de Shippeden.

John del Leeghe, by Robert de Grottone.

Bailiff. William Gardiner offers himself against Philip del Hill. The said Philip, attached by old cloths, value 30ˢ, in the custody of Hugh Viroun and Henry Brounsmith, does not come. Further attachment to be made.

Recognizance. William and John Alayn acknowledge a debt of 10ˢ to John de Burton, and fine 12ᵈ for wrongful detention.

Servient. Judgment pending. The judgment pending between John de Burton, plaintiff, and John le Pynder and Jordan his brother, postponed till next court; and meanwhile enquiry must be made of the lord, because the suitors of court say it is not a matter for them, to give judgment in such a case, because one side is free, and the other, the lord's villeins (nativi).

William Filche, clerk, sues William Hirnyng for a stone of wool, value 6ˢ, which plaintiff bought in the town of Wakefeld from Adam s. of Roger de Sourbi, which was to be delivered last Midsummer day, William Hirnyng being surety, and the present suit is brought in consequence of non-delivery. Defendant acknowledges ½ the stone, and is to pay this; fine, 2ᵈ. The other half he denies, and wages his law. Surety—Richard Withoundes.

Sourbi. Thomas de Heitfeld, 4ᵈ for not prosecuting suit against John s. of Robert de Sourbi.

Stanneley. Eva formerly wife of Symon Tityng who was suing Henry Nelot for her dower in a rood of land in Stanley, comes and acknowledges that she surrendered her dower therein to the lord, through Thomas le Taverner, Bailiff of the free Court, in the time of John de Burton. She is therefore fined 2ᵈ for false claim.

Alvirthorp. John Attebarre sues John Garbot for 10ᵈ for a piece of meadow demised him for a term of years. Defendant acknowledges the same; fine, 2ᵈ; and another 2ᵈ (and damages to be taxed at the next court) for grazing cattle on plaintiff's grass.

John Garbot sues John Attebarre for 18ᵈ for the carriage of timber from the old park to Wakefeld Mill. An inquisition is to be taken; 10ᵈ is found to be owing, which is to be paid; fine 3ᵈ. He also sues said John for 3ᵈ, which he says defendant unlawfully levied from him in the Earl of Lancaster's time for a rent of hens, which he had been accustomed to pay him. John Attebarre says that on account of his losing a sum of money over the rent of hens, plaintiff together with all who held by the same tenure voluntarily paid defendant the said rent a second time to recoop him for his loss. This is confirmed by an inquisition, plaintiff fined 1ᵈ for false claim.

Holne. Richard del Dene sues John del Bothe for obstructing a public path in a place called Littilwodlone. John says the place in question is land he took from the lord in court, and subsequently enclosed. An inquisition is to be taken on this matter, and on John del Bothe's charge against Richard, of throwing down his fences, etc.

Imparlance removed. The imparlance between William Cussing and John de Feri, for carrying away hay, is removed into the Court Burgage in the town of Wakefeld at the petition of the bailiffs of the same, in accordance with their charter, because both parties are burgesses of the said town.

Alvirthorp. Christian formerly wife of Adam de Flanshou, 2ᵈ for false claim against John Attebarre.

An inquisition finds that Henry de Swylington had a right to impound the cattle of Geoffrey and William de Birkinshagh in a place called Brounrode; they are fined 4ᵈ each for false claim. Also that Henry did not impede Geoffrey's access to his land in Brounrode; Geoffrey fined 4ᵈ for false claim; and Henry, 4ᵈ for false claim against Geoffrey for impoundng his cattle in the same place.

. . . John Bulnais and William s. of William de Thornes (6ᵈ) agree.

. . . Robert s. of Ivo (2ᵈ) and William Malyn agree.

William s. of William s. of Thomas, and William Malyn (2ᵈ) agree.

Stanneley. An inquisition find that Thomas Gunne carried corn from the land of Robert s. of Henry Bulle, without his consent; damages 18^d; fine, 6^d

Alvirthorp. John de Fery, by John Garbot, bailiff of Alvirthorp, surrenders a rood of land in Alvirthorp; committed to Alice, wife of John de Grengate; entry, 4^d

John de Grengate surrenders 3 roods in Alvirthorp; committed to Alice his wife; entry, 8^d

Osset. Matilda Cole surrenders 4½ acres in Osset; committed to Henry Alcok; entry, 8^d

Holne. Richard del Dene surrenders 2 acres of meadow in Holne; committed to Robert del Bothe; entry, 12^d

Thornes. Margery formerly wife of Elias de Thornes, surrenders 2¼ acres in Thornes; afterwards re-committed to the said Margery for life, with remainder to Henry her son, who fines 12^d for entry. Similarly, an acre and a quarter in Thornes, with remainder to Robert her son, who fines 6^d; and 3¾ acres, with remainder to William her son, who pays 2^s for entry.

Alverthorp. John Swan surrenders an acre of meadow in Alverthorp; committed to John s. of Robert de Wakefeld, for 12 years after a term of 4 years he already has therein.

Holne. New rent. William Strekais gives 12^d to take an acre of new land in Holne; rent, 4^d

Stanneley. Matilda Bennet, Thomas Gunne, John de St. Swithin, and Thomas Odam's wife, 2^d each; Walter Gunne, 7^d; the wife of William s. of Thomas de Wodehalle, 2^d; William del Spen, 3^d; Richard Poket, 2^d; John Poket, 2^d; Henry s. of Robert, 12^d; John del Bothem, 1^d, and John Dade, 1^d, for dry wood, etc.

Bailiff. John de Burgh, 6^d; John de Heton, 6^d for not coming.

Robert de Grottone, 6^d; John Fraunceis of Warnefeld, 6^d; Robert, servient of the vicar of Warnefeld, 4^d; Robert le Cartewright, 2^d; William de Esshehall, 4^d; Alice Cocus of Warnefeld, 3^d, and Dom John, vicar of Warnefeld, 3^d, for escapes of beasts in Wilbright.

Sandale. James del Okes, 12^d; Agnes de Ripon, 6^d; John Broun, 3^d; John Harpour, 2^d; Amabilla Pecy, 1^d, and Thomas de Milnethorp, 2^d, for escapes and dry wood.

Hiperum. John de Shepley, 2^d; Roger de Brighous, 3^d; John Steven, 2^d; Richard del Hole, 2^d; Thomas del Cliffe, 1^d, for escapes.

Sourbi. William de Wolnronwall, for an escape, 6^d. Surety— Robert his brother.

William de Stainland, 3^d; Hugh s. of Hugh de Northland, —; Peter de Barkesland, 3^d; John del Frith, 1^d; Henry del Lone, 6^d; John de Lighesles, 2^d, and Robert de Benteleyrode, 2^d, for escapes.

Osset. Eva le White, 1^d; John s. of William, 2^d; Thomas Hogge, 1^d; Richard Snart, 1^d; Amabilla Hyrning, 1^d; Magota Long, 1^d; Johanna de Heton, 2^d, and Hugh Dissheforth, 2^d, for escapes and dry wood.

Thornes. Evota Hauke, 3^d for cutting vert.

Wakefeld. Adam Levayn; Robert Willeson; Robert Joseson; Jordan le Maware; the son of Richard Resound; Alice, handmaid of Cecilia le Walker; John de Wolveley; Walter le Sagher; Henry le Netehird; Thomas Sele's wife, and John Tope, 2^d each; Robert Nelot, 3^d; Amabilla, handmaid of Richard de Aula, 3^d; William Erl, 6^d; Robert Swerd, 2^d; John Harihill, 3^d; Richard de Lupesheved, 2^d; Magota Marjoro, 2^d; Robert Capoun, 2^d; John Pollard's son, 6^d; Thomas le Wright's wife, 2^d; Richard de Waterton, 3^d; William le Glover, 3^d; Richard Steel, 3^d; Thomas de Louth, 2^d; Robert Sheep, 2^d; Julian Sibbeson, 1^d; Richard Dikeman, 2^d; Henry Drake, 2^d; Thomas Cussing, 2^d; the son of Thomas s. of Henry, 2^d; Richard de Aula, 6^d; Matilda Tirsy, 2^d; Alice Hoseley, 2^d; Johanna Leget, 2^d; and John Coliceson, 6^d, for dry wood, etc., etc.

Total of this Court—33^s 1^d—and new rent, 4^d

i.e.

Bailiff, 4^s 4^d	Sourbi, 2^s 3^d
Stanley, 3^s 10^d	Thornes, 4^s 7^d
Alverthorp, 3^s 2^d	Osset, 21^d
Holne, 2^s (and new rent, 4^d)	
Sandale, 2^s 2^d	Hyperum, 13^d
Wakefeld, 7^s 9^d	Horbiry, 2^d

COURT held at Halifax on Monday, 27th October, 20 Edw. II [1326]

Sourbi. Thomas del Leghrode sues Adam Migge of Warouley for losing a cow, a steer and 2 heifers, entrusted into his keeping, and worth 30^s. Adam says he gave no warranty to keep the beasts; an inquisition confirms him. Thomas fined 6^d for false claim.

New rents. Thomas del Bothern gives 4^s to take 2 acres of new land in Waroulay; rent, 12^d

Richard Alotson, 12^d to take an acre of new land in Sourbi; rent, 6^d

Thomas s. of Henry de Rieburnedene, gives 2^s 6^d for license to heriot on a messuage and 5 acres in Sourbi, which belonged to his father, whose heir he is.

Adam del Tounende de Miggeley, by William s. of Hugh, bailiff, surrenders 5 acres in Sourbi; committed to Thomas s. of William de Saltonstall, entry, 2^s 6^d

New rents. Richard de Loddyngdene gives 5^s to take 4¼ acres in le Brodehirst; rent 25½^d.

William s. of Hugh de Warlouley, 12^d to take an acre of new land in Warlouley; rent, 6^d

John s. of Elias de Warlouley, 2^s 6^d to take 2 acres of new land in Warlouley; rent, 12^d

John de Elfletburgh, 2^s 6^d to take 2$\frac{1}{2}$ acres of new land in Sourbi; rent, 15^d

Adam s. of Roger, and John his brother, by William s. of Hugh, bailiff, surrender 2 acres in Sourbi; committed to John de Elfletburgh; entry, 2^s

Robert s. of John de Cockecroft, surrenders 3 acres in Stany-dene; committed to Adam s. of William de Northeland; entry, 2^s; also a single acre there; committed to Robert, s. of Wymark; entry, 12^d

Adam. s. of Roger, and John, his brother, surrender 4$\frac{1}{2}$ acres in Sourbi; committed to William del Loyne; entry, 2^s 6^d

New rents. William del Loyne gives 2^s to take an acre of new land in Sourbi; rent, 2^s

William s. of Jordan de Skercote, 12^d to take $\frac{1}{2}$ acre of new land in Warlouley; rent, 3^d

William Mahaud, 12^d for the same.

Adam s. of Alexander, 2^s for 1$\frac{1}{4}$ acre there; rent, 7$\frac{1}{2}$^{d}

Robert de Sothill surrenders 4$\frac{3}{4}$ acres in Warlouley; committed to John Tailliour; entry, 3^d

Bailiff elected. Adam de Coventre is elected bailiff of Sourbi, and is sworn, and is answerable for the farm of the mill of Sourby, etc.

Ivo de Saltonstall sues William Miller of Warlouley, for taking 2^s from Ivo to pay in his name to Hugh de Coppelay, and failing to pay the same. Defendant acknowledges this; fine, 6^d

Adam s. of Roger, surrenders 3 acres in Sourbi; committed to Thomas s. of Julian Wade; entry, 18^d

Total of this Court—40^s—and new rent, 8^s
All from Sourbi.

———

The Sheriff's tourn held there the same day.

12 Jurors. Richard de Waddesworth; Thomas s. of Richard; Robert de Sourbi; Ivo de Saltonstall; Henry de Holgate; John de Rediker; William del Ryding; John de Northland; John s. of Robert de Shesewelley; William del Bothem; Geoffrey de Stodeley and Thomas de Sothill, who say

Bailiff. John s. of Adam de Routonstall, cast his son into a certain well by Lyversege, and held him down (*demersit*) with felonious intent. He is to be taken.

Sourbi. The wives of Bate Dyer of Halifax, of Roger Spil-wod and of Alexander de Hynggandrode, 12^d each for brewing, etc.

Matilda, wife of John Kypas, 12ᵈ for the same.

William, servant of the vicar, 2ˢ for drawing blood from Roger Spilwode and his wife.

Roger Spilwode's wife, from Julian d. of Thomas s. of Cecilia; 12ᵈ

John s. of Richard de Waddesworth, from Thomas Culpoun; 12ᵈ

Margery wife of William s. of Hugh, raised the hue without cause on Hugh Wade; 12ᵈ

Richard s. of Thomas de Ovenden, drew blood from Thomas s. of Alexander; 12ᵈ

Julian d. of Thomas s. of Cecilia, from Roger Spilwode's wife; 12ᵈ

Total of this tourn—10ˢ 6ᵈ—all from Sourbi.

COURT held at Brighous on Tuesday, 28th October, 20 Edw. II [1326].

Hyperum. Alice d. of Matthew de Totehill, sues William de Sondreland for land. Surety—Matthew de Totehill. She pays 3ˢ 4ᵈ to have an inquisition of 24 jurors.

William de Halifax, miller, surrenders ½ acre in Northourum; committed to Bate de Halifax; entry, 6ᵈ

Bailiff. Thomas s. of William de Fekesbi, gives 3ˢ 4ᵈ as a relief on 2 messuages and 2 bovates of land in the toun of Fekesbi.

Rastrik. Thomas s. of Roger del Green, surrenders 10¼ acres and ⅔ rood in Rastrik; committed to Henry del Okes for 10 years; entry only 18ᵈ, because the land is poor and neglected.

William Forester and Agnes his wife, surrender 5¼ acres and ⅓ of a rood in Rastrik; committed to the said Henry for 10 years; entry 8ᵈ because as above.

Agnes wife of John s. of Henry de Fekesbi, sues Henry le Waynwright for 8ˢ, as heir and executor of Henry his late father, who, as bailiff, received 8ˢ from plaintiff, by the hand of Thomas Alayn, bailiff of the Free Court of Wakefeld, for ? an adjournment, (*ad differend dce Agnet*), which he did not effect. An order given for recovery of the 8ˢ; fine, 4ᵈ

Hiperum. William Peck surrenders a messuage and 10 acres in Brighous; committed to John s. of Roger de Brighous; entry, 6ˢ 8ᵈ

The township of Schelf, 12ᵈ for contempt in refusing to elect a constable.

One third of all the lands formerly held by Adam del Bothe in Northourum, to be seized into the lord's hand, because John Sutor bought the said third out of court; and carried the vesture off the said land.

Total of this Court—17ˢ 2ᵈ *i.e.* Services, 3ˢ 4ᵈ
    Rastrik, 2ˢ 4ᵈ   Hyperum, 11ˢ 6ᵈ

The Sheriff's tourn held there the same day.

12 Jurors. Henry de Coldley, William de Lockewod, Richard Couhird, John de Birstall, Thomas de Whitwod, William de Whitacres, John de Shipdene, Richard de Colvirsley, John de Barkesey, Richard del Rokes, Adam de Quernebi and John s. of William.

Rastrik. William del Hill of Berkesland, 12ᵈ for not coming.

Thomas s. of Hugh, and Thomas de Wodheved, 12ᵈ each for drawing blood from one another.

Hiperum. Thomas Miller of Shepden drew blood from Thomas Drake; 12ᵈ

John Drake from John Miller; 12ᵈ

John s. of John Miller, from Thomas Drake; 12ᵈ

Bailiff. Richard de Skurneton, Idonia his wife, and William s. of the said Richard, wilfully killed John de Wraggebi, and carried him away, together with his goods to the value of 40ˢ. They are to be taken.

Hiperum. John de Brighous and John de Skercotes, 12ᵈ each for drawing blood from one another.

Thomas le Waynwright, from John de Brighous; 12ᵈ

John Clareson, from John, servant of the lord of Clifton; 12ᵈ

John Dobson of Southourum, from John de Skercotes; 12ᵈ

John s. of Roger de Brighous, disclosed the council of his associates; fine, 3ˢ 4ᵈ

Rastrik. Roger del Hirst, 12ᵈ for not coming to the court.

Hiperum. John s. of Robert, drew blood from the servant of Richard Tibson; 12ᵈ

Thomas le Taillour and John de Hiperumhirst, 12ᵈ each for not coming.

Total of this Tourn—19ˢ 10ᵈ *i.e.* Rastrik, 4ˢ
                          Hiperum, 15ˢ 10ᵈ

COURT held at Birton on Tuesday, 29th October, 20 Edw. II [1326].

Holne. Richard del Dene fined 12ᵈ, under an inquisition, for fasle claim against John del Bothe for blocking up a public path in Littilwodlone; and 12ᵈ for throwing down John's hedges. Damages taxed at nothing.

Adam le Waynwright sues Richard s. of William, for assault; damages, 100ˢ. Richard acknowledges the assult, and asks taxation of damages; they are assessed at 5ˢ to be paid at once; Adam is wounded in the hand, and it is uncertain whether he will recover the use of his two last fingers; another 5ˢ is therefore to be paid at Whitsuntide, if he does not recover their use; fine, 12ᵈ

Christian de Heppeworth sues Richard Child and Margery his wife, for 4 ells of linen cloth, given to the said Margery to take care of; damages, 12ᵈ. Defendants cannot deny it; Richard is therefore fined 12ᵈ, and ordered to return the linen or pay plaintiff 12ᵈ

Richard s. of William, sues Richard s. of Amabilla, for driving him into his house, by aiming at him with his bow stretched and arrow in position; he is fined, under an inquisition, 6ᵈ for false claim.

Henry s. of Adam, sues Thomas Hebson for 5ˢ, which he paid him on the spot for a stone of wool. Thomas says that for the 5ˢ with which he is charged he paid Henry 10ˢ in usury. Plaintiff fined 12ᵈ for false claim.

Robert Scopard sues Adam del Green and Adam s. of Nicholas Keneward, for 18ˢ 8ᵈ as sureties for Thomas de Wodhous. They acknowledge owing 12ˢ, for which they pay a fine of 2ˢ; the other 2ˢ 8ᵈ, they utterly deny, and beg for an inquisition. Afterwards Robert withdraws his further claim, and is fined 3ᵈ

Thomas s. of Gilbert, surrenders a rood in Alstanley; committed to Adam Broun; entry, 6ᵈ

Matthew son of Gilbert, surrenders another rood; committed to the same; entry, 6ᵈ; and a second rood, committed to Mariota de Wildboreleghe; entry, 6ᵈ

New rent. The said Matthew gives 12ᵈ to take ½ acre of new land in Alstanley; rent, 2ᵈ

Thomas Hebson surrenders an acre in Fogheleston; committed to William de Halumshire; entry 12ᵈ

William Totti surrenders 2½ acres in Fogeleston; committed to Alice, d. of Adam Bensome; entry, 18ᵈ

New rent. Adam de Hogley gives 12ᵈ to take ½ acre of new land in Alstanley; rent, 2ᵈ

Total of this Court—13ˢ 9ᵈ—and new rent, 4ᵈ
All from Holne.

———

The Sheriff's tourn there the same day.

12 Jurors. John de Shepeley, Adam de Heley, William de Rieley, Richard de Thornteley, Robert de Wolwro, Richard de Birton, Richard de Heppeworth, Adam Kenward, Adam del Green, Richard del Bothe, Henry Wade and Henry del Lee, who say

Holne. Agnes del Lee drew blood from John s. of Alan le Pedder, 12ᵈ

Adam de Heley, from John de Shelley; 12ᵈ

Julian Erseward, from Margery le Seuwester, 12ᵈ

Richard s. of Hugh, 2ˢ for not coming.

Bailiff. John s. of the nurse, opened the house-door of Cecilia d. of John Gepsone, entered her house, and stole away cloth, worth 5^s. He is to be taken.

Holne. Richard s. of William, drew blood from Adam le Waynwright; 12^d

Bailiff. Adam de Foulewood, together with some stranger, entered Robert de Wolwro's house, broke open the door of his chamber, and stole clothes and other things, worth 20^s. He is to be taken.

Total of this Tourn—6^s—all from Holne.

COURT held at Wakefeld on Friday, the Vigil of All Saints (Nov. 1) 20 Edw. II [1326].

Essoins. John de Hopton, attorney of Brian de Thornill, by Robert de Mora. Surety—William Templer.

Richard de Birstall, by Thomas de Birstall. Surety—Robert de Grottone.

John de Mora, by William de Mora. Surety—William Grenhod.

William de Birton, by John de Gledeholt. Surety—Richard de Thornteley.

Bailiff. John de Burton, 6^d for not prosecuting suit against John le Pynder and Jordan his brother.

William Hyrnyng makes the law he waged against William Filche, who is fined 4^d for false claim.

Judgment pending between Thomas de Totehill and Ralph de Kerlinghow; defendant is considered to have made no defence because he produces suit instead of waging his law. Thomas is therefore to recover damages. Ralph then asks that damages may be taxed. Thomas submits he is not entitled to taxation, because he made no defence. The suitors are to come to the next court, and decide.

Henry s. of Robert s. of Geoffrey de Stanneley, sues Hugh de Stanneley, for coming to his house in Stannely, 19 Edw. II, and carrying off hay, worth 7^s. Hugh wages his law. Surety—John Attebarre.

Holne. William s. of Gilbert, and John del Hole (12^d) agree.

Bailiff. William Cussyng, and Richard s. of Henry (4^d) agree.

William Cussyng and John Tasshe (4^d) aree.

Suit removed. The imparlance between John Hobsone, plaintiff, and Richard Brounsone for debt, is removed into the Borough Court of the town of Wakefeld, at the petition of the bailiffs of the said town, in accordance with their charter, because both are burgesses of the said town.

Henry s. of Robert de Stanneley, and Robert s. of Roger de Metheley (6^d) agree.

Rastrik. Adam s. of William, sues William del Hill for debt. Surety—Thomas de Scamenden.

Bailiff. Edmund Gates sues John Scot of Deuesbri, senior, and Richard Baicok for trespass. Surety—Richard de Deuesbiri, chaplain.

Thornes. William s. of Thomas de Thornes, and William Malyn (3ᵈ) agree. The said William (4ᵈ) and Richard Proudfot agree.

Holne. An inquisition finds that Thomas de Belleclif, Nicholas s. of Symon and Richard de Elwardhulles owe Adam de Bottirley 66ˢ under a final agreement made between the, touching an indictment made by them upon him. They are to pay the same, and a fine of 2ˢ. They are also fined . . . , for false claim in their suit against him.

. . . An inquisition finds that Robert s. of Richard Peger, assaulted John s. of Elyas de Thornes . . .

[*The end of the membrane is torn away; there are four disjointed fragments tied up with the roll, but not one of them fits on here*].

. . . . . .

. . . ? Thomas Bunney surrenders . . . committed to Richard ? Sicel.

. . . John s. of Hugh de Horbiri, surrenders . . . committed to . . . and

. . . Isabel, d. of William de Whiteacres, to hold to the said Richard and Isabel and their heirs; with remainder, in default, to . . .

Richard Child fined 6ᵈ, and 6ᵈ damages for entering the house of Robert del Clif, and carrying off a napkin.

Matthew Drabel fined 12ᵈ for not coming, when summoned, to answer Richard del Bothe.

Richard de Carteworth sues Henry de Longley for trespass. Surety—Henry de Carteworth.

Bailiff. Henry s. of Robert s. of Geoffrey de Stanley, sues Hugh de Stanley, for driving a cow belonging to plaintiff from Stanley to the Hospitallers' fee, and detaining it there; damages, 7ˢ. Defendant says the animal was grazing on his grass, which plaintiff denies. An inquisition to be taken as to whether defendant is bound to reply, except under the King's writ; as he claims the enclosure as his, and plaintiff claims the grass. An inquisition is to be taken.

Thornes. John s. of Elyas, 6ᵈ for calling John s. of Robert Peger a thief. No damages.

Osset. William Weaver sues Hugh de Dissceford for trespass, in having assaulted him and beaten him 6 years ago, so that his life was despaired of, and he was confined to his bed for nearly 3 years; damages, 100ˢ. Defendant says William set his dog on to a sow of his, and the sow's leg was broken, and for this he beat him lightly with a rod over the back, and had given him compensation as thought right by the neighbours, and he begs an inquisition may be held. They afterwards agree, and Hugh fines 12^d

Thornes. William s. of Elyas, 2^d for false claim against John s. of Elyas de Thornes.

Evota Hauwe and Roger Viron (4^d) agree.

Sandale. A jury finds that Thomas de Holgate, receiver of the fees of the township of Crigleston, wrongfully retains 5^d of the said fees, and suffers others to remain uncollected, whereby the precept is diminished. He is to pay Robert de Grottone the said 5^d; fine, 6^d

Stanley. An inquisition finds that Walter Gunne mowed Robert Lepar's meadow, and carried off the hay; damages, 3^d; fine 4^d

Bailiff. Richard de Deuesbiry, chaplain, 12^d, and Nicholas Faber of Erdeslauwe, 3^d, for escapes in the new park.

Horbiry. John s. of Hugh de Horbiry, 2^d for vert.

Osset. Adam de Gaukethorp, 2^d; Hugh de Dissceford, 4^d; John del Dene, 2^d; Robert Sonman, 2^d; John Mauncel, 1^d; Thomas Hogge, 2^d; and Richard s. of John, 2^d for escapes.

Alvirthorp. Adam Rodde, 1^d for an escape.

Wakefeld. The handmaids of Ralph Bate and William de Mora, 1^d each for dry wood.

Stanley. John s. of Amabilla, 3^d; Robert Peel, 2^d, and John Flacherd's wife, 2^d, for dry wood.

Total of this Court—40^s 3^d *i.e.* Services, 3^s 3^d

Holne 25^s 6^d	Alvirthorp, 9^d
Horbiry, 3^s 6^d	Thornes, 3^s 5^d
Osset, 2^s 3^d	Sandale, 6^d
Stanley, 11^d	Wakefeld, 2^d

The Sheriff's tourn held at Wakefeld on Monday after the Feast of All Saints (Nov. 1). 20 Edw. II [1326].

12 Jurors. Robert de Stodeley; Henry de Chevet; Thomas Gates; Ralph de Kerlinghou; John s. of Richard of Osset; John Pykerd; Adam de Wodesom; German Cay; John de Fery; Robert Ilhore; John Dade and Henry Gantone, who say

Bailiff. John Woderoue's wife brews contrary to the assize; 6^d

The wife of Paulinus de Emley, 12^d; William le Hyne's wife, 12^d; Adam del Cote's wife, 6^d; Robert Miller, 6^d; Alice d. of Stephen, 6^d; Margery le Carter, 6^d, for the same.

John Benneson drew blood from Robert Shirtyng; 12^d

Johanna wife of Robert Shirtyng, from Amabilla d. of Clare; 6^d; and *vice versa*, 12^d

Richard Baicok, John Scot and William s. of William de Deuesbiry, blocked up a certain public path in Deuesbury, which had been made by general assent of all the town; 3^s

John Scot, 12^d for blocking up a path in Algerrode, which is public in open time.

Alice Anegold, 6^d for brewing at $\frac{1}{2}$^{d}

Geoffrey de Erdeslou, 6^d for not coming.

William de Ceyuill drew blood from the wife of John de Heton, 12^d

Stanley. Hugh s. of Hugh Scayff, from the son of John del Haghe; 6^d

Henry Dicar, from Thomas Odam; 6^d

Bailiff. Henry Tasshe, from Thomas Beel's wife; 18^d

Stanley. Elizabet Langshank, Nicholas de Bateley, the wives of Gilbert le Theker, Robert Lepar, Richard Pesci and Hugh Forester, 6^d each for brewing at $\frac{1}{2}$^{d} contrary to assize.

Bailiff. Robert de Boudrode and Henry le Walker, 12^d each for drawing blood from one another.

Alice d. of William de Birkenschagh, raised the hue with cause on Henry le Gardiner, who fines 12^d

Sandale. The wife of Robert Pelleson; of John Payn; of William de Colley; of Jokyn de Bismaran; of John de Wik, and of John s. of Hugh, 6^d each for brewing.

Alexander le Shephird, 12^d for drawing blood from John, his brother.

Thornes. Richard Proudfot drew blood from William s. of Thomas, 6^d

Robert s. of Richard Peger, from Robert de Luppesheved, 12^d

Bailiff. Robert Walker, from John s. of Thomas s. of Henry; 12^d

Robert servant of Philip Damysel, from Johanna d. of Evenild, 6^d

Roger Dunning, from Symon Hors, 18^d; and *vice versa*, 6^d

Walter de Tinglaw, from William Sausemer, 12^d

Henry s. of Robert, from Robert s. of Ivo, and John Barot, 2^s

John s. of Robert Joseson, from Adam Whitphether, 12^d

John s. of Robert Carpenter, from Amabilla Wyles, 12^d

John Wolmer blocked up a public path in front of his house, and prevented the water from flowing, 6^d

Total of this Tourn—36^s *i.e.*   Bailiff, 26^s 6^d
    Stanley, 4^s Thornes, 18^d
    Sandale, 4^s

COURT held at Wakefeld on Friday after the Feast of St. Edmund, (Nov. 22), 20 Edw. II [1326].

Essoins. Richard de Birstall, by Geoffrey de Normantone. Surety—Alan de Mersetone.

William de Birton, by Richard de Birton.

John de la Lighe, by John de Stansfeld. Surety—Richard de Wadworth. (This does not lie, because his tenement is in the lord's hand).

Hugh le Nodder, attorney of John de Nevill, by Richard de Mora. Surety—William Templar.

John Hod, by John Pollard. Surety—William Cussing.

Alvirthorp. Hugh le Barkar and John Garbot (2ᵈ) agree.

Bailiff. Henry s. of Robert s. of Geoffrey, 10ᵈ for not prosecuting suits against Hugh de Stanley.

Alvirthorp. John Attebarre and John Garbot (2ᵈ) agree.

Bailiff. Richard de Thorntley, attorney of Robert de Bello monte, essoins against Richard s. of Hugh, by Richard de Birton. Surety—Hugh de Stanneley.

Richard de Dewesbiry, chaplain, sues Thomas de Ceyuill for 3ˢ, the price of a quarter of oats sold him in 16 Edw. II. Defendant cannot deny, and is fined 4ᵈ

Thomas de Seyuill and Alice formerly wife of John de Heton, (4ᵈ) agree in two matters.

Holne. Richard del Bothe, plaintiff (6ᵈ) and Richard del Den and Matthew Drabel agree.

Thomas s. of John, and Richard del Bothe (12ᵈ) agree in two matters.

Richard de Carteworth (6ᵈ) and Henry de Longley agree.

Robert del Clif, 4ᵈ for not coming, when summoned, to answer Richard Child.

Hiperum. Richard del Thorp essoins against John s. of Jordan, by Thomas de Totehill. Surety—Adam de Heley. John appoints Adam de Sourbi his attorney.

Holne. Richard de Birtone, 6ᵈ for false claim against Adam le Waynwright.

The suit between Alice d. of Matthew de Totehill, of Totehill, and William de Sonderland, for land, is void because she is dead.

Hyperum. Cecilia d. of Matthew de Sheppedene, sues William de Sonderland for land. An inquisition of 24 is to reconsider the verdict of a jury of 12, who are to be distrained to attend the next court.

Thornes. William Nundy sues Robert s. of Richard Peger for 4ˢ 10ᵈ, the price of a horse. Robert acknowledges the debt; fine, 4ᵈ

Stanley. Hugh Forester and Walter [*sic*] (6ᵈ) agree.

Holne. An inquisition finds that Adam le Waynwright assaulted Richard s. of Walter, damages 3ˢ, and trod down his corn, damages, 10ᵈ; fine, 6ᵈ

Bailiff. Thomas Alayn attacher of Henry s. of Robert s. of Geoffrey de Stanley, 4ᵈ for not producing him in court.

The suitors of court decide that Ralph de Kerlinghou, who petitioned at the last court for taxation of damages, shall have no taxation, because he made no defence. Thomas de Totehill is therefore to recover 60^s against the said Ralph for his damages, fine, 6^d

Sourbi. William Wyle of Eland sues John Chapeleyn for debt. Surety—William Parmeter.

Stanley. Thomas Scayff by Robert Leper, bailiff of Alvirthorp, surrenders a rood of land in Ouchthorp in the graveship of Stanneley; committed to William Twentipaire, for 20 years; entry, 6^d

Hugh s. of Hugh Scayff, by Robert de Mora, under-bailiff, surrenders a rood of meadow in Ouchethorp, lying in le Northrode, committed to Thomas Cay for 11 years; entry, 3^d

Hiperum. Adam del Northende surrenders $\frac{1}{3}$ of a messuage and of a bovate in le Bothes, in the graveship of Hyperum; committed to John Sutor, for the term of the life of Eva wife of William de Claiton; entry, 12^d

Holne. New Rent. Thomas Botthecollock gives 18^d to take 1$\frac{1}{2}$ acre of new land in Thwong; rent, 6^d

Hyperum. John s. of Roger de Brighous, surrenders $\frac{1}{2}$ messuage and 5 acres in Hyperum; committed to John s. of Roger, junior; entry, 2^s 6^d

Holne. New rent. Cecilia del Rode gives 12^d to take $\frac{1}{2}$ acre of new land in Hepworth, rent, 2^d

Horbiry. Agnes d. of Robert Modisaule, surrenders $\frac{1}{4}$ of a messuage and of a bovate of land in Horbiry; committed to Robert s. of Robert Modisaule; entry, 2^s

Thornes. Johanna d. of Matilda, sues William s. of Elyas de Thornes for assaulting her in Thornes; damages, 20^s; an inquisition to be taken.

Sourbi. New rent. William s. of Nicholas, gives 2^s to take 1$\frac{1}{4}$ acre of new land in Warloulley wood; rent, 7$\frac{1}{2}$^{d}

Hyperum. New rent. William s. of Roger de Clifton, 12^d to take an acre of new land in Hyperum; rent, 3^d

An inquisition finds that on the day of his death Adam Loveladi was seised of a clearing called Hyrny . . , and that Jordan is his son and next heir, and that the said Jordan's mother paid a heriot on his behalf. The clearing is therefore delivered to Jordan by the steward.

Stanley. Henry s. of Robert, s. of Geoffrey, 12^d for the escape of 3 horses in Wilbight, 12^d, and 12^d for breaking a paling and taking a horse out of the park.

John brother of the said Henry, 12^d for the same.

William del Spen's wife & Matilda Benet, 6^d each; Alice del Spen, 2^d, for dry wood, etc.

Osset. Adam de Gaukethorp, 2^d; John del Dene, 2^d; Henry Sutor's wife, 1^d; Robert s. of Richard Sutor, 1^d; John Mauncel,

1^d; Thomas Hogge, 1^d; William Hyrning, 2^d; John s. of Richard, 1^d; Richard s. of John, 2^d; and Matthew de Shelley, 2^d, for escapes.

Wakefeld. John Richard, 2^d; William Richard, 2^d; Henry le Badger, 1^d; Agnes Hodde's handmaid, 2^d; for dry wood.

John Atteline, for 3 oak saplings in Thurstanhagh, 3^d

William Wright, William Godeheir, John Nelot, John Clement, Thomas le Taverner, William de Castelforth, William Bate, Robert Goldsmith and John de Fery, 6^d each, for not coming to elect the bailiff as they were enjoined.

Sandale. John de Halifax and Matthew de Blacker, 2^d each for vert.

Total of this Court—32^s 9^d and new rent, 18$\frac{1}{2}$^{d}

i.e. Bailiff, 2^s 6^d Alvirthorp 4^d
Holne, 5^s 10^d (and new rent, 8^d)
Thornes, 4^d Stanley, 5^s 5^d
Hiperum, 4^s 6^d (and new rent, 3^d)
Horbiry, 2^s Osset, 16^d
Sourbi, 4^s 11^d (and new rent, 7$\frac{1}{2}$^{d})
Wakefeld, 5^s 4^d Sandale, 4^d

COURT held at Wakefeld on Friday after the Feast of St. Nicholas the Bishop (Dec. 6) 20 Edw. II [1326].

Essoins. Thomas de Thornton, by John de Metheley. Surety— Thomas Alayn.

Brian de Thornhill, by John de Stansfeld. Surety—Hugh le Nodder.

William de Nevill, by the same.

Bailiff. William le Gardiner sues Philip del Hill for 20^s, for which plaintiff was surety to John de Dyneley; Philip undertook to pay the sum at Michaelmas, 16 Edw. II, and failed; whereupon John sued William in the King's Marshalsea at Pontefract, Nov. 17 Edw. II, and recovered the said debt; whilst the proceedings were pending plaintiff went to Philip and begged him to pay the money; Philip denied his responsibility. Defendant says William was never security at his request, and wages his law. Sureties— Thomas Alayn and Elyas de Horbiry. William appoints German Cay his attorney.

Henry s. of John de Heton (2^d) and Alice formerly wife of John de Heton, agree.

Holne. Richard Child sues Robert del Clif for removing Margery his wife, with her goods, from his house, and receiving her, contrary to his wish; damages, 20^s. An inquisition is to be taken.

Hiperum. Adam de Sourbi, attorney of John s. of Jordan, essoins against Richard de Thorp, by John de Stansfeld. Surety— Richard de Waddesworth.

Holne. Adam le Waynwright and William s. of Richard de Fogheleston, (2^d) agree.

Rastrik. Henry de Welda, Richard s. of Peter, Matthew de Totehill, Adam del Rode, Henry s. of Modde, and Henry s. of Henry, sue Elyas le Smyth for 30^s, which he promised to pay them as soon as he sold his land; which he has done in court to Adam del Rode; he now refuses to pay them. Elyas wages his law against them. Sureties—John de Gairgrave and Elyas de Horbiry.

Stanley. Thomas del Spen and Richard Poket (3^d) agree.

Thornes. Avice formerly wife of Ivo le Smyth, 2^d for not coming, when summoned to answer Robert s. of Emma, though she was seen in court.

Horbiry. John s. of Hugh de Horbiry, 3^d under the same circumstances.

Sourbi. John del Stanes, 3^d for not coming to answer William Wyles of Eland.

Thornes. John s. of Matilda and William s. of Elias de Tornes (2^d) agree.

Osset. Alice formerly wife of Robert le Couper, attached to answer Jordan Scot, 5^d for not coming.

Bailiff. Hugh de Stanley, 3^d for not coming to answer John Attebarre.

Alverthorp. Richard del Bothe and Richard de Colley (3^d) agree.

Osset. William s. of John de Gaukethorp, gives 2^s for license to heriot on a messuage and 2½ bovates in Gaukethorp.

Stanley. Richard Scayf surrenders an acre in Stanley; committed to Robert Ilhore for 18 years; entry, 6^d

Holne. William s. of William, surrenders a messuage and 8 acres in Holne; committed to Thomas s. of Thomas de Foeghleston; entry, 5^s

Stanley. Richard Scayf surrenders an acre in Stanley; committed to Henry Nelot, for 18 years; entry, 6^d

Bailiff. Adam Le Hewer is elected bailiff of Stanley.

Hiperum. John s. of Henry de Brighous, surrenders 5¼ acres in Brighous; committed to Adam s. of Roger de Brighous; entry, 3^s

. . . **Bailiff.** John de Flemmyng, 4^s; John de Eland, 2^s; John de Burgh, 4^s; Ralph de Sheffeld, 3^s 4^d; John de Quernebi, 2^s; John de Soland, 18^d; Richard de Crosseland, 18^d; . . . de Rastrik, 12^d; . . ., 18^d . . . [*some lines torn away at the end of the membrane, but none of the four pieces with the bundle fit in; they do not belong to this roll at all*].

[At the head of the membrane, otherwise blank, are two rough jottings, one of which is cut or torn away; the second is much rubbed : . . . which . . . the Prior of Lewes? . . . the lord's steward,? auditor[s]? and bailiffs coming twice in the year to Halifax to hold the tourn there].

COURT held at Wakefeld on Friday after the Feast of the Epiphany (6 Jan.) 20 Edw. II [1326].

Essoins. William de Birton, by Richard de Birton. Surety— William de Castelford.

Thomas de Seyuill, by William de Seyuill. Surety—Robert de Mora.

Brian de Thornhill, by John de Heppetone. Surety—Hugh le Nodder.

William de Nevill, by Hugh le Nodder.

Bailiff. Philip del Hill essoins against William le Gardiner, by John de Wodroue. Surety—Elias de Thorntley.

Adam, bailiff of Sourbi, sues Hugh de Coppeley for preventing him from carrying out his instructions; he is to be distrained to answer for contempt. He afterwards comes, and finds sureties for keeping the peace. Thomas de Totehill and William de Coppeley.

Sourbi. Thomas, vicar of Halifax, 12^d for sundry defaults. Surety—Richard de Waddesworth.

Roger de Grenwod sues Thomas, vicar of Halifax, for not keeping an agreement with regard to a bond for £40 by Richard de Waddesworth and others, given into his hands on the understanding that if an arbitration were not effected regarding a matter at issue between the plaintiff and the said Richard and others by a certain day, the said bond should be given up to plaintiff. Thomas seeks judgment on the ground that plaintiff has not specified for what arbitration was to be made. They are to come to the next court to hear judgment.

Rastrik. Henry de Walda and others, and Elias le Smyth (12^d) agree.

Hiperum. Cecilia d. of Matthew de Shepdene, 12^d for not prosecuting suit against William de Sonderland.

John s. of Jurdan le Milner, 3^d, for the same against Richard de Thorp.

Thornes. Robert s. of Emma, sues Alice formerly wife of Ivo le Smyth, for 8^s 6^d as surety for Thomas de Horbiry. She denies the suretyship. An inquisition to be taken.

Sourby. William Wyles de Eland and John Stanes de Soland (6^d) agree.

Staneley. John Spicer and Richard de Bateley (2^d) agree.

Holne. Magota Jeddoxter surrenders 8½ acres in Wolvedale to the use of Thomas Daweson and herself and their issue; with remainder, in default, to Magota and her heirs.

Osset. Jordan Scotte sues Alice formerly wife of Robert le Couper, for carrying away hay, worth 3^s, from a house at Heton, held by them both in common, Jordan holding ⅔, Alice ⅓. An inquisition to be taken on this, and another matter between them.

Holne. William de Craven sues John del Bothe for not keeping in repair a house, which John received of the plaintiff in exchange for 3 acres of land, and a house, and which was to be kept up for 3 years, at the end of which time the parties had the option of receiving back their former property again. John says the exchange was unconditional. An inquisition is to be taken— John brings a cross suit against William for refusing to carry out what he asserts was a term of the agreement, viz., to come into court, whenever required, and surrender the said 3 acres and a house. An inquisition is to be taken.

Richard Child (6^d) and Robert del Clif agree.

John Ibbot sues Hugh le Shoter for 3^d which he asserts he owes him for service at Daltonebanck. Defendant says he neither owes him any money, nor has received any on his account. An inquisition is ordered.

Thornes. William Bulnais sues William Malyn for 2^s 6^d for a bushel of corn sold him 4 years ago. An inquisition finds for plaintiff. Fine 2^d. Surety—Robert de Mora.

Sandale. John Lorimer and Henry s. of Hugh (2^d) agree.

Sourby. Thomas s. of Julian Wade, 6^d for not coming, when summoned, to answer Thomas de Hadreshelf.

Stanley. Adam le Hewer gives the lord 6^s 8^d in order not to be bailiff of Staneley.

Bailiff. Henry Tasshe, accused of fishing in Richard de Moseley's ponds, which have been taken into the lord's hand, pleads not guilty; an inquisition to be taken.

Holne. Mariota de Wildborleghe took ½ acre of unoccupied land at Anstanley, in bondage; entry, 2^d; rent, 2^d

Hiperum. John le Pynder surrenders a toft and 7¼ acres in Hiperum; committed to Robert s. of Henry de Crumwelbothume; entry, 2^s 6^d

Thornes. Elias Pierson gives 12^d for license not to be bailiff.

Bailiff. William Dolfyn is elected bailiff of Thornes.

William s. of Philip de Thornes, gives 12^d not to be bailiff.

Sandale. John Nalkeson, who held 8 acres from the lord in the town of Crigleston, left the neighbourhood, and the said land is lying uncultivated, and the lord's service is in arrears. Upon this Thomas de Holgate and William de Colley took the said land from the lord; entry, 2^s

Osset. Richard s. of John, 6^d; Matthew de Shellay, 3^d; John s. of Richard, 2^d; Richard Swaynson, 2^d; Thomas Hogge, 2^d and Richard le Wyse, 2^d, for escapes, etc.

Thornes. Robert le Walker's wife, 5^d; Richard Brounsmyth, 2^d, and Robert s. of Ivo, 6^d, for escapes.

Wakefeld. John Tasshe, 6^d; Robert Mareschall, 1^d; Thomas s. of Laurence, 12^d; John Attebarre, 3^d; John Hobson, 1^d; William de Lockwod, 6^d for escapes.

Avirthorp. Eva Tyan, 3^d for escapes.

Thomas Bunny, 6ᵈ for vert.

Stanley. Richard de Bateley, 6ᵈ; Adam s. of John s. of Isabel, 2ᵈ; Robert s. of Walter, 2ᵈ; William Albray, 2ᵈ; Henry de Stanley, 6ᵈ, for vert and ivy.

Richard Pescy, 6ˢ 8ᵈ for carrying away palings.

The handmaid of Thomas le Hidbeer, and John Tytyng's wife, 3ᵈ each for breaking palings.

Wakfeld. Matilda Mous, Margery Liftefast, Matilda Tyrsy, Johanna Archur, Thomas de Louth and Hugh Smerpaytrell, 3ᵈ each for breaking palings.

Jordan le Mauer, 2ᵈ, and John Pollard, 3ᵈ, for dry wood.

Thomas s. of Robert, for breaking the postern, 6ᵈ

Margery Liftefaste, 3ᵈ; Elias Tyrsy's handmaid, 2ᵈ; John Wolmer, 6ᵈ; German Swerd, 6ᵈ; Robert le Wriht, 12ᵈ; Adam le Burdwright, 6ᵈ; John Erle, 6ᵈ; William Wyles, 6ᵈ; Richard de Aula, 6ᵈ; William Goldsmith, 6ᵈ; William del Clogh, 6ᵈ; William Cussyng, 6ᵈ; William Filche, 6ᵈ; John de Wolveley, 6ᵈ; James del Okes, 12ᵈ, for wood, wedges of thorn, etc.

Sworn to by { Robert de Mora, William Templer, William Malyn, John Garbot } Total—43ˢ 11ᵈ— and new rent, 2ᵈ

i.e. Wakefeld 12ˢ 3ᵈ   Stanley, 15ˢ 8ᵈ
Osset, 17ᵈ   Sandale, 3ˢ 2ᵈ
Sourby, 2ˢ   Rastrik, 12ᵈ
Hiperum, 3ˢ 9ᵈ   Thornes, 3ˢ 3ᵈ
Holne, 8ᵈ (and new rent, 2ᵈ)
Alvirthorp, 9ᵈ

COURT held at Wakefeld, Friday, the Morrow of St. Vincent the Martyr (22 Jan.), 20 Edw. II [1327].

Essoins. Hugh de Stanneley, by Robert de Mora. Surety—Thomas Forester.

Thomas de Thornton, by William Templer.

John de Caylli, by Adam de Mideltone.

Essoins. William Scotte of Birthwayte essoins against John de Dronsfeld by William de Wakefeld. Surety—Thomas Alayn.

Philip del Hill, against William le Gardiner by John de Stansfeld.

Thomas, vicar of Halifax, against Roger de Grenwod by Thomas de Totehill. Surety—William de Birton. The said Roger, by Geoffrey de Normanton. Surety—John de Woderoue.

Stanley. Hugh de Stanneley and Henry his brother, are distrained, to answer the lord for several offences, by 10ˢ in the hands of Philip le Sagher; and Henry is fined 4ᵈ

Holne. Richard s. of Hugh, 12ᵈ for sundry defaults.

Robert Beumont and Richard s. of Hugh (4ᵈ) agree.

An inquisition finds that a certain road at Littelwodlone, called le Outelone, is a public way; and John del Bothe enclosed it; fine, 12ᵈ

Bailiff. William de Neville and Brian de Thornhill, 12ᵈ each for respite of suit till Michaelmas.

Sourbi. Thomas s. of Julian de Sourby, sues Adam s. of Roger, for a steer, which defendant says is his own property. An inquisition is to be summoned from Osset and Sourbi for next court.

John de Hadreshelf and Thomas s. of Julian Wade (6ᵈ) agree.

Ossete. Alice formerly wife of John de Heton, 4ᵈ for unjust complaint against Adam del Dene.

Horbiry. Thomas del Spen and Matilda his wife, sue John s. of Hugh de Horbiry, for a stone of wool, which defendant acknowledges. Damages, 2ᵈ; fine, 3ᵈ

Hugh le Shoter, 2ᵈ for unlawfully detaining 3ᵈ from John Ibbote.

Osset. Jordan Scotte and Alice formerly wife of Robert le Couper (4ᵈ) agree.

Thornes. Robert s. of Emma, 6ᵈ, under an inquisition, for false claim against Avice formerly wife of Ivo Smyth.

Sandale. Robert Pelleson and Thomas de Holgate (3ᵈ) agree.

Adam Trubbe, 3ᵈ for not coming to answer said Robert.

Stannely. An inquisition finds that Walter Gunne is unlawfully withholding from Margery formerly wife of William Dolfyn, ⅓ of a bovate of land held by her late husband; she is to recover. Fine, 12ᵈ

Holne. William de Craven (6ᵈ) and John del Bothe (12ᵈ) agree in two matters.

Thornes. William s. of Roger, and Hugh Vyroun (2ᵈ) agree.

Hyperum. Adam s. of Peter de Suthecliff, surrenders 8½ acres in Hyperum, with the reversion of 8½ acres after the death of his father; granted again to the said Adam and Agnes d. of Thomas de Warlouley, and their issue, with remainder, in default, to the heirs of the said Adam; they fine 12ᵈ

Thornes. Hugh Vyroun surrenders a piece of land in Thornes, lying by John Baret's close; committed to the said John Baret; entry, 6ᵈ. Also another 2 acres there; committed to Hugh, s. of Walter le S . . .; entry, 8ᵈ

Holne. William de Craven and John del Bothe exchange two several lots of 3 acres in Littelwode; entry, 12ᵈ each.

Holne. Richard del Dene gives the lord 1ᵈ new rent yearly for a path in Littelwod, called Outelone, so that it may be a public path as heretofore accustomed, and not closed.

John del Bothe surrenders 2½ acres in Lyttelwod; committed to William de Craven; entry, 9ᵈ

Sandale. John Attelme surrenders 22 acres in Crigleston; committed to Robert del Dene (1 acre); Matilda handmaid of Henry del Dene, and John her son (1 acre); Roger s. of William de Donecastre (8 acres); William s. of John (7 acres); Adam Attegrene (2 acres); and Robert s. of John (3 acres). Entry, 2ˢ

Wakefeld. New rent. Thomas s. of Laurence de Wakefeld, takes a piece of unoccupied land in Wakefeld, abutting on his house, close by the house formerly John Cussing's—a piece 18 feet by 10 feet—entry, 12ᵈ; rent, 1½ᵈ

Alice formerly wife of John Cussing, by Robert de Mora, surrenders ⅓ of 8½ acres in Wakefeld; committed to William s. of John Cussyng; entry, 6ᵈ

Holne. Matthew de Ramesden, 3ᵈ; Nicholas s. of Nicholas de Ovenden, 3ᵈ; Nicholas le Dene of Wolvedale, 2ᵈ; Elias s. of Thomas Attewelle, 2ᵈ, and Robert Ster, 1ᵈ, for wood, etc.

Sourby. John de Astey, 6ᵈ; Roger de Grenwod, 3ᵈ; Geoffrey de Crosselegh, 2ᵈ; Adam de Kerkeshagh, 3ᵈ; John Maynard, 3ᵈ; William Horseknave, 3ᵈ, and Robert de Wolronwall, 3ᵈ, for escapes, etc.

Hiperum. John s. of William de Ourum, 2ᵈ; John Somer, 1ᵈ; John de Hilton, 1ᵈ; William le Milner, 1ᵈ; John s. of Henry, 1ᵈ, and John Steven, 1ᵈ for vert.

Wakfeld. John Wolmer, 2ᵈ; Thomas Dubber, 3ᵈ; William de Lockewod, 1ᵈ; Amabilla le Blank, 3ᵈ; William Bate, junior, 3ᵈ, and Robert s. of Isabel, 3ᵈ, for vert.

Ossete. Swayn le Wyse, 2ᵈ; Richard Snarte, 1ᵈ; Robert Scotte, 1ᵈ; Margaret wife of Bate's son, 1ᵈ; Matilda wife of Ralph, 1ᵈ, and Eva le White, 1ᵈ, for escapes.

Stanley. William Arkell, 2ᵈ; John Isabel's son, 1ᵈ, and Johanna wife of Robert de Wodhall, 2ᵈ, for bark.

John Pikebusk and Thomas, s. of Hugh, 2ᵈ for not coming to the castle.

Sworn to by { Robert de Mora / William Templer } Total 24ˢ 9ᵈ— and new rent, 2½ᵈ

4ᵈ too much in the sum total.

i.e. Stanneley, 2ˢ 5ᵈ   Holne, 7ˢ 7ᵈ (and new rent,
Bailiff, 2ˢ   Thornes, 22ᵈ   1ᵈ)
Wakefeld, 2ˢ 9ᵈ (and new rent, 1½ᵈ)
Hyperum, 19ᵈ   Horbiry, 5ᵈ
Sourbyry, 2ˢ 5ᵈ   Ossete, 15ᵈ
Sandale, 2ˢ 6ᵈ

COURT held at Wakefeld on Friday after the Feast of the Purification of the Virgin (Feb. 2), 1 Edw. III [1327].

Essoins. Richard de Birstall, by Geoffrey de Normanton. Surety—Henry de Swilyngtone.

Thomas de Thorntone, by Richard de Grynwod. Surety—Robert de Mora.

John de Cailly, by Richard de Waddesworth.

Bailiff. Essoin. John Attebarre essoins against Hugh de Stanneley, by German Cay. Surety—William Cussyng.

Bailiff. Hugh de Stanneley, 6ᵈ, for sundry defaults. Surety—Thomas Forester.

William le Gardiner, 2ᵈ for not prosecuting his suit against Philip del Hill.

Richard Baycok, 6ᵈ for sundry defaults. Surety—John Scotte.

Hugh de Stanneley puts himself in mercy for sundry offences, in the presence of Dom. Philip de Meuwes; fine, 4ᵈ. Surety—Thomas Forester.

Henry de Stanneley, 3ᵈ for not coming to answer to the lord.

Henry s. of Robert de Stanneley, 3ᵈ, for not coming to answer John Pollard.

Richard Cay, 2ᵈ for not prosecuting his suit against John del Rediker.

Constable. William de Birton is elected constable of Holnefrith.

Sourby. John de Hadreshelf (6ᵈ) and Peter s. of John de Hiperumhirst, agree.

Rastrik. John Couhird, surety for John Steel and Julian his wife, 3ᵈ for not having them in court to answer.

Sandale. Alan Trubbe, 2ᵈ for not coming to answer Robert Pelleson.

Sourby. Adam s. of Roger, 6ᵈ, for detaining a steer belonging to Thomas s. of Julian; damages, 2ˢ

Sandale. Henry le Quarreour, 2ᵈ for not paying Robert Pelleson 3ˢ for 2 quarters of oats bought from him.

Sourby. Roger de Hertelotroide, 12ᵈ for not coming to answer to the lord. for enclosing unoccupied land at Warlouley.

Hugh Wade and Julian his wife, 6ᵈ for contempt by Julian's speaking to the Jury, and 6ᵈ for Hugh's breaking his attachment made by the forester.

Hugh de Helilegh, John Miller, Robert s. of John, John s. of Robert, Adam de Coventre, Peter del Grene, and Henry de Loddingdene, the jurors on the inquisition between Adam s. of Roger, and the said Henry Wade and Julian, 4ᵈ each for taking the said Julian into council.

John s. of Thomas del Feld, 4ᵈ for false claim against Robert s. of John.

The inquisition as to the 3 acres in Sourby exchanged by Adam s. of Roger, with John his brother, for 3 other acres there, and with which he afterwards enfeoffed Thomas s. of Julian, breaking the exchange, whereby, according to the custom of the country 6ˢ 8ᵈ accrues to the lord—postponed for want of jurors.

. . . Eadmund de Barneside, 6^d for $\frac{1}{2}$ acre of unoccupied land at Heppeworth; rent, 2^d

Alvirthorp. Elias s. of Peter Tyrsi of Wakefeld, surrenders 3 roods in the graveship of Alvirthorp; committed to Robert s. of William; entry, 6^d

[**Sourby**]. **New rents.** William de Raupighel takes an acre of unoccupied land in Warlouley, entry, 10^d; rent, 6^d

Robert s. of John, junior, takes an acre of unoccupied land in Sourby, entry, 12^d; rent, 6^d

Sandale. Robert s. of John, surrenders a messuage and 3 acres in Sandale; [committed to] John, s. of Robert Faber of Denby; entry, 18^d

Thornes. Hugh Vyroun, by Thomas Alayn, bailiff of the free Court, surrenders 1$\frac{1}{2}$ acre in Thornes; [committed to] Roger Vyroun; entry, 9^d

Bailiff. A black steer, valued at 2^s, attached as a waif by the bailiff of Sourby, given into the keeping of Thomas Alayn for one year; as long as it is held to be waif; and he is to have it proclaimed for 3 days in Wakefield market.

Holne. New rent. Robert del Bothe takes 7 acres of unoccupied land in le Hadds and 2 acres in le Grentrehed and Dychebrecke; entry, 40^d; rent, 4^d an acre.

Stanley. John Pokett, bailiff of Stanley, 12^d for not presenting the complaint he received from William Filche against Margery del Ker, for debt.

Horbiry. The Abbot of Kirkestall to be distrained to answer by what service he holds 1$\frac{1}{2}$ bovate of land in Horbiry.

Philip Damysel, 12^d; German Swerd, 6^d; Adam s. of Robert, 6^d; William Gardiner, 4^d; John Swerd, 6^d; Robert Marescall, 2^d; John de Grenegate, 6^d; Thomas s. of Laurence, 12^d, and Thomas Hughet, 2^d, for not coming, when summoned, upon the inquisition between the lord and Henry Tasshe. And the bailiff is ordered to summon an equal number for next court; all of the better sort, and most influential men of Wakefeld.

Sworn to by
{ Robert Ra.
  William Brigun
  William Parmenter
  William, s. of Isabel }
Total, 22^{s}6^d, and 4^d new rent, 2^s and 10^d, and 2^s for the waif beast.

i.e. Bailiff, 2^s 2^d and for the waif beast, 2^s
Sandale, 22^d
Holne, 3^s 10^d, and new rent, 22^d
Thornes, 9^d
Wakefeld, 5^s
Stanley, 12^d
Sourby, 7^s 6^d and new rent, 12^d
Rastrick, 3^d
Alvirthorp, 6^d

COURT held at Wakefeld on Friday after the Feast of St. Matthias the Apostle, (Feb. 24) 1 Edw. III [1327].

Essoins. William de Birton, by Robert de Mora.

Richard de Birstall, by John Woderoue.

Henry Wildbor, by Hugh Wildbor.

King's Writ. William Scotte of Birthwaite, who is in the Kings service, essoins against John de Dronsfeld for seizing cattle, by William de Wakefeld. The parties are to appear at Westminster in the Quinzaine of Easter, under the King's writ.

Essoins. John Attebarre essoins against Hugh de Stanneley by William de Lokewod; and Hugh, by John de Stansfeld.

John Theules, against Elias de Thorntley, by Alan de Merston.

Servient. Edmund Gates, 12^d for not prosecuting suit against John Scotte, senior, and 6^d for that against Richard Baicok.

John Pollard sues Henry de Stanneley for taking a cart and 2 horses belonging to him at Stanley; value 20^s. Defendant wages his law. Surety—Hugh de Stanneley.

John Steel, 3^d for not having his wife Julian in court, to answer Thomas de Totehill.

Staneley. Richard Pescy, 2^d for false claim against John Dade.

Horbiry. Thomas de Belhous, 6^d for default.

Sourbi. John Shepherd, 6^d, John Webester, 6^d, and Henry Wright, 6^d for not attending, when summoned, on three inquisitions.

Wakefeld. John de Fery of Wakefeld, 6^d; William de Castelford, 3^d; William s. of ? John (*Js*), 6^d; Adam s. of Robert, 6^d; William Parmenter, 6^d; John de Grengate, 6^d; William le Gardiner, 4^d; Robert de Fery, 4^d; Thomas le Gardiner, 4^d; Robert Marescall, 3^d; William s. of Richard, 6^d; Thomas Hughet, 6^d, and Philip de Castelford, 6^d for not attending, when summoned, on an inquisition.

Staneley. Robert Leper, 6^d; Richard Pescy, 6^d; Gilbert le Theker, 6^d, and Alice Longshanck, 4^d, for weak ale, according to the presentment of the wardens of ale.

Robert Leper, 6^d for not attending on an inquisition.

Rastrik. John de Botherode surrenders 8 acres in Rastrik; committed to Beatrice d. of Henry s. of Margaret; entry, 2^s

Sourby. John del Lumme, by the bailiff of Sourby, surrenders 27 acres in Sourby; committed to Adam s. of John del Legh; entry, 5^s

Wakefeld. William Bate surrenders 1½ acre in Wakefeld; granted to Thomas Roller; entry, 8^d

Sourbi. William Couper takes an acre of unoccupied land at Sourbi; entry, 12^d; rent, 6^d

Richard Bete takes another acre there; entry, 12^d; rent, 6^d

Horbiry. Thomas de Shelley takes from the lord a messuage and 2 bovates at Osset, which tenement he holds by a lease of the time of the Earl of Lancaster until Whitsuntide next, at 4^s

per annum; after which he will pay an additional rent of 8ˢ.
Sureties—Matthew de Shelley and Richard Swaynson.

Thornes. Agnes d. of Henry s. of Alan le Smyth, gives 6ˢ
as a relief on 2¼ acres at Thornes, after the death of Philip her
brother, whose heir she is.

Sandale. Adam Trubbe surrenders an acre at Northerode;
granted to John Lorimer; entry, 6ᵈ

Attachments.

Staneley. Robert Couper, 4ᵈ; Adam le Nethird, 2ᵈ; Robert
Pescy, 1ᵈ, for wood.

Robert Shorte, 5ˢ for a sapling.

Two forges at Erdislauwe, 6ᵈ for breaking palings.

Osset. Adam de Ouchethorp, 3ᵈ; John del Dene, 3ᵈ; Swayn
le Wyse, 1ᵈ, and Robert s. of Ivo, 4ᵈ, for escapes.

Alvirthorp. Alexander Pibridd, 3ᵈ for breaking the gate of
the park.

Sworn to by   { Robert de Mora   }   Total—35ˢ 8ᵈ—and
                { William Templer }   new rent, 9ˢ

i.e. Stanneley, 8ˢ 7ᵈ

     Sourbi, 8ˢ 6ᵈ—and new rent, 12ᵈ

     Bailiff, 21ᵈ

     Horbiry, 6ᵈ—and new rent after Whitsuntide, 8ˢ

     Alvirthorp, 3ᵈ

     Rastrik, 2ˢ

     Thorns, 6ᵈ

     Holne, 6ˢ

     Sandale, 6ᵈ

     Osset, 11ᵈ

     Wakefeld, 6ˢ 2ᵈ

COURT held at Wakefeld on Friday, the Feast of St. Cuthbert
(March 20) 1 Edw. III [1327].

Essoins. Thomas de Ceyuill, by William de Castelford.
Surety—Thomas de Bellehous.

Thomas de Thorntone, by Robert de Mora.

James del Okes, by John de Woderoue. Surety—William
Templer.

Bailiff. Essoin. John s. of Thomas de Heton, against William
de Estwod, by John de Haltone.

Roger de Grenwod, 12ᵈ, and Thomas, Vicar of Halifax,
agree. Surety—Thomas de Thomas de Totehill [*sic*].

Alice de Scriven Prioress of Kyrkeleghes, 3ᵈ for sundry
defaults. Surety—Robert de Mora. Thomas de Totehill has
license to agree with the said Alice.

Thomas le Gardiner, 3ᵈ for not prosecuting suit against
Robert s. of Ivo.

Wakefeld. John Pollard, 2ᵈ for the same against Henry s. of Robert de Stanneley.

Rastrik. Thomas de Totehill, plaintiff, and John Steel and Julian his wife, (3ᵈ) agree.

Sourbi. John de Skercote, 3ᵈ, and William del Loyne, 3ᵈ, for not attending on an inquisition.

Horbiry. The Abbot of Kirkestall is distrained by his rent in the hands of Hugh Modisaule and Thomas de Whitley, viz., 12ˢ, to answer the lord by what service, etc.

Bailiff. The Master of the Hospital del Neuland to be distrained to answer the lord as above.

Alvirthorp. William de Bernby and Agnes his wife, sues Thomas s. of Robert Estreld, for ½ acre at Neutone on le Cliff, saying that William s. of Walter, leased the land to Robert, defendant's father, for 4 years, now expired, and that Thomas continues to hold without right. An inquisition is to be taken.

Bailiff. Robert de Moseley gives 4ᵈ for respite of suit of court till next Michaelmas.

Thornes. Robert le Walker sues William s. of Thomas, for taking an ox belonging to him, worth 10ˢ, out of the new park, and beating it, etc., damages 6ˢ 8ᵈ; an inquisition is to be taken. The said Robert sues the said William for driving an ox to Wakefeld and impounding it, till delivered by Robert de Mora, the bailiff. Defendant says plaintiff and Alice his wife, hold a piece of land in Rodberthorp from the lord, at 1ᵈ rent, now in arrears for 3 years, and he took the ox as the lord's bailiff. Robert says they hold nothing from the lord, neither do they owe any rent. An inquisition is to be taken.

Ossette. Alice d. of Adam de Ossette, sues Thomas Hogge for 3ˢ in silver, which he agreed to pay yearly as profit on a [mark] delivered to him by John s. of Richard, and Hugh Disceford, he being answerable yearly therefor to the plaintiff. He has paid 3ˢ yearly for 3 years, but withholds the fourth payment. Thomas says he took the mark to answer thereon as a mark of silver of the Blessed Mary would answer, and a mark of the said silver would not answer for four years unless . . . He therefore holds he owes nothing. An inquisition is to be taken.

Wakefeld. Adam Bordewright of Wakefeld sues Robert s. of Ivo for debt. Surety—William Cussyng..

Stanley. Henry de Walda sues Hugh s. of Hugh Scayff, for trespass.

Sandale. Thomas de Holgate and William de Colley of Sandale, are to bring John s. of Nalk, to answer to the lord for leaving ½ bovate and 2 acres in Sandale. Thomas de Ketelthorp sues for custody of the land till John comes. It is therefore to be seized into the lord's hand.

Wakefeld. William del Castelford is to answer to the lord for raising an embankment between the great meadow at Wakefeld and his tenement.

John de Grengate, William Gardiner, Thomas Bate and John Tasshe, the same, for making gates, outlets and paths out of their messuage at Wakefeld beyond the lord's great park there.

Thornes. Philip del Hill surrenders ½ messuage and 3½ acres in Snaypthorp; granted to Richard Lew . . .; entry, 12^d

Rastrik. Thomas de Staynland comes into court, and, in the presence of Dom. Philip de Meuwes, begs license to clear and plough 20 acres of unoccupied land which he took of the lord; permission is granted; fine, 13^s 4^d

Sourby. William de Sponer takes ½ acre of moorland at Warlouley; entry, 8^d; rent, 3^d

Ossette. Alice formerly wife of John de Heton, begs the guardianship of Henry s. of John de Heton, and of a bovate of land with a clearing, and a piece of land called Le Pighel, which the said Henry holds in bondage (after his father's death) in the town of Heton, for 6 years; by the wish of the said Henry. And she promises Henry maintenance as long as he will obey her, as he ought to do. She pays the lord 2^s 6^d as a heriot on behalf of said Henry; and 6^d for the custody, etc., doing service for the said Henry.

Sourbi. New Rent. Roger de Hertlotrode takes 3 roods of unoccupied land at Sourbi, rent, 4½^d

Wakefeld. William Wyles surrenders a rood of meadow land in le Baseynges, through John Pollard, bailiff of Wakefeld; committed to Thomas Rose; entry, 6^d

Attachments in the Old Park.

Wakefield. Peter de Acorn, 2^s, and Jordan le Mauer, 12^d, each for a sapling.

Richard de Ledes, 2^d, John Erle, 6^d; Thomas de Colley, 3^d; Thomas le Bordewright, 3^d; Richard Steel, 3^d and William Carpenter, 3^d, for breaking palings and for vert.

Stanley. John [sic] for a sapling, 2^d

Attachments in the New Park.

Ossett. Adam de Gaukethorp, 3^d; Robert Sonneman, 1^d; Richard s. of Sutor de Gaukethorp, 1^d; William Bene, 1^d; Thomas Hogge, 1^d, and Matilda wife of Hugh Pees, 2^d, for escapes.

Wakefeld. Thomas Bate, 2^d; William Parmenter, 2^d; John de Grengate, 6^d; Robert Walker, 2^d, and John de Welles, 2^d, for dry wood, etc.

Attachments in the Great Wood.

Bailiff. Robert le Tailliour, 2^d, and Richard, Chaplain of Deuesbiry, 3^d, for breaking palings.

Stanley. Robert de Wodehall, 1ᵈ; Hugh Cort, 2ᵈ; Richard de Bateley, 2ᵈ; John s. of Amabilla, 2ᵈ; Robert Botone's serving-man, 2ᵈ; Thomas Martyn, 1ᵈ, and German Beel's wife, 1ᵈ, for wood.

Hiperum. William s. of Thomas, 3ᵈ; Thomas s. of Henry, 2ᵈ; Margery del Dene, Thomas del Cliffe, Richard de Thorpe, John del Northende, Symon del Blacker, John le Milner, John le Bercher, Richard del Hole, 2ᵈ each; Roger del Brighous, 3ᵈ; Henry le Taillour, 1ᵈ; Matilda Tyngel, 1ᵈ; Michael Sutor, 2ᵈ, and Adam s. of Peter de Southcliff, 2ᵈ, for vert, etc.

Attachments in the New Park.

Ossette. Richard le Wyse, 1ᵈ; Matthew de Shellay, 2ᵈ; Swayn le Wyse, 3ᵈ; Robert Scotte, 1ᵈ; Henry del Court, 1ᵈ; Jordan Eliot, 2ᵈ; Richard s. of John, 3ᵈ; Richard Passemer, 1ᵈ; Robert s. of Henry de Southwod, 2ᵈ; John Mauncel, 1ᵈ; Hugh de Disceford, 2ᵈ; John del Dene, 1ᵈ; John Moloc's wife, 1ᵈ, and John s. of William 2ᵈ for escapes.

Wakefeld. Henry Dernelove, 2ᵈ; John Morpath, 2ᵈ; Robert Mareschall, 2ᵈ; and William Bruwes, 3ᵈ, for escapes and wood.

Thornes. Roger Vyroun, 1ᵈ; Hugh Vyroun, 1ᵈ; and John Baret, 3ᵈ, for escapes.

Holne. Agnes de Hyngecliff, 3ᵈ; John de Harop, 1ᵈ; Henry de Holnestie, 2ᵈ; John del Bothe, 2ᵈ; Adam s. of William de Foghleston, 2ᵈ, and Robert le Shephird, 1ᵈ, for vert and dry wood.

Sourby. Johanna wife of William, 1ᵈ; John s. of Eva, 2ᵈ; Adam del Shaghe, 6ᵈ; Roger de Grenwod, 12ᵈ and 8ᵈ; John de Rediker, 2ᵈ; Henry de Holgate, 12ᵈ; Robert his son, 2ᵈ; Alice de Shesewelley, 3ᵈ; William West, 2ᵈ; Robert de Benteleyrode, 2ᵈ; William s. of Jordan, 2ᵈ; John Shephird, 1ᵈ; Adam s. of Hugh, 3ᵈ, and William s. of Hugh, 2ᵈ, for escapes, etc.

Sworn to by { John Pollard, Robert de Mora, William Templer }   Total—40ˢ 10ᵈ—and new rent, 7½ᵈ

i.e. Sourby, 6ˢ 2ᵈ and new rent, 7½ᵈ   Thornes, 17ᵈ
Hyperum, 2ˢ 6ᵈ   Holne, 11ᵈ
Wakefeld, 7ˢ 3ᵈ   Bailiff, 2ˢ 3ᵈ
Stanneley, 13ᵈ   Rastrik, 13ˢ 7ᵈ
Ossette, 5ˢ 8ᵈ

COURT held at Wakefeld on the Friday in Easter Week, 1 Edw. III [1327].

Essoins. Thomas de Thornetone, by Robert de Mora. Surety—Thomas Alayn.

William de Birton, by Richard de Birton. Surety—Thomas de Totehill.

Bailiff. John Attebarre sues Hugh de Stanneley for 18ˢ for 6 pigs sold him in Wakefeld 6 years ago. Defendant denies the debt, and wages his law. Surety—Henry de Stannleye.

Elias de Thornteley (4ᵈ) and John Theules agree.

Stanley. Thomas del Ker, 2ᵈ; Robert Leper, 2ᵈ; Philip le Sagher, 2ᵈ; Richard Scayff, 1ᵈ, and Robert s. of Walter, 2ᵈ, for not attending, when summoned, on an inquisition.

Sourby. John del Hole, William s. of Hugh de Warlouley, and Ivo del Hole, 6ᵈ each for the same.

Bailiff. John le Forester and Robert de Mora, 2ᵈ for not having Paulinus de Emeley (for whom they were sureties) in court.

Alvirthorp. Richard de Colley, 3ᵈ for not coming to answer Adam le Heuer.

Holne. Matthew s. of Thomas de Foghleston, sues Elias s. of Henry de Heppeworth, for assaulting him at Foghleston; damages, 6ˢ 8ᵈ. Elyas acknowledges the assult; the damages are taxed at Birton tourn at 6ᵈ; fine, 6ᵈ

Bailiff. Robert de Mora and William Templer, sureties for the Prior of St. Oswald's, 3ᵈ, because he does not come to answer the lord.

The said Robert in the mercy (fine not recorded), for not prosecuting suit against Alice formerly wife of John de Heton.

Thornes. Robert Peger and William s. of Elyas (2ᵈ) agree.

Osset. Alice d. of Adam de Osset, and Thomas Hogge (6ᵈ) agree.

Wakefeld. Adam le Burdewright, 4ᵈ for not prosecuting suit against Robert s. of Ivo.

Thornes. Robert s. of Ivo, 3ᵈ for cutting an oak in the lord's bondage at Snaypthorp. Surety—Robert de Mora.

Stanneley. John del Bothem, 12ᵈ (under an inquisition) for cutting willow in Stanneley wood, worth 6ᵈ

Thornes. Robert s. of Ivo, sues John Baret, because his dog worried to death one of plaintiff's sheep at Snaypthorp; worth 40ᵈ. An inquisition is to be taken.

Robert de Mora, plaintiff, and William Malyn and Agnes Peger (2ᵈ) agree.

Sandale. John Lorimer sues Henry le Quarriour and John de Plegwyk for debt. Henry is in mercy for not coming. John comes, and acknowledges the debt as surety for the said Henry; he is therefore in mercy. Fine [entered in the margin, and not assigned to either], 2ᵈ

Waif. A horse, attached by the bailiff as a waif, is given into the keeping of John Flemyng, to bring to the tourn, etc.

Thornes. Johanna Dade surrenders 2 acres in Thornes; granted to Margery wife of Richard de Luppesheved; entry, 12ᵈ

Robert s. of Ivo, surrenders ½ rood in Snaypthorp; granted to Adam s. of Henry.

Stanley. Thomas Turpyn surrenders ½ acre in Stanley; granted to Walter Gunne; entry, 12^d

Holne. New Rents. Nicholas de Amandene takes an acre of unoccupied land in Carteworth; entry, 10^d; rent, 4^d

Matthew de Ramesdene, the same.

Wakefeld. John Hobbeson, 1^d; Robert Chepe, 1^d; William Cussing, 1^d; Thomas s. of Robert le Wright, 1^d; John Pollard, 2^d; Thomas Cussing, 1^d; Robert Nodger, 1^d; Philip le Sagher, 2^d; Thomas le Walker, 4^d; Thomas Tutche, 1^d; Thomas le Roller, 3^d; John Wolmer, 4^d; Thomas le Bordewright, 6^d; Thomas de Colley, 6^d; Cecilia Pikescull, 2^d; Agnes d. of John de Aula, 3^d; Adam Bordewright and Roger his brother, 6^d; Robert Fraunceys, 4^d; Alice le Tyncker, 3^d; Thomas s. of Laurence, 2^d; John de Grengate, 2^d; John de Welles, 1^d, and Robert Marescall's daughter, 1^d, for escapes, etc.

Thornes. Thomas del Haghe, 2^d, and Henry de Swylington, 1^d, for vert and dry wood.

Stanley. John Dade, 2^d; Walter Gunne, 4^d; Thomas Scayff, 2^d; John s. of Amabilla, 1^d; Richard de Bateley, 2^d; Thomas Belle, 3^d; Robert Short, 12^d; Robert Botone, 12^d; John Hobbeson, 12^d; the servingmen of the two last, 6^d; Johanna wife of William, 1^d; Hugh Cort, 4^d; John Flacherd, 2^d; William Arkel, 2^d; John Isabel, 1^d, and Thomas Martyn, 1^d, for vert, etc.

Ossett, Robert Peny, Adam le Oxhird and Hugh de Disceford, 1^d each; Adam de Gaukethorp, Robert Sonneman, and John del Den, 2^d each, for escapes.

Alvirthorp. Robert de Sharneston; Amabilla Wolf and John Garbot, 1^d each, for ivy, etc.

Sworn to by ⎰ Robert s. of William ⎱ Total—22^s 2^d—
⎱ William de Wakefeld ⎰ and new rent, 8^d

i.e., Bailiff, 9^d Sandale, 2^d
Staneley, 8^s 4^d Holne, 2^s 2^d and new rent, 8^d
Sourby, 18^d Ossett, 15^d
Alvirthorp, 6^d Thornes, 2^s 4^d
Wakefeld, 5^s 2^d

TOURN held at Halifax on Monday before the Feast of St. Mark the Evangelist (Apr. 25) 1 Edw. III [1327].

Agnes wife of Richard Tyncker, drew blood from Cecilia del Grene; 6^d

Magota de Windhill, and the wife of Thomas Hardher of Stansfeld, 6^d each for brewing, etc.

Margery d. of Robert de Skercote, drew blood from Cecilia, d. of Alice le Wasser; 6^d

Richard de Crimblesworth, from William Mauncel; 2^s

The township of Sourby, 40^d for not presenting that Alice del Lone brewed against the assize.

The township of Halifax, 40^d for the same with the wives of Bate Lister and Alexander de Hyngandrode.

The three above women, 6^d each for so brewing.

Robert de Northland, Henry de Holgate, Robert de Wolronwall, William de Lauwe, Richard s. of Bateman, William de Ridyng, John de Rediker, Richard del Brigg, Matthew de Ovenden, Geoffrey de Stodley, John de Cockecroft and John le Harpur of Stodeley, sworn, present that according to custom the Prior of Lewes ought to house the Earl's steward, receiver and all the Earl's bailiffs, when they come to Halifax twice in the year to hold the tourn, and is bound to find all things necessary for them and their horses, as long as they remain there for the purpose of holding the said tourns.

Adam del Munckes and Adam s. of Matilda, stole cattle at Langfeld, and drove them to Blakeburnshire.

Sworn to by   { Adam s. of Roger   } Total—12^s 2^d
                { Robert de Mora   }   —all from Sourby.
                { William Templer   }

COURT held there the same day.

Hugh Wade and Julian his wife, sue Amabilla le Waynwright for calling Julian a sorceress and using other insulting terms, in Sourbi; damages, 20^s. Amabilla pleads guilty, and begs damages may be taxed by the court. They are taxed at 12^d. Fine, 3^d. She is also fined 2^d for false claim against said Henry and Julian, for detaining a chest.

William de Ridyngge sues William de Saltonstall for 17^d, as surety for Roger de Stanbery; defendant acknowledges the debt; fine, 6^d

William s. of Adam de Heptonstall, 6^d for not appearing to answer John de Illingworth.

Richard s. of Alot, surrenders 3 acres in Sourby; granted to Thomas s. of Adam; entry, 12^d

William Mahaud surrenders 3½ acres in Warulley; granted to William le Turnur; entry, 12^d

New Rent. John s. of William took 2 acres of unoccupied land at Sourby; entry, 12^d; rent, 12^d

William Attetounend and Ellen his wife, surrender a messuage and 8½ acres at Sourby; granted to John s. of William Attetounend; he pays the lord 12^d for entry, at the instance of Dom. Philip de Meaus.

Sourbi. John le Piper, 4^d; Thomas de Rothelesset, 6^d; Robert de Warulley, 12^d; John de Elfletburgh, 6^d; John Culpoun, 2^d; William de Saltonstall, 3^d; John de Illyngworth, 2^d; John de Castelstede, 2^d; Thomas le Mercer, 2^d; John de Wolronwall, 6^d;

John Shephird, 2^d; Henry del Banck, 3^d; William de Smalilegh, 6^d, and Jordan del Brigg, 1^d, for vert, escapes, etc.

Sworn as above; Total—10^s 4^d—and new rent, 13^d
All from Sourby.

TOURN held at Brighous on Tuesday before the Feast of St. Mark the Evangelist (Apr. 25), 1 Edw. III [1327].

Rastrik. John de Berkesley, John s. of William de Steynland, William Whitacres, Thomas del Wod, Henry de Coldley, Richard del Rodes, Thomas de Whitwod, Richard Couhird, John de Birstall, William de Steynland, John del Hirst and Adam de Bradeley, sworn, present that John Clerk of Hertesheved stopped up a public spring in Hertesheved; fine, 6^d

Elias Smith of Clifton, 6^d; Richard s. of Cecilia de Clifton, 6^d; Roger Percy of Clifton, and Matthew de Lynthwait, 3^d each, for not coming.

Hiperum. William Milner's wife . . ., Agnes wife of Roger de Brighous, and Thomas Baude's wife, brew and sell contrary to assize. The Jury aforesaid fined 6^s for not presenting these.

Thomas Baude's wife, 3^d; Agnes wife of Roger, 4^d; the wife of Richard le Hyne of Clifton, 4^d, and Roger le Shephird's wife, 3^d for brewing, etc.

The town of Clifton for concealing the two last cases, 12^d

Sworn to by { Robert de Mora } Total—11^s 2^d
             { William le Templer }

i.e., Rastrick, 3^s
       Hiperum 8^s 2^d

COURT held there the same day.

Rastrik. Richard del Shagh sues Agnes formerly wife of John s. of Henry de Fekesby, for debt. Surety—Henry Wright.

Hiperum. Adam de Eland sues Robert de Rissheworth for debt.

Rastrik. John s. of Alcok de Ourum, and Jordan de Hiperum (3^d) agree.

John s. of Jordan, plaintiff, and Robert del Rigge and Symon del Kirkeheud (6^d) agree.

William de Northourum, who held an acre, formerly unoccupied, at Northourum, is dead. His son and heir comes and does fealty, and pays 6^d relief.

Ellen formerly wife of Alan de Rastrik, who held a messuage and 12 acres at Rastrik, by service of 2^s 2^d, and suit of court, is dead. John her son and heir, does fealty and pays 4^s 4^d for a relief.

Sworn as above; Total—5^s 7^d—All from Rastrik.

TOURN held at Birton on Wednesday before the Feast of St. Mark the Evangelist (April 25), 1 Edw. II [1327].

Holne. Jury. William de Riley, Richard de Thornteley, Robert de Wolwro, John s. of John, Richard Hunte, John del Stock, Richard de Birton, Thomas de Billecliff, Adam Keneward, Adam del Grene, Adam Strekais and Henry Wade.

The parson of Birton, 6ᵈ for making a pathway . . . between the towns of Birton and Shelley.

John del Hill's wife, 3ᵈ; William Spicer's wife, 3ᵈ; Amabilla Bagger, 3ᵈ; Robert Lightfot's wife, 3ᵈ; Hugh de Thornteley's wife, 3ᵈ, and Thomas le Smyth's wife, 3ᵈ, for brewing, etc.

Richard de Langley, John Theules, Matthew Drabel and John Ragged, 6ᵈ each for not coming.

Elias s. of Henry de Heppeworth, drew blood from Matthew Drabel, 6ᵈ

John de Holne (6ᵈ) and Thomas de Holne (6ᵈ), from Edward de Hepworth; and the said Edward (12ᵈ), from John de Holne and Thomas, his brother.

Cecilia d. of Avece de Thurstanland, from Hugh s. of Adam (6ᵈ).

William Salter of Lyngyerdes is a common forestaller; 12ᵈ

William Isaud of Almundbury, is a forestaller and sells murrain flesh; 12ᵈ

Thomas Fernoule sells murrain flesh, 6ᵈ

Robert Harward is a forestaller of poultry, 12ᵈ

Robert s. of Elias de Shelley, is a forestaller of meat, 6ᵈ

The jury fined 2ˢ for not presenting that Alan de Merston and William del Mersshe have not come to the tourn.

Sworn as above, Total—13ˢ all from Holne.

Holne. Henry de Cartworth sues Richard Child for 6ˢ 6ᵈ as surety for William del Leegh; Richard acknowledges the debt; fine, 6ᵈ; and 3ᵈ for withholding 2 stones of wool from the said Henry. Henry is fined 3ᵈ for withholding 18ᵈ sheaves of oats from Richard.

Robert del Scoles sues John s. of Matilda del Scoles, for breaking down a wall between their curtilages at le Scoles, and carrying off the stones of the said wall. An inquisition is to be taken.

New Rents. Adam del Grene takes 2 acres of unoccupied land at Cartworth; entry, 18ᵈ; rent, 9ᵈ

Thomas s. of Henry de Wolvedale, takes an acre of unoccupied land at Cartworthmere; entry, 6ᵈ; rent, 4ᵈ

Richard de Hepworth, who held a messuage and 23 acres at Hepworth, by service of 6ˢ 10ᵈ, is dead. Richard his son and heir, does fealty; relief, 4ˢ

Edmund del Bernside surrendes a messuage and 7 acres in Hepworth; granted to William s. of Robert; entry, 3ˢ

William s. of the forester, surrenders 10 acres in Hepworth to John de Ovenden for 12ᵈ; John pays 2ˢ for license to hold.

William s. of Adam del Mere, surrenders ½ rood at Scolemere; granted to John s. of Nicholas de Wolvedale; entry, 4ᵈ

New Rent. Thomas Couper takes a rood of unoccupied land at Carteworth; entry, 3ᵈ; rent, 1½ᵈ

Thomas Drabel surrenders 4 acres in Cartworth; granted to Richard s. of Julian; entry, 6ᵈ

Diota d. of Adam Benne, sues Adam Been, miller, for trespass. Surety—Thomas Attehalle.

Rastrik. John s. of Alexander del Frith, 4ᵈ; John s. of Hugh, 1ᵈ; John del Steghel, 2ᵈ; Thomas del Banck, 1ᵈ, for vert.

Holne. Agnes de Hingecliff, 12ᵈ; Nicholas Wade, 12ᵈ; John s. of Julian, 12ᵈ; and Thomas del Erthe, 4ᵈ, for vert, etc.

Sworn to by   { Robert s. of Robert   } Total—16ˢ 7ᵈ—and new
               { William de Birton   }   rent, 14½ᵈ

i.e., Holne, 15ˢ 11ᵈ—and new rent, 14½ᵈ
      Rastrik, 8ᵈ

————

TOURN held at Wakefeld on Thursday before the Feast of St. Mark the Evangelist (Apr. 25) 1 Edw. III. [1327].

Jury. Edmund de Dronsfeld, John de Mora, Thomas de Belhous, Adam de Wodesom, Richard de Birstall, Thomas Gates, William Cussyng, John Hobson, Thomas s. of Laurence, Thomas s. of Henry, Robert de Stodeley and Robert le Wright of Wakefeld.

Osset. The wife of John s. of Richard de Osset, 6ᵈ; the wives of William de Heton and Richard Passemer, 3ᵈ and 4ᵈ each, for brewing contrary to assize.

Richard Passemer's wife will never send for the tasters; 6ᵈ

Servients. Richard Grayveson's wife and the wife of Henry de Cheesť, 3ᵈ and 4ᵈ for brewing, etc.

Sandale. Alice wife of John Porter, 3ᵈ, and Adam Porter's wife, 4ᵈ, for the same.

Stanneley. The wives of Richard Longshanck and Thomas Beel, 3ᵈ each for the same.

Alvirthorp. Amabilla Wolf drew blood from Johanna serving-maid of Christian de Flansau.

John le Spicer and his wife maliciously impleaded Richard de Colley in Court Christian; 12ᵈ

Bailiff. William Sausemer, from Walter de Tynglauwe; 12ᵈ

Henry and Robert sons of William Wildbor, stole 27 sheep worth 40ˢ from the Abbot of Funtayns at Heton.

Sandale. Matilda d. of John Munck, 12ᵈ, and Alice d. of William de Overhall, 6ᵈ, have been deflowered.

Thomas Pelleson and William del Grene drew blood from one another; 12ᵈ each.

Adam s. of William del Grene, from Thomas s. of Elias de Donecastre, and Adam le Smyth, 6^d

John le Harpur and Thomas le Stobber, from one another; 3^d and 6^d respectively.

Osset. Agnes d. of Henry, from Eva, serving-maid of Henry; 12^d

Thomas s. of William, from Robert Passemer; 12^d

Hugh Wildbor, from Henry his brother, 6^d

Robert Wyldbor, from Robert Wyse, 6^d

John Souter, from Magot de Herthill, 3^d

John Bynne stole a horse from John Walker, and an other from Thomas Gates at Deuesbury.

Thorns. William s. of Elias de Thornes, drew blood from William Malyn; 6^d, and raised the hue without cause on Robert Malynson; 3^d

Stanneley. John s. of John Dade, drew blood from John del Bothem, and from his wife, and impleaded him in Court Christian, 18^d

Walter Gunne, the lord's villein bought a house at Ouchethorp from John del Dale, villein, and sold it to Thomas Tanner, who uprooted it and carried it out of the lord's bondage. Walter is fined 12^d

Hugh de Stanneley, 3^d for appropriating a piece of the common round his close at Stanneley.

John s. of Henry de Whittyngton, killed John Whitheved with a knife in the great wood at Wakefeld.

Wakefeld. Robert le Wright and William his son, were destroying the king's highway at Sherrefforth, by trenches so that carts could not get along; 12^d

William de Burdeux, 6^d, and Henry Raynald, 2^d for blocking up the King's highway in le Westgate.

Philip Damysel and Thomas Mauger, 6^d each for the same.

Thornes. John Bulnais drew blood from William his brother; 12^d

Wakefeld. William Wyles, clerk, made a trench close by John Pollard's house, in the public footway; 6^d

John de Sandale drew blood from William s. of Richard Clerk; 12^d

John Spicer, from Ellen d. of Trik; 12^d

Cecilia de Sandale housed offenders against the assize; 6^d

The town of Wakefeld, 2^s for not presenting that a path had been made by a cart on the east of the town, at the end of a lane leading to the old park, along the lands of John s. of Robert, and William Cussyng, and others.—Also 12^d for not presenting a path had been made through the grass of the lord's tenants, between Wakefeld and the great park.

The above jurors, 12^d for not presenting the non-attendance of John del Dene, villein. They say the township of Stanneley should be responsible for this amercement, because it has not been presented to them.

Sworn to by ⎰ Robert s. of John ⎱   Total 28^s 2^d
                ⎱ William de Osset ⎰

i.e., Bailiff, 4^s 7^d
      Sandale, 5^s 7^d
      Stanneley, 21^d
      Osset, 4^s 10^d
      Thornes, 21^d
      Wakefeld, 9^s 5^d
      Alvirthorp, 3^d

COURT held there the same day.

Sandale. John Lorimer sues James Munck for breaking a fence of his at Crigleston. An inquisition finds defendant guilty; damages, 6^d; fine, 3^d. Surety—William de Osset.

Roger s. of Roger, and John Harpur sue the said James for the same; the same fine and damages in each case.

James Munck sues the two last-named plaintiffs for a similar offence; but afterwards pays 3^d to agree with them.

John Pollard, bailiff, sues Thomas s. of Robert le Wright; who is to be distrained to come.

Osset. Matilda d. of William del Cole, surrenders ½ acre and a house, with a breadth of four feet round the house, at Osset; granted to Richard le Smyth; entry, 6^d

William de Riley sues John de Fery for debt. Surety— Adam de Heley.

Total—18^d *i.e.*, Sandale, 12^d
                    Osset, 6^d

COURT held at Wakefeld on Friday after the Feast of St. John before the Latin Gate (May 6) 1 Edw. III [1327].

Essoins. Richard de Birstall, by Thomas de Birstall. Surety —Robert de Mora, John Hodde, by William Templer. Surety— Thomas Alayn.

Sourbi. Matilda formerly wife of Elias de Warlouley, 3^d for not prosecuting her suit against Amice formerly wife of John de Miggeley.

John de Illyngworth, 3^d for the same against William s. of Adam de Heptonstall.

Hyperum. William Templer, surety for Alexander, servant of John Flemyng, 3^d for not having the said Alexander in court.

Bailiff. The tenants of Thornes, Stanneley, Hyperum, Rastrik, Osset and Wakefeld are to answer the lord at the next court for defaults as to Wakefeld mill-pond.

Holne. Elyas s. of Henry de Hepworth, 3^d for not prosecuting his suit against Matthew s. of Thomas de Foghleston.

Robert del Scoles and John. s. of Matilda (6^d) agree.

Diota d. of **Adam** Benne, and Alan Bene **(6^d) agree.**

Bailiff. William de Estwod and John s. of Thomas de Heton, (6^d) agree.

Hugh de Stanneley essoins against John Attebarre, by John de Stansfeld. Surety—Henry his brother.

Stanley. John Dade, senior, makes his law against John del Bothem, who is fined 2^d

John Dade, junior, fails to make his law against John del Bothem, and requests taxation of damages. John del Bothem says that, according to the custom of the court, there ought to be no taxation of damages. This is to be decided at next court, and all the tenants are to be distrained to be present.

Sandale. Robert de Grottone sues Thomas de Milnethorp and Emma his wife, for half a mark of silver, which they promised him, to have his counsel in a certain plea regarding their daughter. An inquisition is to be made.

Bailiff. Robert de Mora sues John de Mora, who is present, and Agnes his wife, who is not present, for insulting and assaulting him. John wages his law. Surety—John de Gairgrave. Agnes essoins by William de Wakefeld. Surety—William Templer.

Alvirthorp. Adam le Heuar and Richard de Colley (3^d) agree.

Wakefeld. Robert le Walker fined 6^d for false claim against William s. of Thomas.

Bailiff. Amabilla Hannewyf sues Alice formerly wife of John de Heton, for coming and carrying off 7 of Alice's cattle found grazing in plaintiff's ground, when plaintiff was in the act of impounding them. Alice wages her law. Surety—Thomas de Ceyuill.

The said Alice brings a cross suit for damage to her corn by Amabilla's cattle, who acknowledges the same, but says she has always been ready to give compensation at the arbitrament of the neighbours, of which she offers to bring evidence. Alice says she has never been offered satisfaction. An inquisition is to be taken.

Wakefeld. An inquisition finds that the seizure of an ox belonging to Robert le Walker by William s. of Thomas, for arrears of rent [see above] is just; he is to have the ox back; damages taxed at 4^d. Robert fined 6^d for false claim.

Stanneley. Richard Scayff sues Hugh Scayff for land. The said Hugh was seen in court, but withdrew in contempt of court. The 22 acres in dispute to be taken into the lord's hand.

John Erle sues Hugh Bulheved for debt; Hugh is summoned, but does not come. Robert Short and Richard Short are ordered to bring him to the next court.

Thornes. William s. of Thomas, sues Roger Vyroun for insulting him, and preventing him from doing his duty. An inquisition is to be taken.

Hyperum. A sheep found waif, is sold by the bailiff of Hyperum for 12^d

Stanneley. Henry de Stanneley fined 6^d, under an inquisition, for . . . of John Dade, junior, at Stanneley.

[*A few lines at the bottom of the membrane are partly torn away, and the writing partly rubbed off*].

Sourbi. William del Lane surrenders 8 acres in Sourby; granted to Robert s. of Henry; entry, 4^s

New Rents. Hugh de Hileleghe takes 4 acres of unoccupied land at Sourbi; at 6^d an acre; entry, 4^s

Adam s. of William de Northwod, takes ½ acre at Stanyngdene; rent, 3^d; entry, 4^d

Adam de Coventre takes 4 acres at Sourbi; entry, 4^s rent, 6^d

Hyperum. Thomas del Cliffe surrenders a messuage and a bovate of land at Hyperum; granted to William s. of Thomas del Cliff; entry, 4^s.

New Rent. Roger s. of Roger de Clifton, takes an acre of unoccupied land at Hyperum; entry, 12^d; rent, 6^d

Holne. New Rent. John de Brounhill took 2½ acres at Holne; entry, 20^d; rent, 10^d

Hyperum. New Rent. Elias de Sculcotes and William de Hyngandroide take a piece of meadow, hitherto unoccupied, at Haldworthbroke, and pay 4^s 5^d yearly as rent.

Holne. Richard de Elwardhulles surrenders a messuage and 8½ acres at Foghleston; granted to John his brother, after the death of Thomas de Elwardhulles their father; entry, 2^s

New Rent. William del Bothe takes an acre of unoccupied land at Holne; entry, 6^d; rent, 3^d

Thornes. Alvirthorp. Stanley. William s. of William s. of Thomas de Thornes, sues Richard Proudfot for a bovate of land at Thornes, of which John Harloc, plaintiff's kinsman died seised, after whose death the property descended according to the custom of the court to one Thomas his uncle; and after the death of Thomas, to William his son, the plaintiff. Defendant says John Harloc left the land uncultivated for 5 years, whereupon the steward took the land into the lord's hand, and granted it to Richard de Luppesheved, 80 years ago; and that after any land has been granted by the lord to a tenant, and the tenant has held it for 60 years without any question all action is debarred to those who formerly held the land. He begs an inquisition on this point; which is to be taken.

Half a bovate of land held in bondage by Richard le Wayte at Thornes to be seised into the lord's hands; and the bailiff of Thornes distrained to answer why he did not present the death of the said Richard at the last court.

Attachments in the old park.

Stanley. Philip le Sagher, 4ᵈ; William Aubrey, 4ᵈ and Richard Poket, 2ᵈ, for escapes.

Attachments in the new park.

Osset, Jordan Scot, 2ᵈ; the sons of Adam Lovelady, Thomas Hogge and Richard s. of John, 1ᵈ each; Richard, s of Henry Sutor, Gilbert Coker, William Stutt and Thomas Pulter, 2ᵈ each, for vert, etc.

Attachments in the great wood.

Stanley. Richard Proudfot, 4ᵈ, and Roger, servant of William de Wakefeld, 16ᵈ for escapes.

Stanley. William de Ouchethorp, 1ᵈ for dry wood.

John Gamel of Rothewelle, 2ᵈ, and Robert s. of Adam de Carleton, 2ᵈ for escapes.

Sworn to by ⎰ Robert de Wakefeld ⎱ Total, 31ˢ, with the waif
⎰ Henry s. of Thomas ⎱ sheep, 10ᵈ—new rent,
⎰   de Sandale   ⎱ 5ˢ 11ᵈ, rent, 4ˢ 5ᵈ

i.e., Bailiff, 6ᵈ
Stanley, 23ᵈ
Wakefeld, 15ᵈ
Sourbi, 12ˢ 10ᵈ and new rent, 4ˢ 3ᵈ
Osset, 13ᵈ
Thornes, 20ᵈ
Hyperum, 6ˢ 2ᵈ, new rent, 6ᵈ rearrented rent, 4ˢ 5ᵈ
Holne, 5ˢ 5ᵈ and new rent, 14ᵈ
Alvirthorp, 3ᵈ

————

COURT held at Wakefeld on Friday after the Feast of St. Augustine, the Bishop (May 26), 1 Edw. III [1327].

Essoin. Hugh de Staneley, against John Attebarre, by John de Stanesfeld.

Bailiff. John Erle, against Hugh Bulheved, by William Cussyng.

Alvirthorp. William s. of John Rate, sues Henry de Swylington for land.

Rastrik. Roger del Shaghe and Agnes formerly wife of John (3ᵈ) agree.

Thornes. An inquisition finds William s. of William de Thornes, has no right to sue Richard Proudfot for the land in dispute; he is fined, 3ᵈ for false claim.

William s. of Richard le Wayte, does fealty after the death of his father, for ½ bovate of land in Thornes, which his father held in bondage; relief, 4ˢ

Alvirthorp. The inquisition between William de Bernebi and Agnes his wife, plaintiffs, and Thomas s. of Robert Estrild, regarding ½ acre of land at Neuton, finds that William father of Agnes, enfeoffed Robert Estrild defendant's father, therewith; but that William did not surrender the land in court. It is to be taken into the lord's hand until, etc.

Bailiff. John de Burton sues William de Riley for 39ˢ 10ᵈ, part payment for tithes of sheaves sold to him at Deuesbiry, 16 Edw. II. William denies the debt, and wages his law. Surety— Adam de Heley.

The court consider John Dade, junior, fails to make his law against John del Bothem; damages assessed at 6ˢ 8ᵈ; fine, 4ᵈ

Sandale. Robert de Grottone, plaintiff, and Thomas de Milnethorp and Emma his wife (4ᵈ) agree.

Bailiff. Thomas le Taverner, 6ᵈ for not prosecuting his suit against Paulinus de Emeley.

Alice formerly wife of John de Heton, 3ᵈ for not following up her complaint.

Alvirthorp. Geoffrey de Birkenshaghe sues Thomas Thore for assault at Wodhall. An inquisition is òrdered.

Bailiff. Thomas de Whitley sues John de Mora and Agnes his wife, for detaining cattle. Surety—Robert de Mora.

Sourbi. John s. of Roger, sues Hugh Wade and Julian his wife, for 12ᵈ; under an agreement made between them. An inquisition is to be taken.

Sandale. Robert Carpenter of Crigleston to be distrained to answer Thomas Leulyn for debt.

Thornes. William s. of Thomas the bailiff, fined 2ᵈ, under an inquisition, for false claim against Roger Vyroun.

The tenants of Thornes, Stanley, Hyperum, Rastrik, Osset, Sandale and Wakefeld are charged with the banks of the mill-pond not being properly repaired, to the great damage of the lord; they say the fault lies with the earl's bailiffs, not with them; an inquisition is ordered.

Bailiff. Alice, formerly wife of John de Heton, failed to make her law against Amabilla Hannewiffe; fined, 3ᵈ, and to pay damages; she is also fined 3ᵈ for not prosecuting her suit against Amabilla.

Stanneley. Richard Scayff sues Hugh Scayff for 22 acres in Ouchethorp, of which Hugh his father, was seised in fee according to the custom of the court; after whose death the property should descend to plaintiff his son and heir. Defendant says Richard surrendered the land to him in court, after his father's death. An inquisition is ordered.

Grant of the lord's grace. John de Warenne, Earl of Surrey, grants liberty to graze cattle in the new park to Thomas Hogge, William Hyrnyng, Richard s. of John, Richard Passemer, John s. of William, Henry del Court, Thomas le Pynder, Richard Swaynson, John Mauncel, Thomas s. of Moke, and three widows of the said town, at 8ᵈ for an ox, 4ᵈ for a steer, 2ᵈ for a calf, and 12ᵈ for a horse.

. . . John s. of Alice de Rastrik, 15ᵈ for not prosecuting his suits against Amice [*sic*] wife of John le Couhird, Richard s. of Peter, and John s. of Richard.

. . . John s. of Hugh, Thomas Gyge of Horbiry and Henry le Quarriour had custody of the lord's boat on Wakefeld millpond . . . the said boat at the next court.

. . . . . . and William de Colley (. . .ᵈ) agree.

Stanley. An inquisition finds that Margery Poogge enfeoffed Hugh Scayff of a messuage and 22 acres of land in Ouchethorp; and after the death of the said Hugh, Richard his son, surrendered the same to Hugh also son of the said Hugh.

Sourbi. New Rents. Thomas de Haitfeld of Sourbi takes 3 acres of unoccupied land at le Warcokhill in the bounds of Sourbi; entry, 2ˢ; rent, 6ᵈ per acre.

Thomas Culpoun takes 5 acres at the same place, at 6ᵈ; entry, 40ᵈ.

Hyperum. Richard, vicar of Conyngesburgh, surrenders 6 acres at Hyperum, called Ustordrodes, granted to William le Milner and Beatrice, his wife; entry, 12ᵈ

Rastrik. Avice [*sic*] formerly wife of John Couhird, fines 2ˢ for ½ bovate of land at Rastrik, surrendered by John Alot.

Richard s. of Peter, 12ᵈ for ¼ of such bovate.

Henry s. of John, the same.

Henry s. of Henry de Rastrik, 4ᵈ for a rood of the same.

John s. of Henry, 6ᵈ for the same.

Hyperum. Cecilia formerly [*sic*] daughter of Adam s. of Bate, surrenders a bovate and 5 acres at le Bothes; granted to John s. of Henry Faber; entry, 4ˢ

Osset. Richard s. of Adam de Bouderode, surrenders 4½ acres in Bouderode; granted to Henry Sparwe; entry, 12ᵈ

Attachments in the old park.

Stanley. John s. of Walter, 6ᵈ, for not repairing a paling.

Robert Taillour, 6ᵈ; Peter s. of Geoffrey, 2ᵈ; William Attekerk, 2ᵈ; Margery wife of Geoffrey, 2ᵈ; Robert Short's ass-herd, 3ᵈ; William de Calverley, 12ᵈ; Robert servant of Richard Pane, 2ᵈ; Robert Ricard, 2ᵈ; William Attetounende, 2ᵈ; Robert de Mikelfeld, 1ᵈ; William Aubrai, 1ᵈ; William Qwne, 2ᵈ; Henry Chichematĥ, 2ᵈ, and Richard Scayff, 1ᵈ, for escapes and vert.

Sourbi. Geoffrey de Stodeley, 4ᵈ; Adam de Waddesworth, 4ᵈ; John de Rediker, 3ᵈ; John de Elfletburgh, 6ᵈ; Roger de Grenwod,

5^d; Richard de Colveresley, 6^d; Adam Culpoun, 2^d; Thomas Clerk, 6^d; John Culpon, 2^d; Henry de Holgate, 2^d, and William del Lone, 1^d for escapes and vert.

Alvirthorp. William de Ouchethorp, 3^d; Christian de Flansaw, 4^d, and Matilda de Flansaw, 2^d, for dry wood, etc.

Osset. The sons of Thomas Hogge, Richard s. of John, and William de Morley, 1^d each; Gilbert le Smyth's wife; Adam le Orgraver's wife; the sons of Thomas Pees, Jordan Eliot and John Mauncell, 1^d each; Richard Bateson's wife, 1^d; Robert Sonneman, 2^d; John del Clay's handmaid and Robert le Souter's wife, 1^d each, for dry wood.

Wakefeld. John Sculbrok's wife; Thomas s. of Laurence; Henry de Swilyngton, and William de Lockewod, 1^d each for escapes.

Hyperum. Alexander de Ovendene, 6^d; William, his brother, 6^d; John de Astay of Haldworth, . . .^{d}, William de Hyngandrode, John de Holway, John le Milner of Shepdene, Richard le Badger, John del Northende, Jordan le Pynder, John, s. of Roger del Brighous, and William de Sonderland, for vert.

Sworn to by { William s. of William } 52^s 10^d . . . and new
            { Robert de More   }   rent . . .

The true total of this Court is 47^s 1^d [and there are several notes as to the error].

    i.e., Stanneley, 11^s 2^d
          Osset, 2^s 10^d
          Hyperum, 17^d
          Bailiff, 19^d
          Sandale, 7^s

[*The amounts for the other graveships are either torn away, or too much rubbed to read certainly*].

Memorandum, 2^s 2^d for grazing an ox at 8^d, a steer at 4^d . . . between the Feasts of the Invention of the Holy Cross and St. Giles, by grant of the lord.

———

COURT held at Wakefeild on Friday after the Feast of St. John the Baptist (June 24), 1 Edw. III [1327].

Essoins. Thomas de Thorntone, by William Templer.
John de Mora, by William Cussyng.
William s. of Richard de Osset, by Robert de Mora.

Hugh de Stannley fails to make his law against John Attebarre, regarding a debt of 18^s for pigs bought of him; damages, 40^d; fine 8^d; . . . also with regard to a debt of 4^s; damages, 6^d; fine, 6^d

Richard s. of Cecilia, surety for the appearance of the township of Clifton, 3^d because they do not come.

John de Burton, 6ᵈ for false claim against William de Riley, in which William makes his law.

John Tasshe charged with making a footway from outside his messuage at Wakefeld to the lord's great meadow, cannot deny the charge; 3ᵈ fine. Surety—Henry Tasshe.

Thomas Hughet charged with making a similar path from his messuage through his house and garden, denies the charge; an inqusition is ordered.

William de Castleford 3ᵈ for not coming to answer the charge against him.

Adam de Eland, 6ᵈ for not prosecuting his suit against Robert de Rissheworth.

Thomas Leulyn and Robert Alot (3ᵈ) agree.

Geoffrey de Birkenshaghe sues German Beel for assaulting him at Wodhall; damages, 2ˢ. Defendant wages his law. Surety —Robert de Wyrunthorp.

Sourby. John s. of Roger (3ᵈ) and Hugh Wade and Julian his wife, agree.

Alvirthorp. William de Barnby, and Agnes his wife, give 6ᵈ for an inquisition on ½ acre at Neuton, as to whether it was surrendered in court by William, father of Agnes, to Robert, father of Thomas Estrild. The inquisition finds no surrender was made of the said land either in court or out. It is therefore to be taken into the lord's hand.

William de Birkenshagh acknowledges he broke a cattle fence at Wyrunthorp; 3ᵈ. Surety—Geoffrey, his brother.

Geoffrey de Birkenshagh in mercy, under an inquisition, for false claim against Thomas Thore.

Stanley. Richard Scayff, 3ᵈ for false claim against Hugh Scayff.

Hugh Scayff does fealty after the death of Hugh his father, and pays 12ᵈ relief on 22 acres in Stanley.

Alvirthorp. Geoffrey de Birkenshagh, 3ᵈ for offence against German Beal.

Rastrik. Matthew de Tothill, 3ᵈ for not having Thomas de Berkesland in court, for whom he was surety.

Thorns. Robert Peger (3ᵈ) and John Bulnais agree.

William Malyn, 3ᵈ for false claim against John Bulnais.

The towns of Thorns, Stanley, Hiperum, Rastrik, Osset, Sandale and Wakefeld, 40ᵈ each for not repairing Wakefeld mill-pond as they are bound to do.

. . .Thomas de Steynland surrenders 6 acres at Scamedene; granted to John s. of John de Berkesley; entry, 3ˢ—Also another 6 acres there; granted to Roger Atterode; entry, 40ᵈ—An acre, granted to William del Hole; entry, 10ᵈ—Two and a half acres, granted to John Attesteghel; entry, 15ᵈ—Two acres, granted to the same; entry, 12ᵈ—and 1¼ acre, granted to William Turnur; entry, 8ᵈ

[**Holne**]. Thomas Couper surrenders an acre at leker in Holne-frith; granted to Alice formerly wife of Steer; entry, 6ᵈ

[**Sandale**].   Henry Fox surrenders 2½ acres at Crigleston; granted to James Munck; entry, 12ᵈ

. . . Richard del Bothe surrenders 3¾ acres in Wolfdale; granted to Alice d. of Adam; entry, 12ᵈ

Thomas Dawson surrenders 8 acres in Wolvedale to the use of Richard Hogson; entry, 2ˢ

. . . John Baron surrenders 6 acres in Alstanlay to the use of William del Bothem; entry, 2ˢ

Holne. Matthew de Ramesdene surrenders 1½ acre to the use of Adam del Grene; entry, 6ᵈ

Robert s. of Hugh, surrenders 6 acres at Stanley; granted to Robert Leper and Philip Sagher; entry, 2ˢ 6ᵈ

Wakefeld.   John de Pontefract and Thomas de Pontefract, merchants, charged with assaulting Adam le Walker at Wakefeld, in an affray of the whole town, cannot deny the charge; fine, 10ᵈ each.

Philip de Castelford 12ᵈ for the same.   Sureties—William Cussing and Henry Tasshe.

Henry Mason, 3ᵈ.   Sureties—John de Wragby and William Pollard.

William Whugh, 6ᵈ. Surety—Robert Short.

Robert Botoun, 6ᵈ

Adam Grenhod, 6ᵈ for breaking the lord's pound and removing his cattle without a bailiff.

Robert le Roller, 3ᵈ; Thomas Bate, 2ᵈ; William s. of Isabel, 6ᵈ; Philip de Castelford, 6ᵈ; William s. of Robert, 2ᵈ; Henry de Switlyngton, 2ᵈ; Peter de Acom, 2ᵈ, and William le Orfeur, 6ᵈ for the same.

John de Grengate and Thomas Gardiner, 6ᵈ each, for making pathways.   Sureties—John de Fery and Thomas Bate.

Sourbi.   All the lands and tenements, formerly held at Mancanhulles by Peter Swerd, to be taken into the lord's hand, because Henry his son and heir is a minor; the bailiff to answer for the issues.

Wakefeld.   A toft and croft in Wakefeld, formerly held by Agnes Wolf, are delivered as a gift to the said Agnes, by the lord's letters, to hold of the said lord.

Sworn to by { Robert, s. of William } Total—53ˢ 9ᵈ
             { Robert de Mora   }

i.e., Bailiff, 26ˢ 7ᵈ   Alvirthorp, 15ᵈ
      Sourby, 3ᵈ   Wakefeld, 7ˢ 11ᵈ
      Rastrik, 10ˢ 5ᵈ   Thornes, 6ᵈ
      Sandale, 12ᵈ   Stanneley, 3ˢ 9ᵈ
      Hyperum, 6ᵈ   Holne, 18ᵈ

The Earl's mandate received in the following words[1]—John, Earl Warenne, to our dear and faithful John Trehampton, steward of our lands in the county of York, greeting. We charge you to deliver to Agnes Wolf of Wakefeld the land and messuage she used to hold, now taken into your hand, to hold to the said Agnes from us in bondage by the services and customs to the said land appertaining, this letter being your warrant. Given at Clifton, the 4th day of June in the first year, by virtue of which letter the land and tenement were granted to the said Agnes, as above recorded.

_____

COURT held at Wakefeld on Friday after the Feast of the Translation of St. Thomas, the Martyr (July 7), 1 Edw. III [1327].

Essoins. William de Birton, by James del Okes.
Thomas de Belhous, by Robert de Mora.
John de Cailly, by William Templer.

Bailiff. John Erle, 3ᵈ for not prosecuting his suit against Hugh Bulheved.

Waif. The townshipe of Clifton is charged with 18ᵈ for a waif valued at that amount.

The bailiff is ordered to summon a good inquisition from Brighous, with regard to all who brew there, since the tourn, because no one was presented at the last tourn there for brewing.

The lord's charter. A French charter (given verbatim) dated "from our castle at Sandale," 20 May 1 Edw. III, from John, Earl of Surrey, granting to Thomas Alayn and Margaret, his wife, 4 messuages, 4½ bovates and 8 acres of meadow in Horbiry, formerly held by John Kaynock and Robert Atteoke, Gilbert Idey, and Robert, s. of the bailiff of Horbiry, at a rent of 43 sous, *i.e.*, 6 sous for each bovate and 2 sous for each acre of meadow.

Recognizance. Thomas de Whitwod, Richard le Couhird, Thomas Cosyn, Walter le Turnur and John Oliver, summoned to make answer why execution should not be done on them for 54 marks of silver, which John de Burton recovered against them in court last year, say they have already paid 17 marks, 6ˢ and 8ᵈ, and hold John de Burton's receipt for the same; also 12 marks for which they have no receipt, and acknowledge the rest is due. John de Burton denies receiving the 12ˢ; an inquisition is to be taken on this point. At the next court John withdraws on this point.

Thurstanhaghe in Sandale. John Cokewald, 4ᵈ; Thomas Munck, 2ᵈ; James Munck, 2ᵈ; John de Halifax, 1ᵈ; William de Donecastre, 2ᵈ; Roger de Donescastre, 2ᵈ, and Elias Goldhor, 6ᵈ, for vert.

[1] French.

Holne. John s. of Adam, surrenders a bovate of land at le Scoles; granted to William de Littelwod; entry, 4ˢ

Thomas de Steynland gives 4ˢ for license to clear 10 acres of land he holds at Scamendene.

Bailiff. Adam de Everingham to be distrained for arrears of suit of court for tenements at Erdeslawe and Miggeley.

Thomas Drabil surrenders 4 acres in Cartworth; granted to Robert del Bothe; entry, 6ᵈ

Sworn to by   { Robert s. of William   } Total—11ˢ 4ᵈ, with
          { William de Wakfeld   } 18ᵈ for a waif as above.

    i.e., Bailiff, 21ᵈ
        Holne, 8ˢ
        Sandale, 19ᵈ

Memorandum, for grazing fees in the Old Park, till the
    Feast of the Invention of the Holy Cross,   38ˢ 7ᵈ
    For the same in the new park   27ˢ 4ᵈ

                   Total—   65ˢ 11ᵈ
              from Henry de Walda.

CUSTOMARY COURT held at Wakefeld, on Saturday after the Feast of the Translation of St. Thomas the Martyr (July 7), 1 Edw. III [1327].

Osset. Henry s. of John de Heton, 3ᵈ (under an inquisition) for false claim against William s. of Amabilla.

Alice, wife of John de Heton, is constantly having her cattle trespass on her neighbours, and when her cattle were impounded for damages, she broke the pound and drove them off, without making any compensation to those who had impounded the beasts; fine, 12ᵈ

Sandale. Robert s. of John, 6ᵈ; John de Wyk, 6ᵈ; John de Holgate, 6ᵈ; and Adam del Grene, 4ᵈ, for not coming, when summoned, on an inquisition.

Wakefeld. Robert de Fetherstone, 3ᵈ for the same.

Sandale. James Munck, 3ᵈ for not coming to answer Thomas de Ketelthorp.

Holne. Elias s. of Henry, 3ᵈ, for false claim against Matthew Drabel.

Alvirthorp. Geoffrey de Birkenshaghe and German Beel (3ᵈ) agree.

Henry Tasshe sues Geoffrey and William de Birkenshaghe for breaking a cattlefence on land belonging to the lord at Stanneley, in the plaintiff's custody, which enabled several strange beasts to damage the grass in the said Henry's custody, etc. An inquisition is ordered.

Sandale. Thomas Clerk of Crigleston sues William s. of Robert, for blocking up a pathway leading from the town of Crigleston to the fields. An inquisition is ordered.

Osset. Alice formerly wife of John de Heton, 6^d for an offence against Amabilla Hannewyff; and for breaking Adam del Dene's pound, and carrying off her cattle.

Horbiry. John s. of Thomas le Smyth, surrenders 1½ rood at Horbiry; granted to Thomas Bate; entry, 6^d

Wakefeld. New Rent. William Filche, cobbler takes a piece of unoccupied ground, 86 feet by 15 feet, in le Kergate, lying between his tenement on the highroad; entry, 8^d; rent, 1½d.

Horbiry. William s. of John Clerk, takes a messuage and ½ bovate, from land lying unoccupied at Horbiry, called Molebrist; entry, 18^d; rearrented rent, 5^s

Wakefeld. New Rent. William de Sandale takes a piece of unoccupied land, 16 feet by 6 feet, at Bichehill in Wakefeld, between his own tenement and that of Henry Bull, entry, 6^d; rent, 1½^d

Sworn to by $\left\{ \begin{array}{l} \text{William de Horbiry} \\ \text{John de Sandale} \end{array} \right.$ $\left. \begin{array}{l} \text{Total, 7}^s \text{ 6}^d\text{—and new} \\ \text{rent, 3}^d \text{ and rearrented} \\ \text{rent, 5}^s \end{array} \right\}$

i.e., Osset, 21^d
      Sandale, 22^d
      Holne, 3^d
      Alvirthorp, 3^d
      Horbiry, 2^s and re-arrented rent, 5^s
      Wakefeld, 17^d and new rent, 3^d

COURT held at Wakefeld on Friday after the Feast of St. Peter ad Vincula (Aug. 1), 1 Edw. III [1327].

Essoins. Robert de Wyronthorp, by John de Stansfeld.

Thomas de Thorntone, by Robert de Mora.

Bailiff. William de Riley, 6^d for not prosecuting his suit against Roger de Clifton.

Hugh Viroun sues John del Clay for trespass. Surety— Roger Viroun. John does not come; therefore Richard Passemer and Thomas Hogge, his sureties, fined 6^d; and the same for not producing Robert Passemer to answer said Hugh.

Robert de Mora and William Templer, 6^d for not producing Robert le Wright to answer John Hobbeson.

Thomas Halte sues John s. of Thomas de Heton, for trespass. Surety—John de Grengate.

Henry Petche, 3^d for sundry defaults.

Attachments.

Sourbi. Richard de Grenwod, 12ᵈ; John de Elfletburgh, 6ᵈ; John de Rediker, 12ᵈ; Adam s. of Elias, 12ᵈ; Margery de Stodeley, 6ᵈ; John Culpoun, 2ᵈ; Richard s. of Robert, 12ᵈ; John s. of Adam, 6ᵈ; William Milner, 6ᵈ; Thomas del Dene, 2ˢ; Ivo de Saltonstall, 12ᵈ; Richard s. of Richard, 6ᵈ; Richard Attetounend, 6ᵈ; Alice widow, 6ᵈ; Robert del Okes, 6ᵈ; Ivo del Hole, 6ᵈ; William Trist, 6ᵈ; Alice d. of Jordan de Skercotes, 6ᵈ; Henry s. of the Carpenter, 2ˢ; Richard Mist, 6ᵈ; Roger de Calvirley, 3ᵈ; William West and John de Illingworth, 6ᵈ; John Moddre, 3ᵈ; Richard de Ludding-dene, 3ᵈ; Henry de Holgate, 6ᵈ; and Thomas de Halifax, 3ᵈ, for escapes and vert.

Sandale. William s. of Robert, sues John Payn for trespass.

Stanneley. Robert Leper and Philip Sagher surrender a messuage and 7½ acres in Stanneley, which they had by the surrender of Robert s. of Hugh; granted to William Albrai; entry, 2ˢ 6ᵈ

Sworn to by   { John Pollard   } 21ˢ 11ᵈ
           { Robert, s. of William }

i.e., Bailiff 2ˢ 3ᵈ
      Sourbi, 17ˢ 2ᵈ
      Stanley, 2ˢ 6ᵈ

CUSTOMARY COURT there, the Saturday following.

Alvirthorp. John Swan and Margery his wife, 3ᵈ, and Robert Peger agree.

William de Barnby and Agnes his wife, give 4ᵈ for entry into ½ acre of land at Neuton, for which they were sued.

Horbiry. Thomas Gyge, John s. of Hugh, and Henry Quari-our, charged regarding a certain boat at Wakefeld mill, value 5ˢ, which was in their custody and which they have lost, cannot deny the charge. They become sureties for each other for the said 5ˢ

Sandale. An inquisition, taken at the suit of Thomas de Ketelthorpe, finds that William de Plegwyk mortgaged to Robert de Ketilthorp 4 acres of land at Sandale for 33ˢ 4ᵈ, with right to redeem; and after William's death John his son, sold his rights in the land to one Henry de Ketelthorp, who married Elizabeth mother of the said Thomas, and surrendered it to him in court. Thomas therefore has no claim, and is fined 12ᵈ

[**Horbiry**]. An inquisition finds that Thomas Gyge of Horbiry and Henry Quariour of Sandale removed a boat at Horbiry, from a safe place there in which it had been placed by John s. of Hugh de Horbiry, by which the said John incurred [damages], taxed at . . . Fine, . . . Surety—Thomas Alayn.

. . . del Abbay and John Garbot (. . .ᵈ) agree.

[*Three entries at the end of the membrane are so much torn that no connected sense can be made out of them*].

Sandale. William s. of Robert, 6ᵈ, under an inquisition, for blocking up a pathway at Crigleston to the injury of Thomas Clerk; damages, 6ᵈ

Adam s. and heir of Robert del Grene, to be distrained to do fealty at the next court. He afterwards comes and begs for his inheritance as his father's next heir, and pays 3ˢ 4ᵈ as a heriot on a messuage and bovate of land at Sandale.

Stanley. John s. of Simon de Stanneley, 1ᵈ; Thomas Gunne, 3ᵈ; Adam Nouthird, 3ᵈ; William Theker, 2ᵈ; Thomas del Ker, 1ᵈ; Thomas Scayff, 1ᵈ; John Hannecok, 3ᵈ; Richard de Bateley, 2ᵈ; John s. of Iš, 2ᵈ; Adam Heuwar, 4ᵈ; John Flachard, 2ᵈ, and William Cade, 3ᵈ, for default.

Thorns. Robert Piebridd, 1ᵈ; Robert Ters, 3ᵈ; Robert Peger of Thorns, 2ᵈ; William Malyn, 1ᵈ; Robert s. of Richard, 2ᵈ; John Bulnais, 3ᵈ; Richard Proudfot, 3ᵈ; William s. of Philip, 2ᵈ; Robert s. of Ivo, 1ᵈ; Richard Wright, 1ᵈ; John del Haghe, 2ᵈ; Philip s. of Agnes, 1ᵈ; Robert s. of Emma, 2ᵈ; Elias Tirsy, 3ᵈ; Hugh de Stockewelle, 3ᵈ; Thomas de Leptone, 3ᵈ; Ralph Bate, 3ᵈ; Philip Damysel, 4ᵈ; Henry Bull, 4ᵈ; John Dade, 2ᵈ, for the same.

Horbiry. Henry del Hill of Horbiry, 2ᵈ; Thomas s. of Robert, 2ᵈ; Robert de Horbiry, clerk, 1ᵈ; William de Bretwisel, 2ᵈ; Henry Prestman, 2ᵈ; Hugh Modisaul, 2ᵈ; Richard s. of John, 2ᵈ; John s. of Thomas Smyth, 2ᵈ; Adam Godehale, 1ᵈ; John s. of Elias, 1ᵈ; Robert Godehale, 1ᵈ; Hugh del Wro, 2ᵈ; John s. of Henry, 1ᵈ; Peter Modisaul, 1ᵈ; Hugh Cort, 1ᵈ; William Prestknave, 2ᵈ; Thomas Burnel, 2ᵈ, for the same.

Alvirthorp. Thomas s. of Laurence de Alvirthorp, 4ᵈ, and John Wilcok, 3ᵈ, for the same.

Stanneley. The wardens of ale at Stanneley present that the wives of Robert Leper (4ᵈ), Richard Pescy (3ᵈ), Thomas Bunny (4ᵈ) and Richard Langshank (3ᵈ) sell weak beer.

Wakefeld. William Cussyng sues Rosa formerly wife of Roger Prest, for land. Surety—Robert de Mora.

Stanneley. Robert Leper and Philip Sagher surrender a messuage, etc. (as at last court, q.v.).

Sworn to by { Robert s. of John / John de Wakefeld } Total—23ˢ 11ᵈ

i.e. Alvirthorp, 20ᵈ
Horbiry, 7ˢ 6ᵈ
Thorns, 3ˢ 6ᵈ
Sandale, 5ˢ 1ᵈ
Stanneley, 6ˢ 2ᵈ

Attachments by Henry de Welde, forester, on the same day.

Thorns. William Malyn, for breaking a closed gate, 2ˢ
Wakefeld. The serving-man of William Erle, 12ᵈ for the same.

John Harihill, senior and junior, 18ᵈ; German Swerd, 6ᵈ; John de Fery, 6ᵈ; Robert Wright, 6ᵈ; William his son, 6ᵈ; Robert Latter, 6ᵈ; William Barker, 6ᵈ; John Rose's wife, 2ᵈ; Agnes Hogge's handmaid, 2ᵈ; Nicholas Hogge, 2ᵈ; William Hodelyn's wife, Henry Mason's wife, Robert Hoppay, Mariota Fisc, Adam Halffmark, Margaret Symyng, Peter de Stanneley's handmaid, 2ᵈ each; Walter Drake, 3ᵈ; Robert Willeson, 2ᵈ; Robert Jose's son, John Top's handmaid, Robert Chep, John Webester, Henry Broun, Agnes de Ripon, and John Broun, 2ᵈ each; Thomas de Louthe, 3ᵈ, for dry wood and vert.

Stanneley. Thomas Martyn of Stanneley, 3ᵈ for vert.

Osset. Adam de Gaukethorp, 5ᵈ; Adam le Oxehird, 3ᵈ; Richard Passemer, 1ᵈ; Emma wife of Henry, 1ᵈ; Robert Sonneman, 1ᵈ; Richard Barker, 1ᵈ, for dry wood.

Richard, s. of John, Thomas Pees' handmaid, John Mauncel's wife, and Thomas Hogge, 1ᵈ each, for entering the park without license.

John del Dene and Robert Sonneman, 2ᵈ each for dry wood.

Thorns. Hugh Viroun, 2ˢ for breaking a paling.

Robert s. of Emma, 3ᵈ for carrying away paling.

Adam Rudd, 2ᵈ for dry wood and coal.

Wakefeld. Thomas Gardiner, 2ᵈ; Thomas s. of Laurence, 2ᵈ; William de Lockewod, 1ᵈ; Richard Cay, 1ᵈ; the handmaids of William Pollard and William Mille, 1ᵈ each; Agnes Sculbrok, 1ᵈ, and Robert de Fetherston's handmaid, 1ᵈ for escapes.

William del Clogh, for Defford meadow, 10ˢ

Stanneley. Thomas de Lynneley, 6ᵈ; Robert Botone's serving-man, 3ᵈ; Robert Botone, 6ᵈ; William Whugh, 6ᵈ; Adam le Heuwar, 9ᵈ and Thomas Bunny, 6ᵈ, for vert, etc.

Wakefeld. Thomas Wlmer, 2ᵈ; John Hobson, 4ᵈ; Augustus Parmenter, 9ᵈ; William Cussyng, 2ᵈ; John de Grengate, 4ᵈ; William Wright, 4ᵈ and Thomas Cussyng, 3ᵈ

Total—31ˢ 6ᵈ [*The sub-totals for the different graveships are torn away*].

COURT held at Wakefeld on Friday after the Feast of the Assumption of the B.V.M. (Aug. 15), 1 Edw. III [1327].

Essoins. Thomas de Thorntone, by Thomas de Belhous.

William s. of Richard de Osset, by Robert de Mora.

William de Birton, by William Templer.

Bailiff. Richard de Birton and John de Shepley (3ᵈ) agree.

Philip de Castelford, 6ᵈ for not prosecuting his suit against Henry Petche.

Essoins. John de Mora and Agnes his wife, essoin against Thomas de Whitley, by German Cay and William de Wakefeld.

John de Fery, against William de Riley, by Robert de Wakefeld.

Thomas del Gates, surety for the Prior of St. Oswald, 6ᵈ for not having the said Prior in court.

Essoin. Thomas le Halt essoins against John s. of Thomas de Heton, by Richard de Birton, John de Halton and John de Stansfeld.

John del Cley to be distrained to answer Hugh Viroun for trespass.

Richard de Birton and John de Shepley (3ᵈ) agree.

Richard de Birstall essoined; his essoiner fined 2ᵈ for not keeping the day appointed.

James del Okes, 6ᵈ; Henry Wildebor, 3ᵈ, and John Cailly, 3ᵈ, for default.

Rastrik. Adam s. of Henry de Clifton, John Cokewald, William Theules, William s. of Adam de Legh, John del Frith, and Thomas s. of Hugh de Bothemley, 3ᵈ each; Thomas de Lockewod, 4ᵈ; Thomas s. of Thomas de Dalton, 6ᵈ, and Hugh Shepherd, 6ᵈ, for not coming, when summoned, on an inquisition at the tourn at Brighous.

Wakefeld. New Rent. Henry le Diker of Stanneley, took the fishery of the water of Kelder from Aggebrigg brook, to Hewyncliff brook, everybody's rights reserved.

Sworn to by ⎰ Robert s. of Gilbert ⎱ Total—5ˢ 6ᵈ
⎱ William de Wakefeld ⎰ and new rent, 12ᵈ

i.e. Bailiff, 2ˢ 8ᵈ
Rastrik, 2ˢ 10ᵈ
Wakefeld—new rent, 12ᵈ

CUSTOMARY COURT there on Saturday, the following day.

Stanneley. William Twentipair sues Hugh Scayff for carrying off his corn from a piece of land at Ouchethorp, which he had demised to plaintiff for 20 years. Defendant says he had leased him only ⅔, not the whole, of the land. An inquisition is ordered.

Wakefeld. William Gardiner, 6ᵈ for making a pathway towards the great meadow.

Holne. William Wyther, and John s. of Matilda, 6ᵈ each for not coming, when summoned, on an inquisition.

Osset. Alice formerly wife of John de Heton, sues William s. of Amabilla, for assaulting her in her house at Heton. An inquisition to be taken.

Sandale. Thomas Clerk (12ᵈ) and William s. of Robert, agree.

William Erle and Johanna his wife, plaintiffs, and Thomas de Holgate (12ᵈ) agree.

Sourbi. Order given to seize into the lord's hand the lands at Warulley, formerly held by Adam del Wro, beheaded for theft, which lands are held by . . . de Illyngworth; also the lands formerly Peter Swerd's; the bailiff to be answerable for the issues thereof.

Horbiry. Thomas Thoresone offers himself against Elias de Horbiry in a plea of land. Elias is in the King's service, and therefore has a postponement till next court.

Holne. Matthew de Ramesdene, 2^d (under an inquisition) for offence against Matthew Drabel; and the latter, 6^d for false claim against Matthew de Ramesdene.

Thomas Assholff sues John del Scoles, saying they agreed for ½ mark of silver John should . . . and find the said Ellen food and raiment for . . ., but he afterwards drove the said Ellen from his house and beat her, so that she could not remain with him.

John brings a cross-suit against Thomas, saying that when John married Ellen d. of the said Thomas . . . so that the said Ellen removed from his house, with her goods and cattle.

An inquisition is to be taken in both matters.

The community of Holnfirth, 40^d for false claim against Matthew Drabel.

Holne. Richard del Dene, to be distrained to answer why he broke Richard Walais' close, whereby the lord's tenants in Holnfrith lost their goods and cattle. And, at the instance of the said tenants, the said distraint is postponed until the tourn at Birton.

Thorns. Agnes Wolf sues William Malyn for trespass. Surety—Robert de Mora.

Holne. Order given for seizure into the lord's hand of all lands leased in the time of the King and the Earl of Lancaster in the graveships of Sourbi, Holnfrith and Rastrik, until etc.

John s. of Adam del Scoles, sues Thomas Drabel for trespass. Surety—William del Dene.

Adam Waynwright, 3^d; Thomas s. of Richard, 6^d; Nicholas s. of Simon de Hepworth, 6^d; Thomas s. of Thomas Saresone, 6^d; Adam de Butterley, 6^d; William s. of Peter, 6^d; Thomas del Welle, 6^d; Hugh s. of Robert, 6^d; John Michel, 6^d and Thomas Essholff, 6^d, for altering their minds in the verdict between Matthew Drabel and the community of Holnfrith.

Adam Acreland, 6^d, and John del Hole, 4^d for the same.

Sworn to by   { William Templer   } Total—12^s 3^d
              { John Pollard   }

> *i.e.* Wakefeld, 6^d
>   Holne, 10^s 6^d
>   Sandale, 15^d

Memorandum—fees for grazing on the herbage of the
   old park from the Feast of the Invention of the
   Holy Cross to the Feast of St. Oswald . . . . £8 : 16ˢ : 6ᵈ
   The same in the new park   £6 : 3ˢ : 10ᵈ

                              Total   £15 : — : 4ᵈ
   for which Henry de Weld is responsible.

CUSTOMARY COURT held at Wakefeld on Saturday after the
   Feast of the Exaltation of the Holy Cross (Sept. 14), 1
   Edw. III [1327].

   Thorns. Robert s. of Elias 2ᵈ for not prosecuting his suit
against William Malyn.
   John Bulnais, 6ᵈ for withholding a stone of wool from
William Filche, clerk, as surety for Henry Quariour.
   Wakefeld. Thomas Thor and Alan Carlel of Wakefeld (2ᵈ)
agree.
   Stanneley. Henry Diker, 3ᵈ and Thomas Scayff, agree.
   Thorns. Robert s. of Ivo, 3ᵈ for not prosecuting Robert
Bulnais.
   Sandale. Robert Pelleson, 6ᵈ for trespass against James del
Okes, which he acknowledges in court; damages, 6ᵈ
   Stanneley. William Twentipair and Hugh Scaif (2ᵈ) agree.
   Wakefeld. Idonea formerly wife of Adam s. of Laurence,
appears against Master John de Wakefeld, who does not come;
William Filche, his surety, fined 3ᵈ
   Osset. Alice de Heton, 6ᵈ for false claim against William
s. of Amabilla; and Amabilla Hannewyff, 9ᵈ for trespass. (Under
an inquisition). Alice de Heton, 3ᵈ for ploughing part of land
held in bondage by the said Amabilla.
   Wakefeld. William Cussyng (3ᵈ) and Rosa formerly wife
of Roger Prest, agree.
   Horbiry. Thomas Thoreson and Elias de Horbiry (2ᵈ) agree.
   Alvirthorp. The bailiff of Alvirthorp, 2ᵈ for not distraining
Thomas s. of Laurence.
   Rastrik. Thomas Essholff, 6ᵈ for not prosecuting his suit
against John del Scoles.
   Wakefeld. Agnes Wolf (2ᵈ) and William Malyn agree.
   Rastrik. An inquisition finds that Thomas Essholff carried
off goods and chattels belonging to John del Scoles to the amount
of 20ˢ John is to recover damages. Thomas fined 6ᵈ
   Holne. Thomas s. of Matthew Drabel, surrenders 11¼ acres
in Wolvedale; half of which is granted to John le Couper, the
other half to Adam Wade.

Matthew s. of Adam de Wolvedale, by the lord's license, surrenders to John le Couper and Adam s. of Adam, 9 acres, with the houses standing thereon, in Wolvedale, for 5 years. They pay 12ᵈ for license to hold.

Sandale. Nicholas s. of William, 2ᵈ; William de Sandale, mercer, 6ᵈ; William Wright, 2ᵈ; John Shephird, 2ᵈ; John s. of Henry, 2ᵈ; Richard Feldfar, 2ᵈ; Robert s. of Hugh, 2ᵈ; Henry del Dene, 2ᵈ; William s. of John, 2ᵈ; William de Colley, 2ᵈ; John s. of Thomas, 2ᵈ; Nelle de Donecastre, 3ᵈ; John Milner, 2ᵈ; Henry s. of John, 2ᵈ; John Nalkeson, 1ᵈ; Adam Trubbe, 1ᵈ; John s. of Hugh, 6ᵈ; Thomas de Holgate, 6ᵈ; John Lorimer, 2ᵈ, and Henry Fox, 2ᵈ, for default.

John de Halifax, 2ᵈ; James Munck, 2ᵈ; Robert s. of Adam, 2ᵈ; Robert s. of Alot, 2ᵈ, and Adam Dey, 2ᵈ, for the same.

Osset, Thomas Pees, John Mauncel and John de Bradford, 2ᵈ each for the same.

Thorns. John Baret and John del Haghe, 2ᵈ each for the same.

Horbiry. Henry Prestman, Hugh Modisaul, John s. of Thomas, and Adam Gudale, 2ᵈ each; Hugh del Wro, 6ᵈ; Peter Modisaule, 2ᵈ and Hugh Cort, 3ᵈ, for the same.

Wakefeld. Master John de Wakefeld, Thomas s. of Laurence, and Robert Ilhor, 6ᵈ each; John Tuppe, 3ᵈ, for the same.

Horbiry. Thomas Thore surrenders ½ bovate at Horbiry; granted to Elias de Horbiry; he pays 6ᵈ for entry at the instance of Philip de Meaus.

Holne. John s. of Adam, surrenders all his right in 20 acres at le Scoles, which William de Littelwod holds by his surrender in Wakefeld Court; entry, 5ˢ

Alvirthorp. The messuage and 25 acres of land and meadow, formerly held in Alvirthorp by John Bate, were seized into the lord's hand because John was beheaded for theft; and the lord, of his courtesy, grants all the said lands and tenements to Henry de Swilyngton, clerk, and exonerates him and his heirs from duty as bailiff on account of the said lands.

Wakefeld. William Cussing sues Rosa formerly wife of Roger Prest, for 5½ acres in Wakefeld, of which he himself was seised. They agree by Rosa's surrendering the land in court to William, who fines 12ᵈ for entry.

Sworn to by { William de Osset } Total 29ˢ 7ᵈ
            { Robert de Mora }

i.e. Thorns, 15ᵈ   Sandale, 5ˢ 6ᵈ
      Wakefeld, 3ˢ 7ᵈ   Stanneley, 6ᵈ
      Osset, 2ˢ   Horbiry, 2ˢ 3ᵈ
      Alvirthorp, 3ˢ 6ᵈ Rastrik, 12ᵈ
      Holne, 10ˢ

COURT held at Wakefeld on Friday after the Feast of the Exaltation of the Holy Cross (Sept. 14), 1 Edw. III [1327].

Bailiff. Thomas de Whitley, 6ᵈ for not prosecuting his suit against John de Mora.

Essoins. John, serving-man of Thomas de Whitley, essoins against Peter de Whitley, by Thomas de Whitley.

John s. of Thomas de Heton, against Thomas le Halt, by John del Wod and Richard de Birton.

William de Riley, 6ᵈ for false claim against John de Fery.

Alan de Merston, 3ᵈ for several defaults against John de Wirkeley.

Hugh Viroun and Robert Wildbor (3ᵈ) agree. Surety— Thomas de Ceyuill.

Robert Passemer, who at the last court had a love-day in his suit against Hugh Viroun, 3ᵈ for not coming.

Thomas Thore, surety for German Beel, 2ᵈ for not having him in court.

Robert Short, 6ᵈ for not having William Whugh, to answer Margery wife of Simon Hors.

John Hobsone sues Robert le Wright for damages done to his oats at Wakefeld by defendant's cattle. Robert fined 3ᵈ; damages to be assessed.

John de Wirkeley sues Alan de Merston for 7ˢ 6ᵈ for 5 bushels of London barley, bought of plaintiff at Leptone, 16 Edw. II; damages, 10ˢ. Alan acknowledges he owes 18ᵈ, fine 2ᵈ; but wages his law as to the remaining 6ˢ. Surety—Richard s. of Hauwise.

William de Riley sues John de Fery for debt. Surety— Adam Bagger.

Richard s. of Peter, sues Cecilia wife of Thomas del Rode for debt.

Wakefeld. John Pollard is charged with going into the old park, and felling a tree, value 5ˢ; he says it was felled in the lord's service, he places himself on the steward's mercy. The tree is valued at 40ᵈ; fine, 5ˢ

Osset. Hugh de Disceford, villein is indicted for the death of Adam de Gaukethorp. His goods, valued at 35ˢ 2ᵈ, are given into the charge of the bailiff of Osset, to be answerable therefor to the lord, if Hugh shall be convicted. And afterwards the said Hugh was acquitted at York before Dom. Geoffrey le Scrope and others of the Kings justices. Therefore, by the law and custom of England, the said goods are delivered back again to the said Hugh.

Attachments.

Wakefeld. Jordan Mauwar, 3ᵈ; William le Barker, 3ᵈ; William Sweteland, 3ᵈ; William Wright, 3ᵈ; Thomas s. of Robert, 6ᵈ; Robert Latter and his brother, 6ᵈ; Adam Chapeler, 3ᵈ; Adam

Michel, 2^d; Thomas Wright, 12^d; Richard Steel, 2^d; William Glover's son, 2^d; Richard de Waterton's son, 2^d; Henry, his serving-man, 6^d; Thomas de Louthe's handmaid, 2^d; Peter de Stannely, 3^d; Walter Drake, 3^d; Alan le Bocher, 3^d; Thomas Wolmer, 3^d; Agnes de Ripon, 2^d; John Broun's wife, 2^d; German Herward's son, 3^d; Symon Dunning, 3^d; John s. of Robert Carpenter, 2^d; Thomas Scall, carpenter, 3^d; Robert Mareschall, 3^d; John de Morpath and his wife, 4^d; John Wolmer, 2^d, for vert and nuts.

Osset. Willssedene Colier, 2^d; Ralph de Sheffeld, 3^d; William Wynne, 2^d; John de Yarworth, 6^d; William del Ker, 2^d; Robert Snok, 2^d; William le Graver, 1^d; Alan Baillif, 6^d; Thomas Pinder, 6^d; Adam Oxehird, 4^d; for escapes, etc.

John Mauncel, 1^d, and Jordan Scotte, 2^d, for not coming to the lord's hunt.

Wakefeld. Adam Grenehod's serving-maid, 3^d; Philip de Castelford's son, 4^d; for nuts.

Stanneley. John de St. Swithin, 3^d; Thomas Gunne, 3^d, and William Hardi, 2^d for palings.

Wakefeld. William Richaud's wife, and son; John Goldsmyth, and Thomas Molle's wife, 2^d each, for gathering nuts.

Alvirthorp. Avice de Neuton's son, 2^d; John Attebarre, 2^d; Robert Salman, 2^d; John Swan, 2^d, for not coming to the chase.

Henry del Bothem's wife, and Amabilla Wolf, ?1^d each, for escapes.

Stanneley. Richard de Bateley's wife, 2^d; Agnes d. of Thomas, 1^d; Margery wife of Henry, 1^d; Robert Beel, 1^d; Roger le Asiner, 12^d; Robert Botone, 12^d; John del Bothem, 6^d; John Fyndyrn, 12^d; Richeman Colier, and his associates, 2^d; Thomas Gunne's wife, 2^d; William Aubrai's wife, 2^d; John Pikebusk, 1^d; John Horn, 3^d; Hugh Bulheved, 3^d, for nuts and escapes.

John del Bothem, 6^d for not coming to the chase.

Cecilia Botone, 6^d for an escape.

Sandale. Adam del Grene, 2^d; Roger Tropinel, 1^d; James Munck, 1^d, and John Cokewald, 1^d, for dry wood and nuts.

Thornes. Richard Carpenter, for an escape, 3^d

John del Haghe, 2^d; Robert s. of Ivo, 6^d; William del Haghe, 2^d; Robert s. of Emma, 2^d; Philip Damysel, 2^s; Thomas de Leptone, 2^d; John Bulnais, 3^d; William Malyn, 1^d; Margarey wife of Elias [*sic*] 1^d and Philip s. of Richard, 4^d, for not coming to the chase.

Sworn to by { William del Bothem } Total—68^s 2^d—with
{ John s. of Robert } 35^s 2^d for Hugh's goods.

i.e. Osset, 38^s 3^d with the said 35^s 2^d for the cattle of the said Hugh with which the bailiff is not charged in his accounts.

Wakefeld, 14^s Alvirthorp, 22^d

Sandale, 5^d Stanneley, 6^s 8^d

Thorns, 4^s 2^d Bailiff, 2^s 10^d

SHERIFF'S TOURN held at Wakefeld on Thursday after the Feast of St. Leonard November 6, 2 Edw. III [1328].

Bailiff. William servant of the parson of Normanton, 12ᵈ; for shedding the blood of Adam le Welyn.

John Pikard's wife, 6ᵈ, for selling ale at ½ᵈ, contrary to assize.

John Malett, Jordan del Meer and Richard de Metheley, 4ᵈ each for not coming to the tourn.

Adam del Hill, constable of the vill of Eckilshill, 12ᵈ, out of the profit of a swarm of bees.

Robert de Waterton, 6ᵈ for shedding the blood of Richard & William Baycok.

William Baycok, 12ᵈ, for shedding the blood of Robert de Waterton.

Henry s. of Julian, and Richard s. of Alcok, 4ᵈ each for not coming to the tourn.

William s. of Walter, 12ᵈ for shedding the blood of William de Wetherby, chaplain.

Matilda Wyuell, 6ᵈ, for raising the hue wrongfully on Amabilla d. of Thomas.

Margery le Carter and Robert Miller, 6ᵈ each, for selling ale contrary to assize.

Ellota d. of the clerk, and William Baycok's wife, 3ᵈ each, for the same on one occasion.

Robert Schirtyng of Dewesbiry, 12ᵈ for a swarm of bees.

Henry de Chieft and John, bailiff of Emley, 3ᵈ each; Henry le Hyne of Emley and Robert de Bercroft of Crawesthagh 6ᵈ each, for not coming to the tourn.

Henry le Hyne, 12ᵈ for shedding the blood of Henry le Hogge.

John de Worteley's wife and William Broun's wife, 6ᵈ each, William le Hyne's wife, 3ᵈ, for selling ale at 1ᵈ contrary to assize.

Alota d. of Nalle de Emley, 3ᵈ for the same at ½ᵈ

Robert Graunt, 6ᵈ for not coming to the tourn.

Thomas del Bellehous, 12ᵈ for shedding the blood of Elias de Daltone.

Horbiry. Elias de Daltone, 12ᵈ, for shedding the blood of Thomas del Bellehous.

Hugh le Schoter, 6ᵈ for Robert le Webster's blood.

Agnes d. of John de Horbiry, 3ᵈ; Elias de Daltone's wife, & Thomas Gyge's wife, 4ᵈ each, for selling ale at ½ᵈ, etc.

Osset. Johanna de Heton, 3ᵈ; Richard Passemer's wife, 4ᵈ, & Hugh de Disteford's wife, 6ᵈ, for the same.

William Sausmer, Adam Almot and John Fekisby, 3ᵈ each, for not coming to the tourn.

Bailiff. Alice Angold of Erdeslowe, 3ᵈ, and Nicholas le Smyth's wife, 4ᵈ for selling ale at ½ᵈ etc.

John Erkynson's wife, 6^d, for the same at 1^d

German Beel, 2^s, for shedding the blood of Robert Rode and William de Ouchethorpe.

Robert Rode, 12^d, for the blood of John Thore.

William Lacerbadger, William, s. of Gilbert le Tyncler, German Bell and John Thore, 6^d each, for the hue rightly raised on them.

Thomas Bunny's wife, 6^d for selling ale at $\frac{1}{2}$^{d} etc.

Sandale.   Thomas de Milnethorpe, 12^d, for shedding the blood of John del Okes.

Henry le Quarreour, 6^d, for Alexander Miller's blood.

Robert de Sandale, chaplain, 2^s for assaulting Roger Lewelyn, & drawing blood; and 12^d for the blood of Adam de Halifax.

Alice Broun & Christian de le Halle, 4^d each; Thomas Monk's wife, 6^d, for selling ale at $\frac{1}{2}$^{d}, etc.

Adam Grene, who is a common abuser, 18^d; for shedding the blood of Clara d. of Agnes.

The wives of Adam de la Grene, John Payn, John de Wyk and Thomas de Holgate, 6^d each for selling ale at $\frac{1}{2}$^{d}, etc.

William Whitbelt, 3^d for not coming to the tourn.

Beatrice, wife of Adam de Wodusom—for selling ale at $\frac{1}{2}$^{d}, etc.

Stanley.   Agnes de Caupland and Agnes Hawemayden, 6^d each, for shedding one another's blood.

Thomas, s. of Hugh Skayf, 12^d for the blood of Hugh, his brother.

Hugh de Stanneley, 12^d for the blood of Robert de Mickelfeld.

Elizabet de Bateley; Nicholas de Bateley's wife and Robert le Lepar's wife, 6^d each, for brewing at 1^d, etc.

Hugh Forester's wife, 4^d for the same at $\frac{1}{2}$^{d}

Agnes d. of John Isbelł 6^d for lechirwyte.

Thorns.   Robert s. of Ivo, 12^d for drawing the blood of Hugh, his serving-man.

John de Gairgrave, 6^d four times for obstructing 4 paths in Mickilridyng, Beskroyde, le Nuecroft and Cunscroft respectively.

Margery wife of Elias, for raising the hue wrongfully on the neighbours of Thornes, 3^d

Robert Malyn, 6^d for the same on William Nundy & John Kyd.

Bailiff.   Henry s. of Robert s. of Geoffrey, 4^d for not coming to the tourn.

Stanley.   William Whu, 6^d, for shedding Walter Gy's blood.

Servient.   Hugh de Stanneley, 3^d, for not coming to the tourn.

Wakefeld.   William Filche, clerk, and Thomas Kay, 12^d each, for blocking up the road with trunks of trees.

Robert le Mareschal, 4^d, for blocking up the road with a heap of tan.

William de Cliderhowe, chaplain, 2ˢ, for shedding the blood of Richard Withehoundes.

Alvirthorp. Richard Withehoundes, 6ᵈ, for William de Cliderhowe's blood, shed in defending himself.

Wakefeld. Richard le Gardiner, 12ᵈ, for the blood of John s. of Richard le Chapman.

Robert s. of Robert le Couper, 6ᵈ, for the blood of John del Hope and Henry de Long.

Adam Grenehod, 12ᵈ, for Robert Prest's blood.

John Wolmer, 12ᵈ, for entering the lord's park with his cart, and carrying away wood, boards & lathes of other people without right.

Bailiff. Hugh Bulheved 12ᵈ for trespass.

John Pynnyng—for shedding the blood of John de Penerith.

William Wyles, junior, — for making a ditch in the public lane by John Pollard's house in Kergate.

Wakefeld. William Lacerbadger, 6ᵈ, for shedding Elizabeth de Bateley's blood.

William s. of William le Badger, senior, 2ˢ, for the blood of William Isbell.

William Filche, clerk, 6ᵈ, for obstructing the King's highway, with the dust shot from Master John de Wakefeld's oven.

Matilda Tirsi, 6ᵈ for obstructing the road with tree-trunks.

John Goldsmith, 12ᵈ, for shedding the blood of William le Tyncler.

Agnes d. of Robert Rode, and Amabilla Tropinel, 6ᵈ each for shedding one another's blood.

Wakefeld. Henry Peche, 12ᵈ, for shedding the blood of Thomas, carter of William del Clogh.

Hugh Viron, 12ᵈ, for William Hawe's blood.

William de Cliderhowe, 6ᵈ, for not coming to the tourn.

John Sutor, 3ᵈ; Thomas s. of Laurence; William s. of Hugh; Thomas de Louth; William Richaud; John Richaud and Hugh Fox, 6ᵈ each, for the same.

John Graunt and Ralph s. of Laurence, 6ᵈ each, for obstructing the road with a dung-hill.

Thomas le Taverner, 6ᵈ for the same, and with tree-trunks.

Henry Peche & William de Burdeus, 6ᵈ each for the same with timber.

Henry de Swiligtone & William de Lockewod, — for the same.

Robert s. of Ralph, 6ᵈ, for the same with a heap of tan.

William Skinner & John de Grenegate, 12ᵈ each, for the same, with tree-trunks.

William s. of Richard Mille, 6ᵈ; Richard de Byngley, 3ᵈ; Adam s. of Robert, 12ᵈ; John de Wlles, 4ᵈ; Adam Grenehod, 6ᵈ; William s. of Isabel, 6ᵈ; Philip Damysell, 12ᵈ; Thomas Bate, 6ᵈ; and Thomas le Gardiner, 6ᵈ for the same with a heap of tan and tree-trunks.

Henry Fauconberg and Augustine Skinner, 3^d each; Thomas le Flecher, 4^d, for the same, with a dung-heap.

Henry Bul & William Carpenter, 4^d each; John Harihill, junior & John Pollard of Kergate, 6^d each, for the same with tree-trunks.

Thomas Kay, 12^d; Robert Rode, 6^d; William Thrift, 12^d; John Tyd, 6^d; Henry Nelot, 6^d; Robert Wayt, 3^d; John Mous, 6^d; John Nelot, 6^d; Robert Wlf, 6^d; William Filche, clerk, 12^d; Nicholas Hog, 4^d; William Nundy, 6^d; Agnes Hog, 4^d; John Pollard, 6^d; William Pollard, 6^d; William Mariot, 4^d; and Henry Tropinel, 6^d, for baking & selling contrary to assize.

John Harilull, senior, who is a tanner and shoemaker, and sells shoes of sheepskin for oxhide, 3^s 4^d

John, his son, 2^s; William Filche, shoemaker, 3^s 4^d; William s. of Hugh, 18^d; John Tup, 18^d, and Robert Nelot, 18^d for the same.

William Jose, who makes shoes of sheep, horse, calf and dog-skin, and sells them for oxhide; with Henry Broun, for the same, 12^d

William Damysel and Richard de Byngley, 6^d each; Robert Mareschal, & Walter, s. of Walter Cook, 4^d each, for the same.

John Rode's wife, — for brewing & selling at 1^d, contrary to assize.

Thomas Tuche's wife, Ralph Clerk's wife; William Jose's wife, and Elias Tirsi's wife, 6^d each; Robert, s. of Walter's wife, 4^d; Thomas, s. of Henry's wife, 12^d; the wives of William de Fery & Thomas Taverner, 6^d each; the wife of William, s. of Nicholas, 4^d; Matilda del Haghe, 6^d; Hugh de Stokwell's wife, and John Cussing's widow, 4^d each; John Tasshe's wife, 6^d; Thomas Bille's wife, 12^d; Henry Dernelove's wife, 6^d; the wives of William Skinner & John de Grenegate, 12^d each; the wives of William le Gardiner & Robert de Fery, 6^d each; Thomas Bate's wife, 12^d; the wives of Thomas le Gardiner & John le Gode, 8^d each; John Swerd's wife, 12^d; the wives of William Mille, John de Fery & Richard, s. of Henry, 6^d each; the d. of Thomas, s. of Laurence, 12^d; the wives of Richard de Byngeley & William Attelme, 4^d each; John de Welle's wife, 6^d; the wives of Adam de Castelford & William Grenehod, 12^d each; Adam Grenehod's wife, 4^d; the wife of William, s. of Isabel, 6^d; Philip Damysel's wife, 12^d; Thomas Mauger's wife, 4^d; the wives of Thomas de Lepton & German Swerd, 6^d each; Margery Prest, 4^d; Robert de Fetherstone's wife, 12^d; the wives of German Filcok & John Tyd, 4^d each; the wives of Henry Nelot, Peter de Acom & High Bille, 12^d each; Robert Archur's wife & Johanna de Langley, 4^d each; Robert Tars' wife, —; William de Sandale's wife, 12^d; Matilda Tropinel, 4^d; the wife of John Pollard, baker, 6^d ; Agnes Hogge & Nicholas Hog's wife, 4^d each; the wives of William Filche, clerk, & Thomas Kay, 6^d each; the wives of John Hastley, Henry Tropinel, Robert Tropinel, John Hagett & Robert Liftfast, 4^d each; Julian Sabbeson & Matilda Tirsy, 4^d

each; Henry Bul's wife, 12ᵈ; the wives of Michael Carpenter, & William Lacer, 4ᵈ each; Cecilia de Sandale, 4ᵈ; William Richaud's wife, 6ᵈ; Henry le Badger's wife, 12ᵈ; the wife of Richard, servient of Laurence, 4ᵈ; John Goldsmith's wife, 12ᵈ; Robert Rodde's wife, 6ᵈ; John Wilcok's wife, 12ᵈ; the wives of Thomas de Stansfeld & Hugh Fox, 6ᵈ each; Adam le Hewer's wife, 12ᵈ; Alice Torald, 4ᵈ; the wives of William Broun & William Bul, 4ᵈ each; Robert le Roller's wife, 12ᵈ; Robert Capon's wife, 6ᵈ; Juliana de Ripon, 6ᵈ (pardoned by the Steward); John Dade's wife, —; John Clement's wife, 4ᵈ; William Carpenter's wife, 6ᵈ; the wife of John Harihull, junior, 12ᵈ; the wives of John Pollard, Richard de Waterton and William le Glover, 6ᵈ each; the wives of Robert Chop, John de Tanschalt & Adam Leuayn, 4ᵈ each; John de Wolueley's wife, 12ᵈ; John Erl's widow, 6ᵈ; Robert Nelot's wife, 6ᵈ; the wives of Robert le Goldsmith, Robert Swerd & Simon le Turnour, 12ᵈ each; John Broun's wife, 4ᵈ & Richard de Aula's wife, 6ᵈ, for brewing & selling at 1ᵈ contrary to assize.

Henry Drake, 2ˢ for selling unsound meat, & for forestalling fish & meat.

Richard Man, 2ˢ; John Hagett, 12ᵈ; Peter de Stanneley, 6ᵈ; Walter Drake, 12ᵈ; Robert Archur, 6ᵈ; Adam Halvemarke, 6ᵈ; Thomas Wolmer, 12ᵈ; John de Maltone, 12ᵈ and Roberto Liftfast, 6ᵈ for the same.

John de Fery, for blocking the street with tree-trunks and a dung heap, 6ᵈ

Robert le Roller & Robert le Goldsmith, 6ᵈ each; James s. of Walter, & Robert Swerd, 4ᵈ each, for the same.

John s. of John Haribull, 4ᵈ, and John de Maltone, 2ᵈ, for not coming to the tourn.

Total of this tourn—£8 : 11ˢ : 6ᵈ—*i.e.* Bailiff, 23ˢ 4ᵈ
                                                                Sandale, 9ˢ 5ᵈ
                                                                Horbiry, 2ˢ 5ᵈ
                                                                Osset, 22ᵈ
                                                                Thornes, 3ˢ 9ᵈ
                                                                Stanneley, 5ˢ 10ᵈ
                                                                Alvirthorp, 6ᵈ
                                                                Wakefeld, £6 : 4ˢ : 5ᵈ

COURT held at Wakefeld on Friday in Easter Week, 3 Edw. III [1329].

The charge touching Richard le Walker, Adam del Shore, William del Shagh & John s. of Bate, of a deer take in Sourbishire, respited till the next court at Halifax, by security, etc.

All the tenants of Deusbiriwode, summoned as to the tenure of their tenements there, have a day until the Nativity of St. John the Baptist (June 24) next, to shew the warrant and manner of their tenure; and order is given meanwhile that the wood now growing there shall not be cut down by them, nor shall any of them work in the mine there.

William de Crosselee & the other tenants of Brian de Thornhill, named in the Court held at Wakefeld on Friday after the Feast of St. Valentine, have a day till the next tourn at Halifax to answer the lord for contempt in not coming at the lord's summons to the parts about Wircester.

Bailiff. Philip del Hill to be distrained to answer John de Geirgrave for debt.

Master John de Warenne to be distrained to answer Thomas de Totehill for debt.

The charge touching John s. of Robert de Sandale, for drawing the lord's tenants into a plea in the court Christian, in respite till the next tourn at Wakefeld.

Order given, as on several previous occasions, to attach John de Horlastone, Rector of Normanton church, and Roger & William, his servants, to answer Robert de Grotton for trespass.

The imparlance between Henry de Swilingtone, plaintiff, and John de Fery & Amabilla, his wife, for trespass, respited till next court.

Robert Nodgar, complainant against John de Insula, Prior of St. Oswald's, Brother Henry of Abirforth, fellow canon of the said John, & Thomas Pees, for wrongful seizure & detention of cattle, whereon judgment is pending, [essoins] by John Woderoue. Surety—Richard de Birtsall. Defendants appear by attorney; a day is given till next court.

Thomas Torald, defendant against Robert de Mora, [essoins] by Henry Tasshe. Surety—John de Geirgrave.

Thornes. William Bulneis, complainant, & Robert s. of Ivo (2ᵈ) compromise. The imparlance between Henry Tasshe, complainant, & Master Robert de Barneby, Rector of Birton church, respited till the next tourn at Birton.

Bailiff. William de Lancaster & Agnes, his wife, complainants, & William Dammeson (4ᵈ) compromise for debt.

Hugh de Stanneley to be distrained to answer Beatrice formerly wife of Thomas Palfreyman; and John Haget, surety for his appearance at this court, fined 12ᵈ

The imparlance between Richard de Aula & Hugh de Stanneley, for trespass, respited till next court.

Holne. Ralph de Skelmerthorp to be attached to answer the lord for contempt shewn to William de Birton Constable of the peace there.

Thornes. John de Geirgrave complains that Robert s. of Ivo, allowed his cattle to destroy complainant's crops at a place called Wheterode in Snaipethorpe, last February, to the value of 20ˢ Robert makes no defence. John recovers damages; fine, 2ᵈ

The imparlances between John de Geirgrave, complainant, and (1) Robert s. of Ivo, Philip, s. of Roger, William Dolfyn, & William de Mora; and (2) John Baret, Philip s. of Roger & Richard Carpenter, for trespass, respited till next court.

At the request of the parties a love-day is given to John s. of Robert de Crigleston, complainant, & John de Holgate, till next court.

William le Turnour & Rose le Turnour to be attached for making dishes (*disc*) and other small wooden vessels out of the lord's timber, without warrant.

Sourbi. Roger de Grenewod fines 2ˢ for enclosing 6 acres without warrant, and for felling an oak.

Richard de Shakilton to be attached for taking & carrying off the lord's cattle wrongfully.

Bailiff. The imparlance between John de Burtone, complainant, & John s. of Hugh de Horbiry, Henry le Prestknave, John le White, Adam Hepirborn & Elias de Horbiry, regarding an agreement, respited till next court.

Matilda d. of Elias, s. of Peter, complainant (3ᵈ) & Richard Skaif, compromise for debt.

Rastrik. John de Ovingdene to be distrained to answer the lord for a certain stray stirk in his keeping.

Hiperum. John le Pinder to be distrained to answer for enclosing the lord's land without warrant.

Thornes. Richard Proudfot to be distrained to answer Thomas, servant of Sir John de Breuse, for trespass.

The imparlance between the said Thomas, complainant, & William Dolfyn & Agnes Peger, for trespass, respited till next court.

Roger le Siveman, complainant 3ᵈ & Simon s. of Thomas, compromise for trespass.

The said Roger, complainant, & Richard Brounsmith & Matilda, his wife (4ᵈ) compromise for trespass.

Osset. John s. of Evota, complainant, & Amabilla, formerly wife of Henry Goos 4ᵈ compromise for trespass.

Alvirthorp. The imparlance between Philip Damisel, complainant, & Richard Withoundes, for debt, respited till next court.

Thornes. Robert Malyn, senior, & William Bulneis, 2ᵈ compromise with respect to an agreement.

Bailiff. Richard Roscelyn to be distrained to answer William Hirning for debt.

Thornes. An inquisition finds that Robert Malin, senior, is detaining 2ˢ from Robert Malin, junior, the price of a cart; he is ordered to pay the 2ˢ; fine, 2ᵈ

Bailiff. Henry Sparu to be distrained to answer William Hirning for debt.

Sourbi.   Adam s. of Roger, complainant against Matilda formerly wife of Richard de Waddesworth, for debt, fined 6ᵈ with his surety, for not prosecuting.

Holne.   The charge touching John del Bothe & William de Craven for exchanging land without license from the court, is respited till next court.

Osset.   A messuage & a bovate of land, formerly held by Jordan Campion in Osset, for his life, by demise of John, s. of Ralph de Horbiry, are demised to John Campion, son of the said Jordan, to hold according to custom, etc. Entry, 10ˢ to be paid on June 24th.

Holne.   Thomas s. of Gilbert de Alstanley, gives 20ᵈ for license to take 3 acres of the lord's unoccupied land next Alstanley; to hold according to custom, etc. Rent, 4ᵈ an acre.

Sourbi.   John de Illingworth, 20ᵈ, for 2 acres of unoccupied land in Werlulley, at le Withinheued, to hold as above; rent, 6ᵈ an acre.

Holne.   William s. of Richard de Hepworth, surrenders an acre in Hepworth; demised to Edmund del Barndside, to hold as above; entry, 6ᵈ

Hyperum.   John s. of Roger del Brighous to be distrained to be at next court to make a fine for entry into 16 acres, which John de Shapeley demised him out of court.

Thornes.   Robert Malyn surrenders an acre in Thornes, on Ravenshow; demised to John s. of Robert, to hold according to custom, etc.; entry, 6ᵈ

Alvirthorp.   Robert Bulneis surrenders ½ acre in Alvirthorp; demised to Roger Dunnyng, to hold as above; entry, 3ᵈ

Richard Withundes surrenders a messuage in Alvirthorp; demised to Roger Dunning as above; entry, 3ᵈ

Thornes.   Robert Malyn surrenders ½ bovate in Thornes; demised to John Bulneys, to hold as above. Entry, 2ˢ

Sourbi.   Thomas Culpoun gives 12ᵈ for license to take an acre of the lord's unoccupied land in Sourby, between the paling & the water; & ½ acre of unoccupied land at le Mareshagh. To hold. etc. Rent, 6ᵈ per acre. The said acre lies cornerwise between le Redikerforth & le Driettungge.

Holne.   John Drabyl gives 12ᵈ for an acre of unoccupied land at Holnelee; to hold, etc. Rent, 4ᵈ

Adam de Holne gives 2ˢ 6ᵈ for 2½ acres at Holnlee; to hold, etc. Rent, 4ᵈ an acre.

Sandale.   John le Nailer surrenders 3⅜ acres in the graveship of Sandale; demised to William de Donecaster; to hold, etc. Entry, 18ᵈ

Osset.   Julian, d. of Ralph de Northwode, surrenders 4½ acres in Osset, which are afterwards demised to William, s. of Christian, for 12 years; entry, 12ᵈ

Total of this Court—29ˢ 6ᵈ. And new rent, 3ˢ 11ᵈ a year.

i.e. Bailiff, 2ˢ 2ᵈ
Thornes, 3ˢ 2ᵈ
Sourby, 5ˢ 2ᵈ   New rent, 21ᵈ
Osset, 11ˢ 4ᵈ
Holn, 5ˢ 8ᵈ   New rent, 2ˢ 2ᵈ
Alvirthorp, 6ᵈ
Sandale, 18ᵈ

COURT held at Wakefeld on Friday, the 12th of May, 3 Edw. III [1329].

Essoin. Thomas de Thorntone by Henry Tasshe. Surety— Robert de Mora.

Sandale. Nigel de Doncaster who had a day by previous assignment to be at this court to declare the truth between John, s. of Robert de Sandale, & John de Holgate, in a plea of detaining cattle, does not come. Fine, 6ᵈ.

Henry Shakelok, 4ᵈ for the same.

Bailiff. Robert Nodger, 12ᵈ for not prosecuting suit against John de Insula, Prior of St. Oswald's, Brother Henry of Abirforth & Thomas Pees.

Robert de Mora, complainant, & Thomas Torald, compromise for trespass. Robert's fine pardoned by the Steward.

Hugh de Stanneley, distrained to answer Beatrice, formerly wife of Thomas le Palfreyman, by 3 oxen in the custody of Thomas Alayn, bailiff, does not come. Better distraint to be made, to answer said Beatrice, & the lord for default.

Sandale. The inquisition of twelve jurors to which John, s. of Robert de Sandale, & John de Holgate, referred themselves, finds that John de Holgate is not detaining any of the complainant's goods or chattels. Fine, 3ᵈ for false claim.

Thornes. John de Geirgrave sues Robert s. of Ivo, Philip s. of Roger, William Dolfyn & William de Mora, for making wrongful presentment of sundry trespasses, as committed by complainant, at the last tourn at Wakefeld, to wit for obstructing 3 paths at Snaipthorp, on which he was fined 2ˢ. Defendants maintain their presentment was true. All parties refer themselves to an inquisition; and John de la More, Robert de Wyronthorpe, Thomas del Belhous, John, s. of Richard de Osset, Robert de Stodeley, Thomas, s. of Adam de Southwode, John, s. of Hugh de Horbiry, Elias de Dalton, Richard Pasmer, Thomas Hog, Richard Withoundes & Richard de Collay, sworn upon this inquisition, have a day till next court to shew verdict in the premises.

John de Geirgrave complains of Philip s. of Roger, Richard Carpenter & John Baret, that last autumn they allowed their cattle to feed upon his corn, growing & in sheaves, in Belkrode & at le Ryerodeheued, damages, ½ mark. Defendants say that complainant's carter entered the said places with complainant's cart & horses on several occasions, and broke down the hedges & the fence, so that their cattle got in by complainant's own default. It was afterwards found that complainant estimated his damages at 5 thraves of oats, these he is to recover, & defendants are fined 3^d for wrongful detention.

The inquisition touching William de Sundirland, as to the oak felled by him in Hyperum wood without warrant, respited till the tourn at Rastrik.

The same with the inquisition on William, late forester of Hyperum, for felling and giving out sundry oaks without warrant.

John le Pinder accused of enclosing land without warrant, is afterwards found not guilty.

Bailiff. Thomas, servant of Sir John de Breuse, complainant, & Hugh, s. of Katherine (4^d), compromise for trespass.

[*This entry is crossed through, "because in the court of the Borough."*]

Osset. William Hirning, 3^d for false claim against Henry Sparu for withholding rent.

Thornes. The inquisition to which Thomas, servant of Sir John de Breuse, complainant, & Richard Proudfot, William Dolfyn & Agnes Peger, referred themselves, respecting the charge of cutting & carrying away the said Sir John's hedges, find Richard & William not guilty; they say Agnes's children carried away wood from the said hedges to the value of 2^d. She is to pay 2^d damages to Sir John, & 2^d fine.

Robert Malyn, senior (3^d), & Matilda, formerly wife of William Malyn, compromise by license on the plea of detaining goods.

Stanley. Thomas, servant of Sir John de Breuse, complainant, & Richard de Bateley (6^d) compromise on three pleas for trespass.

Bailiff. Robert de Sandale, chaplain, & John le Taylur, chaplain, to be attached to answer Robert de Grotton for trespass.

Essoin. William del Okes essoins against John de Geirgrave, Bailiff of Wakefeld in a plea of trespass, by Henry Tasshe.

Thornes. Robert s. of Ivo, summoned to answer William Bulneis for debt, fined 2^d for not coming.

Stanley. An inquisition to be summoned for next court between Agnes d. of Richard del Ker, complainant, & Robert s. of Robert le Leper, on a charge of assault.

Sandale. Thomas s. of Roger acknowledges he cut down thorn wood belonging to Adam Trubbe in Sandale, to Adam's damages, 12^d; he is to pay damages, & 2^d fine.

Alvirthorp. Richard Withoundes surrenders a messuage & 13 acres of land & meadow in Alvirthorp; the messuage formerly belonged to Philip Torald. They are afterwards demised to Matilda dau. of Thomas de Kerlinghow, to hold to herself & the heirs begotten between herself & the said Richard; with remainder, in default, to the right heirs of Richard; to hold according to the custom of the manor. Entry, 2ˢ

Sourby. Agnes d. of Henry de Soland, & William her son, to be summoned to answer Thomas de Fakesby for trespass.

Bailiff. Master Robert de Barneby, Rector of Birton church, to be attached to answer Henry Nelot, who appoints William de Locwode his attorney.

Recognizance of John de Shepeley. John de Shepeley comes into court, & acknowledges he is bound to Alice formerly wife of Hugh del Hole, in 16ˢ 8ᵈ, to be paid half next Michaelmas, the other half at the following Feast of the Purification. Sureties— John le Couper & Hugh de Thorntley.

Holne. The whole community of the vill of Foulestone sues Adam le Waynwriht & Richard Michel for debt.

William Cade, charged with villeinage, comes & fines 13ˢ 4ᵈ to have a respite till next Michaelmas, unless the Earl comes into the neighbourhood before then. Nevertheless his tenements are seized into the lord's hands.

Total of this Court—42ˢ 3ᵈ

i.e. Sandale, 15ᵈ
Thornes, 2ˢ
Bailiff, 14ˢ 4ᵈ
Alvirthorp, 2ˢ
Stanneley, 2ˢ
Ossett.

———

SHERIFF'S TOURN held at Wakefeld on Friday, the 12th of May, 3 Edw. III [1329].

Alvirthorp. John Swan, — Siluing & Robert de Sharnestone, 4ᵈ each for not coming to the tourn.

Thomas Bunny's wife, 6ᵈ for ale contrary to assize.

Bailiff. Richard le Carter, 12ᵈ twice, & Henry le Hocher, 12ᵈ twice, for bloodshed.

John de Wortley's wife & Matilda Broun, 6ᵈ each; William le Hyne's wife, 4ᵈ, for ale against the assize.

John Malet, 6ᵈ for not coming to the tourn.

Horbiry. Robert le Webster, 3ᵈ; John Broun & John Eliot, 4ᵈ each for not coming.

Agnes d. of John s. of Hugh, 4ᵈ for ale contrary to assize.

John s. of Alice de Horbiry, 12ᵈ for bloodshed.

Bailiff. John le Shepehird of Waltone & Adam le Wriht, 6ᵈ each for not coming.

John de Sandale's wife, 6ᵈ for ale against the assize.

Robert s. of William de Deusbiry, 3ᵈ & Richard s. of Alexander de Bouderode, 4ᵈ, for not coming.

John de Bouderode's wife, 6^d; Margery le Carter & Elizabet de Deusbiry, 4^d each; John Erkyn's wife, 6^d for ale contrary to assize.

William Popet 4^d for not coming.

Agnes Nangold & Nicholas Faber's wife, 6^d for ale contrary to assize.

Sandale. Henry Hudson, 3^d; James Monk, John Hancok & Richard le Yonge, 6^d each, for not coming.

John Broun's wife, Cecilia, sister of John Taylur, and Christian de Aula, 3^d each; Robert Pelleson's wife, 6^d, for ale contrary to assize.

Thomas s. of John de Sandale, & John his brother, 12^d each for bloodshed.

Bailiff. John Tagon, 3^d for not coming.

Adam del Cok's wife, 2^d, & the wife of William de Fourneis, 12^d for ale contrary to assize.

Thomas le Grubber, Richard de Floketone & Beatrice de Ouirhalle, 12^d each, for bloodshed.

Sandale. John Dande & Henry del Dene, 4^d each; John Moliner, 6^d; John le Nayler, Henry Shakelok, Richard Feldfare & William Eliot, 3^d each, for not coming.

Henry le Quarreur's wife, 3^d; the wives of John de Wyk, John s. of William, Adam del Grene & John Payn, 4^d each for ale contrary to assize.

Elias de Donecaster's wife, 2^d for the same twice.

Adam del Grene, sawyer, 12^d for bloodshed.

Stephen Erkyn, 12^d for raising the hue wrongfully.

Stanneley. John s. of Amabilla, Walter Gye & Robert de la Wodehalle, 3^d each, for not coming.

Thomas Martin, 6^d for the same.

Bailiff. Hugh de Stanneley, 12^d for shedding the blood of William de Lenton.

Stanneley. Robert le Leper, junior, & Agnes del Ker, 12^d each, for shedding each other's blood.

Richard Pesci's wife; Nicholas de Bateley & Richard Longshanks' wife, 3^d each; Hugh Forester's wife, 2^d, for ale contrary to the assize.

Bailiff. John Robin for impleading the lord's bondsmen in the court Christian.

Osset. Richard, s. of Cecilia de Osset, & William de Bouderode, 12^d each for bloodshed.

The wives of Richard Pasmer, Hugh de Disceforth & William de Heton, 4^d each for ale contrary, etc.

Wakefeld. John Tup & Robert Nelot, for making a path without right, 6^d each.

John s. of Philip de Castilforth, 12^d for bloodshed.

Bailiff. Hugh de Stanneley, the same.

Wakefeld. John s. of Richard Kay; Alice, wife of Thomas Wolmer, & Adam, s. of William Filche, the same.

William Filche, clerk, for blocking up the road with tree-trunks & dust, 12^d

Alexander the doctor, 3^d; Philip de Castilforth, 6^d; William Maynard, 2^d; John de Wragby, Adam de Castilforth & William Bate, senior, 3^d each, for not coming.

Custance Whittunt, 6^d & Mariota, d. of Alan, 12^d for bloodshed.

Stanneley. The townships of Ouchethorp & Stanneley, 40^d for making a path without right.

Wakefeld. John Hagget's wife, 6^d for raising the hue wrongfully.

Robert le Gardiner, 12^d for bloodshed.

Simon Fox, 6^d for carrying off pieces of lime.

John s. of Philip de Castilforth, 2^s, for the hue rightly raised on him.

John Margeri, 6^d, for the same.

Robert Capoun & John Clement, 2^d each for blocking up the king's highway with dung.

William s. of Hugh, for blocking up the road with a heap of tan.

William le Barker, Richard Kade, John Fotistik, Hugh Fox, William le Badger, John Permenter & Richard Kay, 3^d each, & William Michel, 2^d, for not coming.

John le Graunt, William s. of Margery & John his brother, 3^s for a tanned hide worth 3^s, which they found in the demesne.

Thomas Kay, 6^d for baking & selling bread contrary to assize.

Robert Rood, 3^d; William Thrift, 6^d; John Tyde, 3^d; Henry Nelot, 3^d; Robert le Wayt, 2^d; the wife of John Mous, 2^d; John Nelot, 3^d; Robert Wolf, 3^d; William Filche, 6^d; Nicholas Hogge, 2^d; William Nundy, 3^d; Agnes Hogge, 2^d; John Pollard, 3^d; William Pollard, 3^d; William Mariot, 2^d & Henry Tropinel, 2^d for the same.

John Harilull, senior, for tanning hides & making shoes of them, & also of skins of calves, sheep, dogs & horses, 40^d

John his son, 2^s; William Filche, 40^d; William s. of Hugh, 18^d; John Tup, 18^d; Robert Nelot, 18^d; William Jose, 6^d; Henry Broun, 6^d; William Damisele, 6^d; Richard de Binggeley, 6^d; Robert le Maresshalle, 4^d & Walter s. of Walter Cook, 4^d, for the same.

Henry Drake, 2^s for selling unsound meat, & for forestalling meat & fish.

Richard Man, 2^s; John Haget, 12^d; Peter de Stanneley, 6^d; Walter Drake, 12^d; Robert Archur, 6^d; Adam Halmark, 6^d; Thomas Wolmer, 12^d; John de Maltone, 12^d and Robert Liftfast, 12^d, for the same.

The wives of John Hood, Thomas Tutche, Ralph Clerk, William Jose and Elias Tirsy, 3ᵈ each; the wife of Robert s. of Walter, 2ᵈ; the wife of Thomas s. of Henry, 6ᵈ; the wives of William de Fery & Thomas le Taverner, 3ᵈ each; the wives of William s. of Nicholas, Hugh de Stokwell & John Tasshe, 2ᵈ each; the wives of William de Castilforth & Henry del Stokkis, 3ᵈ each; Alice formerly wife of John Cussing, 2ᵈ; the wives of Thomas Bille, William Skinner, John de Grenegate, Thomas Bate, John Swerd, Adam de Castilforth, William Grenehod, Philip Damisel, Robert de Fethirstone, Henry Nelot, Peter de Acom, Hugh Bille, William de Sandale, Henry Bul, Henry le Badger, John Goldsmith, John Wilcoks & Thomas le Roller, 6ᵈ each; the wives of Henry Dernelove, William le Gardiner, Robert de Fery, William Mille, John de Fery, Richard, s. of Henry, German Swerd, Thomas del Leptone, Robert s. of Ralph, John Pollard, baker, William Filche, clerk, Thomas Kay, William Richaud & Robert Rodde, 3ᵈ each; the wives of Thomas le Gardiner & John le Gode, 4ᵈ each; the wives of Richard de Byngley, William Attelme, Adam Grenehod, William s. of Isabel, John de Welles, Thomas Mauger, German Filcoks, John Tyde, Robert Archur, 2ᵈ each; Johanna de Langley, Matilda Tropynel & Agnes Hogge, 2ᵈ each; the wives of Nicholas Hogge, John de Hastley, Henry Tropinel, Robert Tropinel, John Haget, Robert Liftfast, Michael Carpenter & Richard, servant of Laurence de Castley, 2ᵈ each; Julian Sibson, Matilda Tirsy, Amabilla Lacer & Cecilia de Sandale, 2ᵈ each, for ale contrary to assize.

Wakefeld. The wives of Hugh Fox, Adam le Heuwer, Robert le Roller, William Filche, shoemaker, John Harihill, junior, Robert Carpenter, John de Wolveley, Robert le Goldsmith, Robert Swerd & Simon le Turnour, 6ᵈ each; the wives of Robert Ilhoor, William Broun, William Bull, John Clement, Thomas de Stansfeld, Robert Cheep, John de Tanshall, Adam Levayn & John Broun, 2ᵈ each; Alice Torald, 2ᵈ; the wives of Robert Capoun, William Carpenter, John Pollard, Richard de Watirton, William le Glover, Robert Nelot & Richard de Aula, 3ᵈ each; Johanna formerly wife of John Erl, 3ᵈ, for ale contrary to assize.

Total of this tourn—£6 : 2ˢ : 10ᵈ

i.e. Bailiff, 17ˢ 8ᵈ   Alvirthorp, 18ᵈ
Horbiry, 2ˢ 3ᵈ   Osset, 3ˢ
Sandale, 10ˢ 11ᵈ   Wakefeld, £4.
Stanneley, 7ˢ 6ᵈ

COURT held at Wakefeld on Friday the Feast of SS. Peter & Paul (June 29) 3 Edw. III [1329].

Essoins. John de Ceyuill, by Thomas de Ceyuill. Surety—Thomas de Whitteley.

Thomas de Thorntone, by John de Thorntone.

William de Birtone, by Robert de Mora. Surety— Richard de Birton.

A day is given to the tenants of Dewesbiriwode to shew the manner of their tenure at next court.

William de Locwod to be distrained to answer Roger de Grenewode for debt, & for default in not appearing when summoned.

The inquisition between Roger de Grenewode, complainant & Peter s. of John de Whitil, for trespass, respited till the sheriff's tourn.

Robert Scut, Thomas le Pinder, Richard Swaynson, Swayn le Wise, William de Heton's wife, Adam Coo, Hugh de Disceford, Henry Sutor's wife, John Lonman, John del Dene, Adam del Dene, & Alice formerly wife of John de Heton, have a day at the sheriff's tourn to answer the lord for multure withdrawn, etc.

Thornes. John Peger complains of William Lolly, for assaulting him, & beating him with a stick; damages, 40ˢ. William does not deny; is ordered to pay damages, & fine, 6ᵈ

Rastrik. Half a rood of land in Rastrik, which Thomas s. of Julian, holds without license from the court, is taken into the lord's hand. It is sown with oats, & the bailiff is to answer for the issues.

Alvirthorp. The inquisition between Richard Withoundes, complainant & William de Birkinshagh & Geoffrey his brother, for trespass respited until the sheriff's tourn.

The same with the inquisitions for trespass between William de Birkinshagh & Adam s. of Robert de Castilforth; & the latter & Richard Withoundes, respectively.

Osset. William Hirning, complainant sues Thomas de Shelley for 3ˢ for ploughing 4 acres in Osset; Thomas denies the debt; both parties demand an inquisition; to come at the sheriff's tourn. William also claims from Thomas 3 bushels of corn, the vesture of a rood of land in Osset, value 21ᵈ. An inquisition to be taken as above.

John le White, complainant, demands from Thomas de Shelley a messuage & 2 bovates in Osset, from which he is ousting him, and which he says ought by right to descend to him, complainant, after the death of William le White his father, whose heir he is. Thomas says he had a term of 30 years in the tenements by demise of Sir John de Horbiry, formerly lord there, who during that term alienated the property to the Earl of Warenne, & Thomas took the same, to himself & his heirs, from the Earl, here in Court. Inquisition ordered as above.

Alvirthorp. Thomas s. of Richard Clerk, to be distrained to answer Adam s. of John Isbel, in a plea of land.

Bailiff. Elias de Cartworth to be attached to answer Thomas de Whitteley, for trespass.

Thomas le Taverner to be distrained to answer William de Scargill, for debt.

Alvirthorp. Thomas Cussing, 8ᵈ for not coming, when summoned, to answer Margery formerly wife of Robert Gerbod, in a plea of dower.

Adam le Heuwer, 12ᵈ for the same.

Servient. John le Taillur, 6ᵈ for not prosecuting suit for trespass against John Flemyng of Daltone.

Thornes. Agnes Wolf demands 5ˢ against John s. of Elias, & William Dolfyn, under an agreement with regard to a messuage & half a bovate in Thornes. Defendants do not deny, they are to satisfy complainant & 2ᵈ fine.

Alvirthorp. John Attebarre complainant & Adam le Bordwriht, William de Birkinshagh, Geoffrey his brother, Richard de Collay & John Swan, have a day till the Sheriff's tourn, regarding the debt of 5 marks for which John sues them.

Servient. The imparlance between Goscelin le Stedeman, complainant, & William le Glover, for trespass, respited as above.

Sandale. John Nalk to be summoned again to answer Adam Trubbe for debt.

Alvirthorp. The imparlance between Robert Hood of Neutone, & John Swan, for debt, respited till the tourn.

Thornes. Agnes Peger to be summoned again to answer Michael Carpenter for debt.

William Grenehod to be distrained to answer Margery, formerly wife of Robert Gerbod, in a plea of dower.

Adam le Bordwriht, Robert de Mora, Thomas, s. of Richard Clerk, German Swerd, Thomas le Roller & John Pollard, the same.

Bailiff. The tenants of Dewesbiriwode, charged as to the manner of their tenure, fine 13ˢ 4ᵈ for a respite till the lord comes into the neighbourhood.

William le Templer gives 40ᵈ for license to take a pit in Wyrunthorplone to dig for coals, on condition that he will refill the said pit before next Michaelmas.

Total of this Court—19ˢ 6ᵈ.

> *i.e.* Thornes, 8ᵈ
> Alverthorp, 20ᵈ
> Bailiff, 17ˢ 2ᵈ

———

HALMOTE held at Wakefeld on Wednesday after the Feast of St. Swithin (July 2) 3 Edw. III [1329].

Alvirthorp. John Attebarre sues Adam le Bordwriht for 5 marks of silver, under an agreement with regard to 10 acres in Alvirthorp, bought by Adam of John. Adam acknowledges the debt, which he is to pay; 6ᵈ fine.

Thomas Cussing to be distrained to answer Margery formerly wife of Robert Gerbod, in a plea of dower. The 10 acres in Inetrode in which Margery claims dower, to be taken into the lord's hand. The bailiff to answer for the issues, till Thomas comes to answer Margery.

Stanneley. The said Margery sues Adam le Heuwer for her dower in an acre in Neutone field, which her late husband alienated to Adam. Adam acknowledges the fact. The grave of Stanneley is ordered to cause livery to the said Margery of her dower therein; Adam fined 6ᵈ

Rastrik. Richard s. of Adam de Rastrik, surrenders a messuage & ½ bovate in Rastrik; afterwards demised to Peter s. of Adam, to hold, etc., according to the custom, etc. Fine for entry, 3ˢ 4ᵈ

Alvirthorp. Adam s. of John Isbel, complains that Thomas s. of Richard Clerk, is ousting him from an acre of land in Neutone field, which he claims in right of Agnes, his wife. Thomas says he is not bound to reply, because his account does not tally with his complaint because Agnes his wife, is not mentioned in the complaint. Adam therefore recovers nothing; fine, 6ᵈ for false claim.

Rastrik. John de Rastrik sues Thomas s. of Julian, & Julian his mother, for trespass. Surety—the grave.

William le Badger charged with villeinage says he is a free man & of free condition, and pays — fine for respite until the lord's coming, so that he may have the lord's letter to his Steward of Wakefeld, to make inquiry as to his condition.

Henry le Badger, charged as above, fines as above.

Alvirthorp. Margery formerly wife of Robert Gerbod, demands against Adam le Bordwriht her dower in 10 acres in Alvirthorp, sold by her late husband to John Attebarre, & by him to the said Adam. Adam calls John Attebarre to warranty, who says he surrendered the 10 acres here in court to the use of Adam, & that from that time he was not held to warranty, & that such is the custom of the manor. Adam & John demand an inquisition, which is taken by the oath of twelve jurors from 4 townships, who say the custom of the manor is that from the time when any tenant by the rod sells or alienates any of his land so held, from that time forth he is not responsible for any dower whatsoever in such land so alienated, and cannot be called to warranty for livery of dower. Adam, who now holds the 10 acres is therefore to deliver her dower therein to the said Margery; fine, 6ᵈ. John Attebarre is acquitted.

The said twelve jurors find that the community of the vill of Wyronthorp felled an ash, growing on the unoccupied land of the said vill, valued by the jurors at 6ᵈ. They are to satisfy the lord for the 6ᵈ, & 12ᵈ fine.

The verdict of the inquisition as to the houses of villeins in the lordship, sold & removed; as to certain trespasses committed within the lordship, for which the lord has as yet received no amends; as to stone carried off from Wakefeld mill-pond to lay on the flax; & who have offended in these respects—postponed till next court.

Thomas s. of Adam Spink sues Robert del Hill for land. Surety—Nicholas de Bateley.

An inquisition finds that Johanna, d. of William de Osset, carried off 2 loads of grass, value 2ᵈ, from Sandale orchard, worth 2ᵈ. The said William fined 6ᵈ for receiving her.

Johanna serving-maid of John s. of Geoffrey, did the same. The said John is to satisfy the lord for the trespass, & 6ᵈ fine for receiving her.

Agnes Wilkis did the same. Alice Sceet, who received her, is to satisfy the lord, & 6ᵈ fine.

All the tenants in Dewesbiriwode to be distrained to satisfy the lord for wood cut & carried off there & in Hetonbank.

Alvirthorp.   William de Ouchethorp surrenders a rood of land in Swannildene in Alvirthorp; demised to William le Templer, to hold, etc. according to the custom, etc. Entry, 6ᵈ

Stanneley.   John Pollard of Kergate surrenders an acre in Ouchethorp field in the graveship of Stanneley, demised to John Hobson of Wakefeld, to hold as above. Entry, 6ᵈ

Adam, s. of Robert de Castilforth, Thomas Bate, John de Grengate, William Goldsmith, John Pollard, John Harihill, junior, Robert . . . Robert Ilhoor, summoned to answer for sundry defaults . . ., do not come. Fine, 2ˢ

The twelve jurors at the sheriff's tourn—for concealing insults, etc. offered . . . at the chapel of St. Swithin's . . . at Wakefeld.

John Swerd . . ., Robert Swerd, 6ᵈ, Philip Damysel, 6ˢ 8ᵈ . . . for contempt, for . . . presenting defaults at the tourn with others.

John le Goldsmith, William del Clo . . ., Henry Drake, William Fil[che] . . ., 12ᵈ

Robert Goldsmith for contempt . . . in not coming to the tourn, 12ᵈ

[Total . . .]

i.e. Rastrik, 15ᵈ	Sandale, 2ˢ
Stanneley, 2ˢ 3ᵈ	The farmers of the vill, 5ˢ 6ᵈ
Alvirthorp, 2ˢ	

SHERIFF'S TOURN held at Wakefeld on Wednesday after St. Swithin's day (July 2) 3 Edw. III [1329].

William Syne . . . . . .? Deye, Adam . . . of Emmeley, 6ᵈ
John Spink of Holand, 12ᵈ, Richard, s. of Robert, of Wironthorp,
2ˢ for bloodshed.
Richard, s. of John Bullok, . . . for the same from Peter
Go . . .
Robert de Galbar . . . for the same.
• • •
Nicholas . . . for the same from . . . Monk . . .
Thomas de Milnethurp's wife, 12ᵈ for bloodshed.
Robert s. of John Scissor, & Walter s. of John Scissor, 12ᵈ
each for the same.
William Lolly, 12ᵈ; William de Shrefeld, 12ᵈ; Thomas de
Gounton, . . .; John Tyting, William Gurdon, Avice . . . of
Robert Tyting; Matilda, handmaid of John Grengate, 12ᵈ each
for the same.
John Suetighid, 2ᵈ; Robert del Ripon, 12ᵈ; . . ., 12ᵈ; Richard
Withoundes, 6ᵈ, for the same.
Richard Withoundes 6ᵈ for raising the hue wrongfully, &
6ᵈ for homesoken.
Geoffrey de Birkinshagh for blood . . .
Richard Withoundes for shedding his daughter's blood . . .
John s. of Philip de Castilforth, for bloodshed . . .
. . . Roscelin, junior, for the same ? 6ᵈ
Richard Shore, for the same, 12ᵈ
Hugh de C . . ., 40ᵈ
Sir William de Ceyuill, 40ᵈ for the same.
Agnes Hagge, senior & junior, 12ᵈ each; John s. of Robert
Preest & John s. of Philip de Castilford, 12ᵈ each for the same.
William s. of Hugh, 12ᵈ for the hue rightly raised on him.
John Erl, 6ᵈ; Ralph de Fery, 12ᵈ; Robert s. of Elias del
Cliff, 12ᵈ, for blood.
The wife of John Pollard of Kergate, 12ᵈ for the hue, & 12ᵈ
for blood.
John s. of John de Fery, 12ᵈ for blood.
Robert le Couper, for the hue justly raised on him, 12ᵈ
Thomas de Colley, 2ˢ; William Lacer Badger, 12ᵈ, for blood.
Hugh Forester's wife, for brewing contrary to assize at ½ᵈ,
& Nicholas de Bateley for the same, 4ᵈ each.
Elizabeth de Bateley, for brewing at 1ᵈ, 3ᵈ
Thomas Bunny's wife, 6ᵈ for the same.
William de Barneby's wife, 3ᵈ for the same twice.
Adam le Bordwriht's wife for the same several times, 6ᵈ
Walter Carpenter, 6ᵈ for not coming.
William, s. of Mariota, 6ᵈ for forestalling hens, eggs & butter.
Russel of Pontefract, 6ᵈ for the same.
Peter de Stanneley, 6ᵈ for selling flesh of . . .
Walter Drake, 6ᵈ for the same.
Henry Sutor of Pontefract, 6ᵈ for forestalling fish.

Robert Liftfast & Richard Man, 6ᵈ each, for selling unsound meat.

William Filche, shoemaker, because he is a shoemaker and tanner, 12ᵈ

John Harilul shoemaker, John his son, John Tup, Robert Nelot & William Jose shoemakers, 12ᵈ each for the same.

Richard de Binggeley, 6ᵈ for shoes of horse, calf & dog-skin.

Robert le Marshal, William Damysel, Henry Broun, Walter Batty & Geoffrey de Bradeforth, 6ᵈ each for the same.

John Erkin's wife, 8ᵈ for brewing ale at 1ᵈ contrary to assize.

. . ., 4ᵈ; Margery d. of Thomas Erkin, . . .; Robert Miller of Dewesbiry, 6ᵈ; Margery le Carter, 4ᵈ; John de . . .'s wife, 4ᵈ Johanna formerly wife of Robert Clerk, 6ᵈ; the wife of Thomas s. of Robert Clerk, 6ᵈ; ?Christian de Aula, 4ᵈ; Cecilia . . ., 4ᵈ; Adam Colet's wife, 4ᵈ pardoned because a servant; Adam Leubyn's wife, 4ᵈ; Hugh de Disceford's wife, 4ᵈ; the wives of John Alayn, Richard Pasmer, Thomas Pees, Margery de Holgate, Adam de la Grene, & Henry Gunne, 4ᵈ each; the wives of Thomas Monk, John de Holgate, John de Wyk, William de la Grene, Richard Pescy, Robert le Leper & John le Rede, 6ᵈ each; Emma d. of Robert s. of Walter, 6ᵈ; Henry Wildbor, Johanna de Heton, 3ᵈ each for ale contrary to assize.

John Hereward, John Tastard, Simon Dunnyng, Richard Scott, Robert s. of Elias del Cliffe, 12ᵈ each; Ralph de Fery, 40ᵈ, for bloodshed.

Henry de Stanneley, John his brother, & Thomas de Colley, 40ᵈ each, for contumely at St. Swithin's chapel.

John Tyting & Adam s. of Robert Watson, 12ᵈ each for the same.

William s. of Hugh, 6ᵈ for blocking up the road.

William Carpenter, 4ᵈ; Thomas Rose, 2ᵈ; Augustine Skinner, Philip Damysel & Thomas s. of Laurence, 6ᵈ each; Adam Grenehod, 3ᵈ for the same.

Total of this tourn :—105ˢ 5ᵈ   Bailiff, 47ˢ 8ᵈ

Farmers of the town, 57ˢ 9ᵈ

COURT held at Wakefeld on Friday after the Feast of St. Leonard, (Nov. 6) 4 Edw. III [1330].

Essoins. Richard de Hosit by Robert de Mora. Surety— William le Templer.

Hugh de Stanneley, by Thomas Alayn.

John del Rode of Soland, by Robert de Mora. Surety— William de La Lone.

Adam de Stayncliff, by John de Shipdene.

Sir John le Fleming, by Thomas de Totille. Surety—John de Dronsfeld.

Brian de Thornhille, by Robert de Stodley. Surety—
Thomas Alayn.

Thomas de Thorntoun, by William le Templer.

Thomas de Burgh, by Robert de Mora.

Sourby. John de Hadirshelf, complainant, essoins against
John Clerk, by Adam s. of Roger. Surety—William de la Lone.

Rastrik. The whole graveship of Rastrik, 2ˢ for not coming.

Hiperum. The graveship of Hiperum 2ˢ for not coming.

Stanneley. Henry de Stanley, defendant, essoins against
Philip le Sagher in a plea of land, by John Attebarre. Surety—
William le Templer.

Wakefeld. The whole graveship of Wakefeld, except John
Nelot & William Cussing, fined 2ˢ for not coming.

Rastrik. John Steel, grave of Rastrik, 12ᵈ for not coming to
do his duty as grave.

Richard de Botherode to be distrained, as previously ordered
to answer Thomas de Tothille for trespass; & the lord for default.

Thomas s. of Julian, complainant, essoins against John s. of
Henry de Rastrik, by Thomas de Totille. Surety—William de
Lokwod.

Bailiff. William Cussing, complainant, against Robert de
Wyrunthorp, by Robert de Mora. Surety—William le Templer.

Stanley. All the lord's tenants who are bound to elect the
grave of Stanley 2ˢ for not coming; the following excepted—
Walter Gunne, Robert Ricard, John le Sagher, John Poket,
William Albray, Robert Leper, Thomas Gunne, Robert de Mikkel-
feld & Henry Pokett.

Bailiff. Thomas s. of German Filcok, to be distrained to
answer John de Gairgrave & his fellows, farmers of the vill of
Wakefeld, for trespass.

Sandale. Thomas de Milnethorp & Emma his wife, complainants, & James del Okis & Agnes his wife, have a day till
next court.

Bailiff. John le Goldsmith, Philip Damysel & John Attebarre to be distrained to answer John de Breous for trespass.

John de Ryley to be attached to answer John de Dronsfeld
for trespass.

Bailiff. John de Ryley to be attached to answer Robert de
Altoftes for trespass.

Alvirthorp. Geoffrey de Birkynshaghe complains that on a
certain day Richard Withehoundes entered complainant's house
against the peace, & beat his wife, his son & his serving-maid, to
his damage, &c. Richard acknowledges the fact; damages taxed
at 2ᵈ. Fine, 3ᵈ

Stanley. Robert Ricard to be attached to answer Robert
Aubray for trespass.

Thomas del Ker & Margaret, his mother, to answer John del
Halle, for trespass.

Grave of Sourby. William de Saltonstalle is elected grave of Sourby, received & sworn.

Alvirthorp. John Swan, who was elected grave of Alvirthorp, & had a day at this court to swear & receive office, 3ᵈ for not coming.

Robert Shiluing & Johanna his wife, to be summoned to answer Robert Malyn in a plea of land.

Bailiff. Thomas s. of German Filcok, to be attached to answer Robert de Wyrunthorp for trespass.

John de Caylye, 6ᵈ for not coming to do his suit.

William s. of Richard de Osset, in mercy for the same; fine not recorded.

John de Querneby & John s. of Ellen de Rastrik, 6ᵈ each for the same.

William de Birtoun, 4ᵈ; & Thomas del Bellehous, 3ᵈ, for the same; their fines pardoned.

Sandale. John Tubbing surrenders a messuage & 5½ acres in Sandale; demised to Matthew de Shipdene, for 12 years, according, &c. Entry, 2ˢ

Total of this Court—26ˢ 10ᵈ *i.e.,*

Rastrik, 3ˢ	Bailiff, 18ᵈ
Hiperum, 5ˢ 8ᵈ	Sandale, 2ˢ
Wakefeld, 2ˢ	Holne, 3ˢ 10ᵈ
Stanley, 7ˢ 6ᵈ	Horbiry, 10ᵈ
Alvirthorp, 6ᵈ	

———

COURT held at Wakefeld on Friday, the Feast of St. Andrew the Apostle (Nov. 30) 4 Edw. III [1330].

Essoins. Thomas de Thorntoun, by Thomas de Totehille. Surety—Robert de Mora.

Richard de Birstal, by William Templer.

Hugh de Stanley, by Henry Tasshe.

Bailiff. William Cussing, complainant, essoins against Robert de Wyronthorp by Henry Tasshe. Surety—German Kay.

William Cade charged with a state of bondage fines 20ˢ to have favour.

Sourby. John de Hadirshelf, complainant, offers himself against John Clerk, complaining that on Tuesday after Martinmas, 1 Edw. III, he received from complainant 10ˢ to pay Hugh de Totehill, in discharge of a debt owed by complainant; but defendant never paid the money, & Hugh distrained on complainant for the amount; damages, 10ˢ. John Clerk comes & does not defend in the words of the Court; complainant is therefore to recover the 10ˢ against him; fine, 3ᵈ

Alvirthorp. The imparlance between Margery, formerly wife of Richard Gerbod, complainant, & William Grenehod, for dower, respited until William s. of said William, comes to this Court.

Bailiff. Whereas John de Shepeley on a previous occasion acknowledged in this court that he was bound to Adam de Kelingley in 55ˢ to be paid last Martinmas, he now comes & finds surety for paying the said sum before next Epiphany; to wit, William de Birtoun.

William de Totehille, complainant, by his attorney, Thomas de Totehille, offers himself against John s. of Thomas de Halifax; John, distrained the first time by two oxen, then by four, now in the grave's custody, does not come. Everything is to be taken in distraint.

Sourby. A young stray black ox is sold to John de Soland for 3ˢ. Surety—Roger de Grenewod.

Bailiff. Hugh del Hill, 4ᵈ for not having John de Ryley, for whom he was surety, to answer John de Dronesfeld. John de Ryley to be distrained for next court. And another 4ᵈ for not having him to answer Robert de Altoftes, who appoints John de Dronesfeld his attorney.

Thomas Abbot & Matilda his wife, complainants (3ᵈ) & John de Shepeley compromise for debt, & John fines 3ᵈ in a second matter.

William Templer to be summoned to answer John s. of Thomas de Wakefeld, in a plea of land.

Stanneley. Henry de Stanneley, 4ᵈ for not coming when summoned, to answer Philip le Sagher in a plea of land.

Hiperum. The whole graveship of Hiperum, 40ᵈ for not having elected a grave to serve the lord.

Rastrik. Thomas de Totehille, complainant & Richard s. of Peter, & John de Rastrik (8ᵈ) compromise for debt.

An inquisition to come to next court to try whether John s. of Henry de Rastrik, wrongfully took beasts belonging to Thomas s. of Julian, in a place called Oustyrode, & impounded them, damages 6ˢ 8ᵈ; or whether he took them by right in le Birfeld, as John avows.

Stanley. The whole graveship of Stanneley sues Hugh de Stanneley for trespass, to wit that by default of Hugh they cannot keep Birlaghe. He is to be attached.

Sandale. An inquisition to come next court to try whether James del Okis & Agnes his wife, wrongfully killed a pig belonging to Thomas de Milnthorp, worth 18ᵈ, & whether James committed an offence against Emma, wife of said Thomas, by following her violently with an iron fork into the said Thomas's barn.

Holne. John le Couper acknowledges he took away fern that Ellen del Knol had cut to cover her house, to the damage of said Ellen; damage to be taxed at Birtoun tourn; (afterwards taxed at 2ᵈ) John fined 4ᵈ

Ellen del Knol sues William Wethir & Adam Wade for the same trespass; damages, 12^d. Defendants deny; an inquisition to be taken at the tourn.

Margery Strekeyse sues William Withir for 3^s 6^d, her wages for the last half year. William says Margery withdrew herself from his service for a fortnight for no cause, & he therefore engaged another serving-maid in her place. An inqusition to be taken at Birtoun tourn.

Stanneley. An inquisition to come next court to try whether Robert Ricard carried off the vesture of a piece of meadow belonging to Robert Aubray in the vill of Stanneley; value, 6^d; damages, 12^d; the which defendant denies. Afterwards the grave comes & says that Robert's wife carried off the hay after he had put the lord's prohibition upon it; she acknowledges this. Robert fines 12^d for the trespass.

Johanna de la Halle complains that Thomas del Ker's cattle destroyed & trampled 4 thraves of her oats in Stanneley field, each thrave worth 18^d; damages, 40^d. Thomas acknowledges it; Johanna to recover both principle & damages.

John Pollard surrenders ½ acre in Stanneley; demised to William Twentipair; to hold, according &c. after the term of 4 years that William s. of Nicholas has therein. Entry, 12^d

Johanna de la Halle sues Richard Ricard for wrongfully carrying off & making away with a cartload of hay worth 5^s, from a piece of meadow-land belonging to her, called Stanbrigsyk; damages, 6^s 8^d. Richard says he did no injury by taking the hay, because Richard de la Halle, husband of the said Johanna, had carried off a cartload of his hay the previous year; upon which the said Richard, Johanna & himself had agreed that he should take the vesture of this piece of meadow as compensation for his hay. He demands an inquisition.

Alvirthorp. Robert Shiluing & Johanna his wife, to be summoned to answer Robert Malyn in a plea of land.

Bailiff. Thomas s. of German Filcok, to be attached to answer Robert de Wyronthorp for trespass.

Adam s. of Robert s. of Walter, to be distrained to answer Robert le Leper for trespass.

Thomas Odam to be summoned to answer Thomas s. of German Filcok for taking a horse.

Stanneley. Richard Skaif surrenders an acre in Stanneley; demised to Robert s. of Ralph de Wakefeld, for 18 years. Entry, 12^d

Richard Skaif surrenders 1⅙ acre in Stanneley; demised to Henry Poket, junior, for 12 years. Entry, 2^s

Horbiry. Adam s. of John de Horbiry, surrenders a toft with buildings thereon in Horbiry, containing ½ acre; demised to Margery formerly wife of Robert Gerbod; to hold, according &c. Entry, 12^d

Christian de la Halle of Sandale; Alice wife of Adam Leulyn & Magota wife of Thomas Clerk, 2ᵈ each for weak ale.

Stanneley. Nicholas de Bateley; Emma d. of Robert s. of Walter; & the wives of Richard Pescy & Robert le Leper, 2ᵈ each, for brewing and not sending for the tasters.

Bailiff. Agnes de Coupland to be summoned again to answer William le Badger for debt.

Sandale. John Payn to be summoned again to answer John Brand for debt.

Horbiry. Robert Clerk of Horbiry & Elias de Horbiry to be summoned again to answer John de Geirgrave respecting an agreement.

Sourby. John s. of Thomas de Skircok, to be summoned to answer Thomas de Totehill for debt.

Michael Sourmilk to be summoned to answer the same.

Holne. A stray sow sold to Adam de Holne for 12ᵈ. Afterwards came William Ay & claimed the said sow "three-handed," & it was delivered to him.

Bailiff. John de Grenegate, who was summoned to come before the Steward on an inquisition on sundry customs regarding the millers & the mills at Wakefeld, 12ᵈ for not coming.

Adam de Castilforth, John Hobbeson, Thomas Filcok, Robert Swerd & Henry le Badger; William Filche, Ralph Malleson, Thomas Gardiner, John de Wolveley, John Wilcok, Henry le Smith del Hagh, John Clement, William Glover, Robert Nelot, John s. of Hugh le Chapman, & Henry Bul, 4ᵈ each for the same.

Total of this Court—40ˢ 9ᵈ. And for strays, 3ˢ

Bailiff, 28ˢ 4ᵈ
Sourby, 3ᵈ   And for a stray, 3ˢ
Stanley, 6ˢ 4ᵈ
Holne, 4ᵈ
Horbyry, 12ᵈ
Sandale, 6ᵈ
Rastrik, 8ᵈ
Hiperum, 40ᵈ

HALMOTE held at Birtoun on Tuesday after St. Andrew's day (Nov. 30) 4 Edw. III [1330]

Holne. Thomas Fernoule surrenders a messuage & 12½ acres in Foulestoun, demised to John Fernoule his son; to hold, according &c. Entry, 6ˢ 8ᵈ.

Thomas s. of Thomas Drabil, gives 13ˢ 4ᵈ as a heriot on a messuage & 26 acres lying in Shaghley & the vill of Wolvedale, the latter being new land, after the death of his father whose heir he is. Thomas is 6 months of age; the land is meanwhile committed to the custody of Margery, his mother.

Alice d. of Nelle, comes & proves three-handed that Michael Drabil & John Drabil, executors of Thomas Drabyl, are withholding from her 3ˢ 4ᵈ, for a stone of wool which the said Alice bought of Thomas, last year, when he was alive.   They are to make the same good.   Fine, 8ᵈ

William, serving-man of Robert de Wades, acknowledges he defrauded the lord of toll on 2 young oxen & 3 sheep after Michaelmas; fine, 6ᵈ

The farmer of the vill of Wakefeld to be attached to come to next court at Wakefeld.

Thomas del Rode surrenders 4¾ acres in Hepworthe; demised to Amabilla d. of John del Scoles; to hold, according &c.   Entry, 2ˢ.   Surety—Thomas de H . . .

An inquisition finds that Margery Strekeyse had no right to claim 3ˢ 6ᵈ wages from William Withir, because she withdrew from his service; fine, 6ᵈ for false claim.

They find that William Wethir & Adam Wade did not carry off fern belonging to Ellen Knol, as she charged against them; her fine forgiven.

Alice d. of John de Billecliff, surrenders 5¾ acres in Wolvedale; demised to Emma d. of John de Billecliff, to hold, according &c. Entry, 3ˢ

Total of this Halmote—27ˢ 10ᵈ.   All from Holne.

———

SHERIFF'S TOURN there the same day.

William del Okis, 12ᵈ for bloodshed; fine forgiven by the Steward.

Peter Coket, Roger Tepel & his wife, 12ᵈ each for the same.

Alice wife of John; & the wives of Thomas de Foulestoun & John del Mersh, 12ᵈ each, for brewing contrary to assize.

The township of Combreworth, 12ᵈ for concealing John Withir.

The township of Birtoun, 12ᵈ for concealing John Licster.

Richard Child, 2ᵈ for not coming.

Adam Strekeyse, indicted at this present tourn by twelve jurors for usury, comes & fines with the lord for this trespass & for all other counts of trespasses in any wise to be charged against him up to this moment by the lord—£10 silver; to be paid in equal parts at the next Feasts of the Purification, Whitsuntide & Michaelmas; with the stipulation that if the said Adam should be convicted again of committing the crime of usury against any specified person for any specified sum, from the day of his present fine, then Adam confesses & allows that he shall be bound to the Earl in another sum of £10 silver payable at the lord's pleasure *sine die*.

Total of this tourn—£11: 5ˢ: 8ᵈ: *i.e.*, Holne 25ˢ 8ᵈ

Bailiff £10, payable at the Purification & Easter next.

COURT held at Wakefeld on Friday after the Feast of St. Lucy the Virgin (Dec. 13), 4 Edw. III [1330].

Thornes. Robert de Lupsete surrenders a rood in Thornes abutting on to le Kirkegate in le Netherfeld; demised to John Tasshe of Wakefeld; to hold, according &c. Entry, 6ᵈ

Wakefeld. William s. of William s. of Hugh, surrenders an acre in Wakefeld by Haseeng; demised to John Harilul, junior; to hold, according &c. Entry, 12ᵈ

Holne. Thomas del Boure surrenders 3⅜ acres in Hepworth; demised to Thomas s. of Thomas. Entry, 12ᵈ

Stanley. Isabel Spink to be distrained for breaking the Bailiff's attachment of 2ˢ, arrested by the Bailiff in her hands.

Adam s. of Robert de Stanneley, to be distrained to answer Margery d. of William s. of Bateman, for trespass.

Holne. Thomas le Couper surrenders an acre in Cartworth; demised to Thomas s. of Matilda; according &c. Entry, 6ᵈ

Alvirthorp. Richard Bunny, instructed to come before the Steward, 12ᵈ for not coming.

Wakefeld. Thomas s. of Laurence, charged with bondage, fines 20ˢ to have an inquisition on that point.

Adam le Heuwer, 13ˢ 4ᵈ for the same.

John Tup, 5ˢ for the same.

Henry, John & Robert Nelot, 10ˢ; Robert s. of Ralph, 2ˢ; John Pollard, baker, 12ᵈ, & Henry le Badger, 2ˢ for the same.

The fourth part of a burgage in the vill of Wakefeld in le Westgate, which Alice formerly wife of Hugh Talp, held there for her life, with remainder to the right heirs of said Hugh, & which was seised into the lord's hand because said Hugh died without heir of his blood, is demised to Henry s. of John Bul, to hold to him & his heirs by the services thereon due & accustomed. Entry, 10ˢ

Wakefeld. Matilda Tirsy, charged with bondage, comes & acknowledges she is the lord's born bondwoman & of servile condition, & gives the lord 3ᵈ a year as recognition.

Alice Tirsy acknowledges she is the lord's born bondwoman by blood; & gives 3ᵈ a year as above.

Bailiff. Adam de Everingham, to be distrained to make a fine for sundry defaults of suit of court, which he owes every 3 weeks for tenements in Erdeslow.

William, s. of William de Sandale, charged with bondage, fines 13ˢ 4ᵈ, on condition of being free for the whole of Earl Warenne's lifetime, & during the whole of that time not being charged or molested for bondage or servile condition.

Alvirthorp. Walter Gunne sues Richard Bunny for 2 messuages & a bovate of land in the hamlet of Neutoun in the graveship of Alverthorp, from which he states he is ousting him, & wrongfully so, in that Robert Gunne, father of the said Walter, whose heir he is, recovered the property against Richard as his right & inheritance, by an inquisition at a court held at Wakefeld in John de Donecaster's stewardship.

The which jurors in the "gross" of their verdict before the said Steward said that Henry Gunne, grandfather of plaintiff Walter, was for some time seised of the said tenements in his demesne as of fee, & demised them to one Walter de Northwode for 10 years, & that Robert Bunny, father of Richard, the present tenant, wrongfully recovered the same against Walter de Northwode, the lessee, under an inquisition during Henry Gunne's absence. Wherefore it was afterwards given that Robert Gunne, complainant's father, should recover the said tenements against Richard Bunny, and Walter demands an inquisition as to his right as above. Richard Bunny defends, & says he is not bound to answer this count, because on another occasion, at a court held at Wakefeld during the stewardship of William de Wakefeld, it was found by an attaint of 24 jurors on the abovesaid jury of 12, that the latter had made a false oath, and Richard was accordingly to recover seisin of the tenements. He also says it is not consonant with the law, nor the custom of the manor, to make further inquisition in pleas of land than by an attaint of 24; & he demands judgment thereon. Walter says that with land held in bondage at the will of the lord, the lord of his special grace, notwithstanding the common law, can grant to such tenants at will an attaint on an attaint to enquire more truly regarding the tenants' right. And thereupon he produces a certain close letter from Earl Warenne, directed to Sir Simon de Baldrestoun, Steward of his lands, in co. York, in these words—John, Earl of Warenne & of Surrey, Lord of Bromfeld & of Yale, to our dear & faithful Sir Simon de Baldrestoun, Steward of our lands in the North, greeting. Whereas Richard Bunny is in possession of two messuages & a bovate of our new land in the vill of Neutoun, by judgement given on the verdict of an inquisition of 24 jurors; nevertheless we have heard that Walter Gunne, our born bondsman of Stanneley, ought rightly to have the said two messuages & the bovate of land; wherefore we command you, on hearing the complaint of the said Walter to summon before you eight & forty of those who best know the truth of the matter, & put them on their oath on the . . . right of the said Walter; & if you find by their verdict that the said Walter has a right to the tenements, then give him seisin according to right of the said messuages & land, to hold from us according to the custom of the manor. And do not omit this. We commit you to God. Given at our Castle of Sandale, the 5th day of November in the fourth year. By virtue of which command order is given for 48 men of the nearest graveships to come to the next court to enquire as above.

Total of this Court—107ˢ 2ᵈ, & in recognizances from bondsmen, 6ᵈ

i.e.,   Wakefeld, 64^s 10^d & in recognizances, 6^d
Stanneley, 18^d
Alvirthorp, 2^s
Bailiff, 23^s
Sandale, 6^d
Rastrik, 5^d
Hiperum, 2^d
Holne, 2^s
Osset, 7^s 1^d
Thornes, 5^s 8^d

HALMOTE held at Halifax on Tuesday after the Feast of the Epiphany (Jan. 6), 4 Edw. III [1331].

Whereas, by his close letter directed to Sir Simon de Baldrestoun, his Steward in the Northern parts, Earl Warenne had directed the said Steward to certify him as to the true value of the pastures of Withnes, Turmleemosse & Mankanhuls, and if it would be to his damage if the said pasture was let to farm for the term of a life, or not—by virtue of this mandate twelve jurors, to wit Ivo de Saltonstal, Thomas de Rochilsete, Richard . . ., Thomas de Halifax, Richard de Saltonstal, Thomas Chapman, Roger de Grenewode, Peter del Greene, Thomas de Heitfeld, Henry de Holgate, Thomas de Saltonstal & Henry, s. of the Carpenter, say upon their oath that in common years the said pasture, in all its issues, is worth 26^s 8^d; & that if let to farm for the term of a life, it would be no damage to the Earl.

The same inquisition finds that all the tenants who owe suit to the mills at Werlulley & Soland will give multure of their groats of the twentieth vessel, & that they will give no multure of the flour produced from the groats.

Matthew de Illingworth, in the mercy for an uproar in the halmote; fine forgiven by the Steward.

William del Leeghrode demands against Thomas le Mercer, Richard le Smith & Amabilla del Langhrode, ½ bovate (locality not given) from which he says they are ousting him. They acknowledge the disseisin; he is to recover the same; damages, 2^s 3^d; fine, 12^d

John s. of William de Sotehill, fines 8^d for license to take 1½ acre of unoccupied land between the water of Keldre & the park-paling of Ayrikdene; according, &c. Rent, 6^d an acre.

An inquisition finds that Thomas de Rochilsete & William Miller of Halifax were not sureties for Amabilla del Leeghrode against Thomas le Mercer & Richard le Smith, for 13^s 4^d, as charged with being by said Thomas & Richard, who are fined 6^d for false claim.

William Miller, charged with trespass on the lord's venison on suspicion, gives the lord 12^d to have an inquisition at this halmote. Surety—William del Louwe.

Adam del Shaghe & John & Henry his sons, charged with the same, give 2^s as above.

Roger de Bentleyrode sues Thomas s. of Henry, for withholding from him wrongfully the vesture of 2½ acres in Sourby, sown with oats; worth 20^s. Thomas, by Thomas le Preest, his attorney, whose words the said Thomas s. of Henry avowed in the halmote, denied the trespass. Both parties demand an inquisition. And Robert s. of John, John del Hole, Elias le Couper, Thomas s. of Henry de Luddingdene, Adam s. of Alexander, & Thomas del Bothom, jurors, say defendant is withholding only half the vesture, which they value at 5^s; this Roger is to recover; both fined 3^d

Total of this Halmote—6^s 8^d. And new rent, 9^d.

All from Sourby.

———

SHERIFF'S TOURN there the same day.

Sourbi. The wives of Alexander del Hingandrode & Adam s. of Margaret, 4^d each for brewing constantly at ½^d

The wife of Richard Clerk of Heptonstal, & Matilda de Kipask, 4^d each for brewing sometimes at ½^d

John Maynard of Stansfeld, 3^d for not coming to the tourn.

Michael del Ewod's wife, 4^d for ale, three times at ½^d

William s. of Wilcok de Langfeld, 3^d, & Henry Miller, 4^d, for not coming to the tourn.

John s. of Elias de Waddesworth, 12^d for the blood of Elias his brother.

John Ward, 3^d, & John del Bothom of Rissheworth, 6^d, for not coming.

The wife of Richard Faber of Werlulley, 4^d for brewing commonly at ½^d

Alice del Lone of Sourby, 2^d for brewing at ½^d

Total of this tourn—14^s 9^d. All from Sourby.

———

COURT held at Wakefeld on Friday after the Epiphany, (Jan. 6) 4 Edw. III, [1331].

Bailiff. William Cussing & his surety, in the mercy for not prosecuting suit for trespass against Robert de Wyronthorp. Fine forgiven by the Steward.

John Attebarre, complainant, essoins against Hugh de Stanneley, by Henry Tasshe. Surety—German Kay. Hugh to be summoned again.

Sourby. William de Totehille, by Thomas de Totehille, his attorney, complains against John s. of Thomas de Halifax, that on Wednesday after the Feast of SS. Peter & Paul, (June 29) this 4th year, defendant's cattle, chiefly oxen & cows, grazed & trampled on a piece of meadow belonging to complainant, in a place called Threpcroft in the vill of Ovendene, to the value of 39ˢ 11ᵈ; damages, 39ˢ. Defendant comes & does not defend in the words of the court, as he ought He is therefore to satisfy William both for principal & damages; fine, 12ᵈ

Bailiff. John de Dronesfeld, 3ᵈ for not prosecuting suit for trespass against John de Ryley.

Robert de Altoftes, 3ᵈ for the same.

Bailiff. John de Burtoun, complainant, & William de Birtoun compromise for debt, William acknowledging that he owes the said John 20ˢ silver, to be paid half at the Feast of the Purification & half at the Feast of the Annunciation, under penalty of seizure of his goods by the Earl's bailiffs. William fines 2ᵈ for license to agree.

Sourby. John de Baliden to be distrained to answer Thomas de Totehille in a plea of debt. They afterwards compromise, John fining 2ᵈ

Holne. Adam de Holne, grave, for making a false answer before the Steward, 12ᵈ

Rastrik. Matthew de Totehille & John s. of Ellen, to be distrained to answer Thomas de Totehill for debt.

Sourbi. Thomas de Totehille & Richard de Grenewode compromise for debt. Richard pays 6ᵈ

The said Thomas also compromises for debt with Richard de Fouside ;& Thomas de Rochilsete, who pay 6ᵈ each; also with Oto de Haldworth, 3ᵈ

Bailiff. Johanna de la Halle, complainant (3ᵈ) & Robert del Spen compromise for trespass.

Sourby. John de Skircote to be distrained to answer Thomas de Totehille for debt.

Alvirthorp. John Attebarre, complainant [essoins] against Hugh de Stanneley by German Kay. Surety—Robert de Mora; & in a second suit against the same, by Thomas Torald.

Rastrik. Thomas del Wodheved, complainant, & Henry s. of Hugh (6ᵈ) compromise for carrying away oats. Damages taxed at 6ᵈ

Bailiff. At the request of the parties a love-day is given to Robert de Wyronthorp, complainant, & Thomas s. of German Filcok, at next court without essoin.

John de Geirgrave, complainant, & Robert Clerk & Elias de Horbiry, (3ᵈ) compromise regarding an agreement.

Horbiry. Hugh Gyge & Thomas Gyge (4ᵈ) compromise respecting land.

Stanley. Isabella Spink arraigned for 2ˢ arrested in her hands due to Agnes de Coupland, who is impleaded by William Badger for debt, because the said Isabella broke the arrest contrary to the bailiff's prohibition, comes & acknowledges this trespass. She is to be answerable to the bailiff for the said 2ˢ; fine, 2ᵈ

Stanneley. Walter Gunne, in mercy for not prosecuting his suit for land against Richard Bunny. Richard to go *sine die.* Walter's fine forgiven.

Alvirthorp. Robert Malin demands against Robert Shiluing & Johanna his wife, ½ a messuage in Flanshow in the graveship of Alvirthorp, from which they are ousting him, wrongfully, he says, in that Johanna d. of John de Flanshow, gave and delivered the said tenement here in court in the time of John de Trihampton. Defendants say that Robert s. of Simon de Flanshow, grandfather of the said Johanna, bought the tenement from the said John de Flanshow, & took it here in court before John de Donecaster, then Steward; & the said Robert gave the same to the said Johanna in the time of Henry de Walda, formerly Steward. Both parties demand an inquisition. Defendants appoint Thomas Torald their attorney.

Thornes. Robert s. of Ivo, Richard Carpenter, Henry Shiluing, William Houwe, Thomas del Haghe & John le Hine, to be attached to answer John de Geirgrave for trespass.

Bailiff. Johanna formerly wife of German Filcok, to be attached to answer John de Geirgrave & the community of the vill of Wakefeld for trespass.

Thornes. William s. of Richard le Wayte, surrenders ½ bovate in Thornes; afterwards demised to Henry, s. of Thomas Bate; according &c. Entry, 6ˢ

Stanley. Edusa Preste surrenders 1¾ acres of land & meadow in Stanneley; demised to Johanna her daughter; according, &c. Entry, 12ᵈ

Thomas Skaif surrenders 3 roods in Stannelei; demised to Robert Ilhoor; according &c. Entry, 6ᵈ

Richard Skaif surrenders a rood in Stanneley; demised to William Attetounend of Stanley, for 13 years; Entry, 6ᵈ

Alice Poket surrenders ⅛ of a rood in Stanneley; demised to Alice Albray; according &c. Entry, 6ᵈ

Thornes. Richard de Finchdene surrenders 8 acres in Snaipthorp, in a place called Euerode, in the graveship of Thornes; demised to Thomas, s. of Master Robert Carpenter; according &c. Entry, 4ˢ

Sandale. John Tubbing surrenders 4 acres in Criglestoun, in the North part of a place called Rourode; demised to Henry Fox; according &c. Entry, 2ˢ

John Tubbing surrenders 5½ acres in Criglestoun, in the South part of the aforesaid place; demised to Matthew de Shipdene; according &c. Entry, 2ˢ

Sandale. Matthew de Shipdene surrenders 3 acres in Criglestoun, in Westrowerode; demised to John Tubbing; according &c. Entry, 12ᵈ

Sourbi. The grave of Sourbi ordered to make attachments of all tenants by the rod in his graveship who keep hand-mills in their houses, to the lord's damage.

Holne. Richard Childson of Cartworth surrenders a messuage & 13 acres in Cartworth; demised to Robert de Botha; according &c. Entry, 40ᵈ

John de Grenegate acknowledges he owes the Earl 18ˢ to be paid at the will of the lord whensoever he may be convicted of disobedient behaviour to the lord or any of his servants.

Total of this Court, 37ˢ 3ᵈ. (*sic*) *i.e.*, Rastrik, 6ᵈ
             Thornes, 10ˢ
             Horbiry, 4ᵈ
             Sourby, 3ˢ 7ᵈ
             Holne, 4ˢ 4ᵈ
             Stanneley, 6ˢ 4ᵈ
             Sandale, 5ˢ
             Bailiff, 14ᵈ
             Hiperum, 5ˢ 5ᵈ

SHERIFF'S TOURN held there the same day.

Bailiff. The township of Eccleshille, 12ᵈ for not coming to the tourn.

The wife of Nicholas Faber of Erdeslowe, 6ᵈ for brewing at ½ᵈ

Matilda Broun of Emmeley, 6ᵈ for brewing at 1ᵈ

Robert le Milner, 4ᵈ for the same occasionally.

Robert Clerk's wife, 2ᵈ for the same once.

Osset. Thomas Pasmer 18ᵈ, for blood with a stick.

Richard Swaynson, 12ᵈ for blood.

Bailiff. Stephen del Wodhouse, Adam Gylmin, Adam le Carter, John le Baker, Silvester del Wodhouse & Jordan de la Mere, presented for not coming; their fines respited.

Horbiry. Rosa formerly wife of Hugh s. of Thomas, 6ᵈ for the hue.

Hugh Broun of Shitlington, 4ᵈ for not coming.

Thornes. John Truepak of Snaipthorp, 12ᵈ for blood.

Sandale. Ingusia d. of Walter Belle, & Johanna wife of Adam de Halifax, 12ᵈ each for blood.

Sandale. The wife of Thomas Clerk of Waltoun, 3ᵈ for brewing occasionally at 1ᵈ

Adam Leulyn's wife, 6ᵈ for brewing at ¾ᵈ

The wife of Thomas, brother of Robert de Sandale, chaplain, 6^d; & Christian de Hall, 3^d for brewing at 1^d

Alvirthorp. Thomas Bunny's wife, 12^d for brewing at 1^d

Bailiff. Thomas s. of Matilda Hog, for the hue rightly raised on him, 6^d

Thomas de Louthe, 6^d for raising the hue wrongfully.

Richard Withoundes' fine, for the hue rightly raised on him, is forgiven.

John Burnel, William Atte Elm, John s. of Ralph Malle, Robert le Couper of Kergate & Gilbert Filche, 12^d each for blood.

Richard de Watirtoun's wife, 6^d; John s. of Nicholas de Bateley, & Thomas s. of Richard Clerk, 12^d each, for blood.

Richard Steel, 2^s for forestalling oats.

Total of this tourn—41^s 8^d *i.e.*, Osset, 3^s
                               Alvirthorp, 2^s
                               Bailiff, 20^s 3^d
                               Stanneley, 9^s 6^d
                               Horbiry, 10^d
                               Thornes, 12^d
                               Sandale, 5^s 1^d

HALMOTE held at Brighouse on Wednesday after the Epiphany, (Jan. 6), 4 Edw. III [1331].

Hiperum. William del Hingandrode, arraigned in full halmote for resisting the lord's grave in collecting the tenants' amercements, comes & cannot deny the same. Fine, 6^d

Rastrik. William s. of William del Hirst, arraigned for stealing away & carrying off 2 mares arrested as strays, in the keeping of Thomas de Stainland, acknowledges the fact, & says they are his; but he is fined 12^d for removing them without the Bailiff's license; & 6^d for cutting hay in the said Thomas's enclosure, against the owner's will, which he acknowledges doing. Surety—Thomas, s. of John de Locwode.

William del Wade acknowledges he removed a mare, placed as a stray in Thomas de Stainland's custody; fine, 12^d

Thomas de Whitacres, senior, acknowledges he has not paid the lord's bailiff for grazing a mare in Scammandene; fine, 6^d Surety—Thomas de Whitacres, junior.

Thomas Faber of Stainland gives 6^s 8^d for license to cultivate & plough 5 acres of the lord's unoccupied land in Scammandene, previously arrented to the said Thomas amongst other acres that he took from the lord in Scammandene.

Hiperum. Simon s. of William Batemanson, surrenders 2 acres in a place called Elynrode in the bounds of Northourum; demised to Henry s. of William de Halifax; according, &c. Entry, 2^s

William s. of Adam del Bothe, gives 4^s as a heriot on a messuage & 8 acres at le Bothes in the graveship of Hiperum, on the death of his father, whose heir he is; to hold, according &c. Surety—Henry de Luddingdene.

Richard de Wynhille sues John de Shipdene for 5^s 6^d, which he owes him as surety for John Oteson; damages, 12^d. John acknowledges & is to pay the debt. Fine, 4^d

Rastrik. Thomas s. of Julian, in mercy for quitting the Halmote in contempt of the lord; his fine pardoned.

An inquisition finds that the said Thomas allowed his cattle to graze on the herbage of the Birefeld, contrary to the custom of Bireleghe; his fine forgiven.

Hiperum. Robert de Rissheworthe acknowledges he delivered two stirk given into his keeping as strays, to a certain man of Bradeforth, without license from the Bailiff. Fine, 12^d. Surety— Thomas le Waynwriht.

Order given to attach Ivo le Webster, Avice del Brooke, Thomas del Rokis, Robert s. of Alexander, Thomas de Brerehey & John Miller del Bothis, to answer the lord for withdrawing multure from the lord's mill. They all come except Avice, & acknowledge the trespass. Fine, 18^d, and they are to satisfy the miller in addition. John Miller is acquitted by an inquisition.

Thomas le Waynwriht surrenders 5 acres in Prestley, in the graveship of Hiperum; afterwards demised to Henry del Rokis; according &c. Entry, 3^s

Geoffrey de Shelf, who had a stirk committed to his keeping as a stray, which he afterwards gave up without license from the Bailiff, fines 6^d for the trespass.

Ivo le Webster, 6^d for false claim against Henry Horn & his associate, millers of Rastrik mill.

A stray brown stirk & a stray hogget valued by a jury at 2^s 10^d, are sold for that sum to Henry de la Weeld, he being answerable for them or their value, if called for before next All Saints' day.

Rastrik. Thomas del Wodheved sues Henry s. of Hugh de Bothomley, for carrying off oats, value 20^s. Surety—John Steel.

Hiperum. William s. of John de Sundirland, surrenders 2 acres in Shipdene, in the graveship of Hiperum; demised to Henry his brother; according &c. Entry, 2^s

Total of this halmote—27^s 8^d Rastrik, 9^s 8^d
Hiperum, 18^s

Rastrik mill demised to farm to Henry Horn & John s. of William Miller, for 24 merks, from Michaelmas last until next Michaelmas. Sureties—Adam del Rode, Roger Spillewode, John s. of Henry de Rastrik, Alexander de Rastrik, Adam de Bradeley, Thomas s. of Roger, William s. of Thomas de Hiperum, John s. of Walter de Aldrichegate, Simon del Dene & William de Sundirland.

SHERIFF'S TOURN there the same day.

Rastrik. Margaret Flemming & Agnes, d. of Cecilia de Linley, 6^d each; Johanna Scot, 4^d, for brewing at $\frac{1}{2}$^{d}

Hiperum. The wives of John de Birstal, Simon s. of Jordan, & John del Cliff, 6^d each; Julian, wife of Walter's son, 6^d, for brewing at $\frac{1}{2}$^{d}

The wife of Roger del Brighous, senior, 2^d for brewing contrary to assize.

Matilda sister of John del Brighouse, 12^d; Thomas Baude's wife, 6^d; William de Whalley's wife, 3^d; William Miller's wife, 2^d; John de Helles' wife, forgiven; & the wife of Robert Faber of Bairestowe, 6^d, for brewing commonly at 1^d

Rastrik. Agnes Tyngil, 4^d for brewing at $\frac{1}{2}$^{d}

William de Abirforth's wife, for the same three times, 4^d

John del Haliwelle, John del Brig & William s. of Beatrice, 12^d each for blood.

Total of this tourn—24^s 3^d Rastrik, 10^s 2^d
                                      Hiperum, 14^s 1^d

COURT held at Wakefeld on Friday, the Feast of St. Peter in Cathedra (Feb. 22), 5 Edw. III [1331]

Essoins. Hugh de Stanneley, the second time, by Henry Tasshe. Surety—Robert de Mora.

Thomas de Thorntoun, the second time, by John de Thorntoun. Surety—Thomas Alayn.

Bailiff. Order repeated, as many times before, to distrain Philip del Hill to answer John de Geirgrave for debt, and the lord for divers defaults; and to retain 5 horses, worth 10^s, by which the said Philip is distrained, in the custody of Thomas Alayn, bailiff.

Alvirthorp. The imparlance between Margery formerly wife of Robert Gerbod, complainant, & William Grenehod, for land, respited till William s. of the said William, comes to the neighbourhood.

Holne. Julian formerly wife of William le Specer, charged with baking bread for sale at her own oven, without license of the court, & attached by Nicholas Wade to appear at this court, does not come. Nicholas fined 2^d; Julian to be distrained for next court.

John le Badger, arraigned in court for the same, left the court in contempt of the lord, 2^d; order given for distraint.

Sourbi. Richard Faber of Werlulley & Thomas le Mercer, complainants, & William del Leghrode (2^d) compromise for debt.

Bailiff. Thomas, s. of German Filcok, 2^d for not prosecuting his suit against Thomas Odam for impounding a horse; Thomas Odam is to have the horse, valued at 9^s, returned.

John de Wyke to be summoned to answer William de Hacforthe for debt. William appoints Robert de Mora his attorney.

Hugh de Stanneley to be distrained to answer John Attebarre for debt.

Thomas, s. of German Filcok to be distrained to answer Robert de Wyronthorp for trespass.

An inquisition of six freemen & six bondmen to come [to decide] between the farmers of the vill of Wakefeld & Richard Palmer, as to the toll to be paid the said farmers.

Holne. William de Bramwith, arraigned in Court for trespass & despite to the lord in removing & throwing down stalls of the merchants at Birtoun, comes & cannot deny the fact, and puts himself in the lord's grace for 20^s if he offends again in like manner, & takes an oath with his hand on the Gospels that from henceforth he will not offend in this way. Fine, 12^d

Bailiff. Amabilla wife of Henry le Nouthird, fines 6^d for having impleaded bondmen in the Court Christian.

Holne. Matthew s. of Gilbert, gives 10^s to have an aid & favour.

Osset. Order given to distrain John s. of Richard de Osset, Matthew de Osset, Henry Wildbor, Hugh Wildbor, Swayn le Wise, William s. of Richard, Jordan Eliot & Reginald Snart, to answer the farmers of the vill of Wakefeld for withdrawing suit to the mill.

Thornes. John de Geirgrave, complainant, & Robert s. of Ivo, Richard Carpenter, William Howe, Thomas del Haghe & John le Hyne (5^d) compromise for breaking complainant's paling at Snaipthorp, on condition that they duly repair the said paling.

Bailiff. Stephen Erkyn, William de la Chaumbre & William Cort, defendants, essoin against John Brand of Brettoun, for trespass, by Adam de Orkeney, William Templer & Robert de Mora, respectively. Surety for all—Adam Sprigonelle.

Adam Sprigonel gives 6^d to have an inquisition respecting a certain yearly rent of 12^d withheld from him in the graveship of Sandale.

Thornes. John s. of Mariota, gives 6^d for license to exchange ½ acre in Thornes with John Bulneys for another ½ acre there; to hold, according &c. Because John Bulneis will not fine with the lord for the exchange of the other ½ acre, the land is ordered to be seised into the lord's hand. Afterwards he comes & fines 6^d for the exchange.

Osset. Matilda d. of William Cool, surrenders a messuage & 4 acres in Osset; demised to Thomas Passemer; according, &c. Entry, 18^d

Hiperum. Ivo le Webster, accused of felling and working 100 oaks in different years, from which the lord has never received any profit, says he is not guilty, & demands an inquisition.

Bailiff. Thomas Gates & Ralph de Kerlinghou to be summoned again to answer Thomas Alayn for debt, in five complaints.

Sandale. Johanna formerly wife of William de Castilforthe, surrenders ½ acre in Sandale; demised to John de Wolveley; according, &c. Entry, 6ᵈ

Wakefeld. Henry le Dyker comes to court & takes from the lord the fishery of the water of Keldre, between Agbrigbroke & le Hewenclifbroke, for 2 years, at 2ˢ yearly rent, Henry having previously paid 12ᵈ a year for the same.

Stanneley. An inquisition finds that John del Bothom cut down an elm in Wakefeld wood, & carried it off without warrant; he is to pay the lord the value thereof, estimated by the jurors at 6ᵈ; fine, 2ᵈ

They find also that Robert Wastneis, forester in Stanneley wood, sold an oak in his bailiwick, worth 4ˢ, without warrant. He is to make good the 4ˢ; fine, 2ᵈ

Robert le Leper comes & acknowledges that he carried off a young ash, worth 3ᵈ; this he is to make good; fine, 3ᵈ

John Pollard surrenders 1¼ acre in Stanneley; demised to Richard Man of Wakefeld; according &c. Entry, 6ᵈ

Assessors—Elias de Horbiry.
Richard Withoundes.
Robert le Leper.

Total of this Court—21ˢ 8ᵈ. And increase of farm rent, 12ᵈ
Stanneley, 5ˢ [7ᵈ]
Holne, 11ˢ [4ᵈ]
Sourby, 2ᵈ
Sandale, 6ᵈ
Thornes, 17ᵈ
Wakefeld . . .
Osset, [18ᵈ]
Bailiff, [14ᵈ]

COURT held at Wakefeld on Friday after the Feast of St. Gregory the Pope (March 12), 5 Edw. III [1331].

Essoins. William de Birtoun, by Richard de Mora. Surety—William Templer.

Richard de Birstalle, by Geoffrey Picard. Surety—John Attebarre.

Bailiff. Julian formerly wife of William le Spicer, 2ᵈ for baking bread for sale in her own oven without license.

Holne. John le Badger to be distrained for the same. He afterwards satisfies the Bailiffs, & puts himself in mercy; 2ᵈ

Sourby. Thomas de Tothille, complainant, & John del Toun (3ᵈ) compromise for debt. Surety—Richard del Wode.

The said Thomas & John de Waddesworth 3ᵈ compromise as above; also Thomas & John de Skircote 2ᵈ

Osset. An inquisition finds that Alice formerly wife of Robert le Couper, removed multure from Horbiry mill, to wit, ½ bushel of corn to the value of 5ᵈ. Fine, 2ᵈ. Also Alice formerly wife of John de Hetoun, the same; fine, 2ᵈ; & Richard le Barker, 3 dishes of corn, worth 1ᵈ; fine, 2ᵈ. They are all to make loss good to the farmers of the vill of Wakefeld.

Bailiff. Stephen Erkyn, William de la Chaumbre & William Cort, defendants, essoin against John Brand of Brettoun, by Robert de Grottoun. Sureties—Thomas, William & Adam Pelleson, respectively.

Holne. Richard Child complainant, 2ᵈ & Henry Wade compromise for detention of a cow.

Sandale. John de Holgate, Henry Fox & Elias de Donecaster to be summoned again to answer Robert del Holgate for debt.

Thornes. An inquisition to come to next court to try whether William de Biltoun & Emma, his wife, are wrongfully detaining from Agnes Pegar 3 roods of land in Thornes, which she claims to hold by way of dower.

Bailiff. Alice de Skrevyn, Prioress of Kirkeleghs, by her attorney, offers herself against John Cokewald of Hertesheved in a plea of trespass. John does not come. Agnes Tyngil, his surety for appearing at this court, 2ᵈ. John to be distrained to answer the said Prioress.

The said Prioress offers herself against Agnes Tyngil & Thomas, her son, for trespass, They do not come. John Cokewald, their surety, 2ᵈ as above.

Thornes. William de Biltoun & Emma his wife, demand against Agnes Pegar, 2ˢ silver which she owed the said Emma before her marriage. Agnes denies the debt. An inquisition to come to the next court to decide this, & also whether Agnes rased, felled & sold a barn & 4 ashes, that belonged to the said Emma before her marriage.

Holne. A messuage & 52 acres of land & meadow in Overthong, which formerly belonged to Adam Strekeyse, with remainder after his death to William Strekeyse, his brother & heir, are granted to the said William, according &c. The fines 20ˢ for a heriot.

Wakefeld. Three acres & a perch of land on le Falbank of the lord's demesne, which William Filche, clerk, holds for a term of years, demised to the said William, to hold for his life by the services, &c., & after his decease, to Adam & William his sons; to hold, according &c. Entry, 6ˢ 8ᵈ

Sourby. Robert de Bentleyrode, Henry de Lodingdene, Robert s. of John, junior, William del Lone, Henry del Lone, Thomas Forester, Adam Nellesoun, John de Skircote, John s. of Thomas de Skircote, John de Hirst, Hugh de Helileghe, Hugh Fampel & Elias Couper, mainpernours of Adam s. of Richard, for keeping the peace with Thomas de Heytfeld, slain by the said

Adam & .... his brother, give the lord 26ˢ 8ᵈ as a fine to have a respite till next Easter.

Süreties for Thomas de Lodingdene, for keeping the peace with the Earl's tenants, & that he will not stir up strange malefactors to enter the Earl's lordship to the hurt or damage of any tenant within the lordship, to wit, Henry de Lodingdene & William del Lone. And a certain mare belonging to the said Thomas, in the hands of the said Henry & William, is to be kept safe, and they are accountable for the same, or for the price thereof, if Thomas be convicted again of any trespass against any of the lord's tenants in the manner abovesaid.

Total of this Court—65ˢ 6ᵈ *i.e.* Holne, 20ˢ 6ᵈ
Bailiff, 6ᵈ
Sourby, 37ˢ 4ᵈ
Osset, 6ᵈ
Wakefeud, 6ˢ 8ᵈ

COURT held at Wakefeld on Friday, 5th April, 5 Edw. III [1331].

Essoin. John Attebarre, complainant, essoins, against Hugh de Stanneley by William Cussing. Surety—Richard Withoundes. And in a second matter, by Henry Tasshe; in a third, by Robert de Mora.

Stanneley. Henry le Nouthird & Amabilla his wife, complainants, & William Attetounend & John Tyting (4ᵈ) compromise for debt.

The imparlance between Robert de Wyronthorp, complainant, & Thomas s. of German Filcok, removed into the Burgesses Court of the town of Wakefeld, because the said Thomas is a burgess.

Bailiff. John Brand of Brettoun, complainant, offers himself against William de la Chaumbre, who does not come. William Pelleson, surety on his essoin at the last court, 4ᵈ. William de la Chaumbre to be distrained for next court.

Bailiff. Alice de Skrevyn, Prioress of Kirklees, complainant, compromises severally with John Cokewald of Hertesheved (2ᵈ) and Agnes Tyngil & her son Thomas (2ᵈ), for trespass.

Alexander del Brighous & Adam de la Rode come at the suit of Henry de la Weld & acknowledge they broke the fence of a certain inclosure belonging to the said Henry in Rastrik. They are to pay damages, taxed at 1ᵈ; fine, 2ᵈ

Alice, formerly wife of John de Heton, to be summoned to answer Agnes formerly wife of Robert de Beaumont, knight, for debt.

Sandale. John s. of William de Ovirhalle, gives 5ˢ as a heriot on a messuage & a bovate of land in Sandale, on the death of his father whose heir he is; according, &c.

Bailiff. Thomas s. of German Filcok, sues Thomas Odam for detaining a horse. Surety—William Cussing.

Alvirthorp. Robert de Fery, by John Attebarre, the grave, surrenders 1¾ acres in Alvirthorp; demised to William de Fery; according &c. Entry, 12^d

Thornes. Robert de Lupesset surrenders an acre in Thornes; demised to Thomas de Leptoun; according, &c. Entry, 8^d

Robert de Lupsete surrenders ½ acre in Thornes; demised to William s. of William s. of Thomas; according, &c. Entry, 6^d

Wakefield. John Dade, senior, by Thomas Alayn, bailiff of the free Court of Wakefeld, surrenders 2 acres in Wakefeld, lying in a place called Codlingcroft; afterwards demised to William Filche, clerk, for his life, with remainder to Adam & William, his sons; according &c. Entry, 18^d

Total of this Court—10^s 7^d *i.e.*, Sandale, 5^s 8^d
                               Bailiff, 9^d
                               Thornes, 14^d
                               Wakefeld, 18^d
                               Stanneley, 4^d
                               Rastrik, 2^d
                               Alvirthorp, 12^d

John de Geyrgrave sues William s. of Philip de Mora & William Dolfyn for seizing cattle. Surety—John de Fery.

COURT held at Wakefeld on Friday, the Morrow of St. Mark the Evangelist (April 25) 5 Edw. III [1331].

Essoins. William de Birtoun, by Robert de Mora. Surety—William le Templer.

Hugh de Stanneley, by William le Templer.

Thornes. An inquisition of jurors finds that Agnes Peger owes, and is wrongfully withholding, 2^s silver from William de Biltoun & Emma, his wife, this she is to pay; fine, 2^d. Also that the said William & Emma are not deforcing Agnes from 3 roods of land, which she claims against them as dower. Agnes fined 2^d for false claim; & William & Emma, 4^d for false claim against Agnes, for cutting down ashes.

Holne. William de Craven, Thomas Attewelle, Heghmagge, & Margery le Halt, 4^d each; William de Hudresfeld, Thomas Hancock, Nicholas de Anondene, Agḡ de Cartworth, Amabilla Cuthound & Richard del Morehous, 2^d each; Adam Strekeys, 12^d; Henry de Holnest & Thomas Fairberd, 6^d each for vert.

Wakefield. John s. of Hugh, & William Kik, 3^d each; Simon Hors, 4^d. for vert.

Stanley. William Arkel 2^d. for vert & wood.

Osset. Robert Peny, William Carpenter (twice) & Thomas le Pinder, Adam de Goukthorp, & Henry de Goukthorp's wife, John Sonman, & Robert Sutor, 2ᵈ each; Adam de Goukthorp & Adam le Oxbird, 4ᵈ each for escapes & wood.

Stanley. John del Rode, 3ᵈ for escape of sheep.

William del Spen, 6ᵈ for the old paling.

Sandale. Adam ,s. of Robert del Neubigging, gives 4ˢ as a heriot on a messuage & 1½ bovate of land in Sandale in le Nubigging, after the death of Robert his brother, whose heir he is; to hold, according &c.

Thomas de Milnthorp & Emma, his wife, surrender three roods of land in Sandale; demised to Robert s. of Hugh de Wakefeld, according, &c. Entry, 18ᵈ

Holne. Margery formerly wife of Thomas Drabil, guardian of Thomas s. & heir of the said Thomas, aged one year, surrenders ½ messuage & 13 acres in Wolvedale in the graveship of Holne; demised to Simon del Cote, for 12 years; entry, 40ᵈ

Wakefeld. John s. of Philip de Castilforth; Johanna Swerd; Rosa Preest; John Nelot, Nicholas Hog & William Thrift's handmaid, 2ᵈ each for dry wood.

William Twentipair, 3ᵈ for breaking the paling.

Thomas s. of Robert Carpenter, surrenders ½ acre in Wakefeld demised to William s. of Robert Carpenter; according &c. Entry, 6ᵈ

Total of this Court—33ˢ 1ᵈ Thornes, 8ᵈ
            Sandale, 5ˢ 6ᵈ
            Bailiff, 3ᵈ
            Osset, 3ˢ 1ᵈ
            Holne, 8ˢ 6ᵈ
            Wakefeld, 12ˢ 3ᵈ
            Stanneley, 2ˢ 10ᵈ

Adam de Kelingley of Pontefract sues Robert de Wyronthorp, Thomas Alayn, John de Dronesfeld & William de Birtoun severally for debt. Surety—Thomas Torald.

———

COURT held at Wakefeld on Friday, 17th May, 5 Edw. III [1331].

Essoins. Hugh de Stanneley, by William Cussing. Surety—Robert de Mora.

Thomas s. of German Filcok, against Thomas Odam, by William Cussing Surety—John s. of Mariota.

Edusa Preste, defendant, against Robert Ricard & Elizabeth his wife, by William Cussing. Surety—William Albray.

Bailiff. Henry Fox, defendant, against Robert de Holgate, by William Cussing. Surety—John Attebarre.

Robert de Holgate, who is a freeman, came to court & did not make his charge against Elias de Donecaster in the words of the court, as he ought in a plea of debt; he is therefore to recover nothing by his complaint; fined 6ᵈ for not prosecuting.

Stanneley. Robert s. of Ralph, sues William Attetounend, junior, for 3ˢ 6ᵈ for a mare bought by him of complainant; damages, 2ˢ. William acknowledges he bought the mare, but says Robert has not yet delivered it. Robert replies the said mare died in Stanneley pasture, in the custody of William. Both parties demand an inquisition.

Thomas de Totehille, complainant, offers himself against William de la Leegh, complaining that on Thursday after Easter, this 5th year, William, with his two dogs, chased 6 pigs belonging to complainant (worth 3ˢ each) in the ville of Lynneley, in a place called Lynleybank; whereby Thomas lost the said pigs; damages, 39ˢ. William comes and does not defend by the words of court; he is therefore attainted both of principle & damages; fine, 3ᵈ

Holne. Richard de Todholme gives 40ᵈ to have favour respecting a certain trespass with which he is charged. He finds a surety to abide the inquisition at the tourn, to wit William de Birtoun.

Alvirthorp. Robert Malyn, complainant, offers himself against William de Birkinshaghe. William is a born bondman, and does not come when summoned; fine, 4ᵈ. To be distrained for next court.

Hugh de Stanneley, defendant, essoins against John del Bothom, by Henry Tasshe. Surety—William Templer.

An inquisition to come to try whether William Strikeise made an agreement with Robert de Botha regarding the reversion of a tenement that belonged to Adam Strikeise in Holne.

Hiperum. William de Sundirland surrenders a messuage, ½ bovate & 5 acres of Rodeland in the graveship of Hiperum; demised to Matthew de Ovendene, for 20 years from next Michaelmas; according, &c. Entry, 3ˢ

Holne. Thomas s. of William de Alstanley, surrenders a messuage & 1¾ acre in Alstanley in the graveship of Holne; demised to Alice formerly wife of Robert de Alstanley; according, &c. Entry, 12ᵈ

Alice del Storthes surrenders an acre in Foulestoun; demised to John le Couper; according &c. Entry, 8ᵈ

Thornes. Richard de Otteley & Alice his wife, surrender 1½ rood of meadow in Thornes, in a place called Wolmerrode; demised to Thomas Bate & William s. of Isabel de Wakefeld, for 6 years; according &c. Thomas fines 6ᵈ for entry.

Total of this Court—11ˢ 2ᵈ.   Bailiff, 17ᵈ   Alvirthorp, 6ᵈ
                                 Thornes, 12ᵈ   Holne, 5ˢ 3ᵈ
                                 Hiperum, 3ˢ

COURT held at Wakefeld on Friday, 8th June, 5 Edw. III [1331].

Essoins. Thomas de Thorntoun, by John de Thorntoune. Surety—Thomas Alayn.

Richard de Birstal, by Henry Tasshe. Surety—William Templer.

Bailiff. John Attebarre, complainant, & Hugh de Stanneley (2ᵈ) compromise for debt, Hugh acknowledging he owes John 2ˢ 10ᵈ. Hugh fines 2ᵈ again to compromise respecting a second debt with John.

Alvirthorp. The said John, 2ᵈ, to compromise with Hugh for a third debt.

Bailiff. Henry Nelot, serjeant of the Court of the Borough of Wakefeld, 6ᵈ for contempt to the lord in refusing to do his office at the command of the Steward.

Bailiff. John Brand of Brettoun, 2ᵈ for not prosecuting his suit for trespass against William de la Chaumbre.

Essoin. Edusa Preste, defendant, against Robert Ricard & Elizabeth, his wife, by William Cussing. Surety—William Albray.

Bailiff. Ralph de Sheffeld, who cut down an oak in the outer wood of Wakefeld without warrant, found sureties for making satisfaction therefore, to wit Henry de Galeway & William Roscelin, senior; fine, 40ᵈ

William Roscelin, senior, for 2 oaks, finds sureties—Ralph de Sheffeld & Henry de Galeway. Fine, 4ˢ

Sandale. The whole township of Sandale, except the grave, 2ˢ for not coming to the court.

Bailiff. Thomas s. of German Filcok, offers himself against Thomas Odam, complaining that on Monday after Sept. 8, 1330 said Thomas took a horse of complainant's in the high street in Stanley, in a place called Lunsdlade, & drove it to his house in Stanley, where he impounded it, until delivery was made by the lord's bailiff; damages, 20ˢ. Defendant justifes the impounding the horse, because he found him grazing & doing damage in an enclosure belonging to defendant, called le Flattes; he therefore followed the horse, & came up with & took him in the high street; & he demands return of the said horse. And as complainant cannot oppose this avowry in this court without the King's writ, Odam is to have return of the said horse; complainant fined 12ᵈ for false claim.

Holne. William Strekeise, executor of Margery Strekeise, gives 13ˢ 4ᵈ for an aid to levy the debts due to said Margery within the lordship, to the amount of 60ˢ 5ᵈ

Adam de Holne, grave, 6ᵈ for making a false presentment of a summons upon William, s. of Hugh.

Bailiff. Thomas Alayn, 6ᵈ for not having Thomas s. of German Filcok, whom he attached, to answer Robert de Mora.

Henry de Stanneley essoins against Robert s of Walter, grave of Stanneley, by John de Castilforth. Surety—John de Stanneley.

Alvirthorp. An inquisition to come to Wakefeld tourn to try whether William de Birkinshaghe undertook the custody of 22 sheep belonging to Robert Malyn, and that 2 sheep, worth 5ˢ, died by his default.

Stanley. John Tyting to be distrained to answer William de Sandale & Johanna, his wife, for debt.

Thornes. Henry Shiluing acknowledges he entered John de Geirgrave's house in Snaipthorp, & carried off an axe worth 18ᵈ. He is to make this good; fine, 4ᵈ

Horbiry. An inquisition to come to Wakefeld tourn to try whether Thomas Gyge & Agnes his wife, wrongfully allowed their cattle to graze on Hugh del Wro's corn; damages, 6ˢ 8ᵈ; & whether Hugh assaulted Agnes; damages, 20ˢ

Thomas Gyge acknowledges he laid low Hugh del Wro's hedge in Horbiry, together with the ladder belonging to it; damages, 2ˢ. This he is to make good. Fine, 6ᵈ

Sandale. Thomas s. of Peter, to be attached to answer Adam Leulyn & Alice, his wife, for trespass.

Thornes. John s. of Mariota, has not prosecuted his suit for trespass against Robert Malyn. He & William Templer, surety for the prosecution, in the mercy; fine, 3ᵈ

Bailiff. John Couper & William Templer, surety 2ᵈ for not prosecuting suit for debt against Richard de Bateley.

Horbiry. John s. of Hugh de Horbiry, & Richard his son, to be summoned to answer Cecilia d. of German Hudelyn, for debt.

Robert s. of William de Horbiry, 2ᵈ for not prosecuting his suit for trespass against Hugh le Shoter.

Alvirthorp. John Gerbod, Matilda his wife, & Alice & Cecilia daughters of John Torald, to be attached to answer Thomas le Roller for trespass.

Bailiff. Henry Bul & Agnes his wife, to be attached to answer Walter Gunne for trespass.

Osset. Johanna d. of Richard s. of John, gives 6ˢ 8ᵈ for license to marry William s. of John Faber, outside the lordship.

Bailiff. John de Stanneley comes in full court & acknowledges he owes Thomas le Roller 70ˢ, to be paid at the next tourn at Wakefeld. Surety—William Baillif.

Stanneley. John Pollard of Kergate surrenders 2 acres in Stanneley; demised to William Twentipair; according &c. Entry, 18ᵈ

Osset. Alice formerly wife of John de Hetoun, 6ᵈ for offering opposition to the Birelaghe.

Thornes. Robert Malyn surrenders a rood in Thornes; demised to Thomas de Leptoun; according &c. Entry, 6ᵈ

Horbiry. An inquisition to come to Wakefeld tourn to try whether Thomas Gyge, when he was grave, concealed a complaint by Agnes d. of William, against Hugh Gyge, & another against the same by Hugh le Shoter; & also if he removed without right a certain beam found in Horbiry field. He was afterwards acquitted by the inquisition.

Richard, s. of John, for the pannage of a sow & 3 hogs, without grazing rights, 5^d. Fine, 6^d

Thomas Hog, 3 hogs, 3^d. Fine, 3^d

Hugh de Disceforth, for 2 sows & 4 hogs, 8^d. Fine, 6^d

William Carpenter, for 4 hogs, 4^d. Fine, 4^d

Osset. Robert Stut, Richard Passemer, John s. of William, Johanna de Hetoun & Adam s. of Adam, 4^d each for not coming to answer the lord for their pigs as above. To be distrained for next court.

Stanley. John del Bothom, 4^d pannage for 2 pigs. Fine, 4^d

Richard Pesci, 11^d for 2 pigs & 7 hogs. Fine, 2^d

Philip le Sagher, 9^d for 1 sow & 7 young pigs; fine, 2^d

Walter Gunne, 3^d for 3 young pigs. Fine, 2^d

Robert de Wyronthorp, 6^d for 6 hogs. Fine forgiven.

Nicholas de Bateley, 15^d for 3 pigs & 9 hogs; fine, 3^d

Sibilla formerly wife of Hugh Skaif; Robert le Leper; Henry Poket; John Hancok & Thomas Thore, 2^d each for not coming to answer for their pigs as above. To be distrained for next court.

Sourbi. Robert s. of John & John s. of Robert, mainpernors of Adam s. of Roger, for keeping the peace with Thomas de . . . fine 5^s to have a respite till the Earl comes.

Total of this Court—64^s 1^d *i.e.*, Stanneley, 7^s 6^d
Sandale, 2^s
Thornes, 2^s
Osset, 12^s 1^d
Alvirthorp, 7^d
Holne, 13^s 10^d
Sourby, 5^s
Bailiff, 13^s 4^d
Horbiry, 8^d
Hiperum, 7^s 1^d

HALMOTE held at Birtoun on Thursday after the Feast of St. Barnabas the Apostle (June 11) in the year abovesaid. [1331].

Holne. Gilbert de la More, 3^d for not prosecuting his suit for debt against William de Houley. He & his surety, Henry del Weld, in mercy.

An inquisition finds that Matthew & John Drabil, executors of Thomas Drabil, are unlawfully withholding from Margery, formerly wife of the said Thomas, 9ᵈ out of that part of Thomas's goods that falls to her; & 9ᵈ out of her son's portion; they are to pay her the 18ᵈ. Fine, 8ᵈ.

Robert de la Bothe complainant, & William Benet Strekeise (3ᵈ) compromise regarding an agreement.

An inquisition finds that Thomas Undirlangley chased Robert Chobard's cattle with his dogs; damages, 12ᵈ. Fine 3ᵈ. They find sureties for keeping the peace; Thomas de Hiengecliff for Thomas; Thomas de Billecliff for Robert; under a penalty of 6ˢ 8ᵈ

John de Brounhill, complainant & John s. of Thomas Shepherd (2ᵈ) compromise for debt.

Alice Kenward (2ᵈ) complainant, & Thomas her son, compromise in a plea of land.

John de Shepeley, Robert de Langley, Thomas Faber of Shepeley & Adam s. of Roger, acknowledge they owe Sir William de Sancto Albino, rector of the church of Almanbiry £6 silver, to be paid 20ˢ at the Feast of St. Oswald next; 20ˢ at Martinmas; 20ˢ at the next Feast of the Purification; 20ˢ at Easter; 20ˢ at the Nativity of St. John the Baptist, & 20ˢ at the following feast of St. Oswald; if they fail therein the Earl's bailiffs to make distress, &c. And Sir William pays 10ˢ for an aid to levy the said debt.

Sureties for Thomas s. of John Kenward, that he will be reconciled with Agnes his wife, & will treat her well—William Wade, Nicholas de Ananden, Adam Wade & John Couper. And if he fails & should be convicted, the sureties bind themselves to the lord in 40ˢ

Matthew Drabil gives 5ˢ to be allowed to prove the debts that Thomas Drabil his son, owed him at the date of his death.

Alice Kenward surrenders a messuage & a bovate of land in Wolvedale; demised to Thomas s. of Henry de Wolvedale; according, &c. Entry, 5ˢ

William del Wade gives 6ˢ 8ᵈ to be allowed to purge himself by an inquisition of twelve jurors of a disgrace laid to his charge.

Richard Michel surrenders 7 acres in Foulestoun; demised to John s. of Richard, s. of Michael; according, &c. Entry, 3ˢ

Stephen le Halt surrenders 8 acres in Hepworthmere; demised to Richard de Alstonley & Alice his daughter; according &c. Entry, 3ˢ

Total of this Halmote—34ˢ 11ᵈ. All from Holne.

———

TOURN held there the same day.

Holne. Adam le Badger's wife, 3ᵈ, & Julia Specer, 6ᵈ for brewing, &c. The said Julian, 3ᵈ for baking contrary to assize.

Margery wife of John del Hill, 6ᵈ, & Agnes wife of William del Okis, 3ᵈ, for brewing, &c.

John s. of Stephen de Combreworth, 4ᵈ for not coming.

Thomas s. of Simon, 12ᵈ for deflecting the water of Brodwelle. to the detriment of his neighbours.

Total of this tourn, 4ˢ 4ᵈ. All from Holne.

HALMOTE held at Halifax on Tuesday, 14th June, 5 Edw. III [1331].

Sourby. Elias de Hadirshelf, complainant, & Adam de Horbiry (2ᵈ) compromise for debt.

Adam de Horbiry, complainant (2ᵈ) & Elias de Hadirshelf compromise for trespass.

Geoffrey de Stodeley, complainant, & William del Lomme (2ᵈ) compromise for debt.

An inquisition to which Richard s. of Simon, complainant, & Adam s. of Nigel, referred themselves, finds that Adam is wrongfully ousting Richard from 3 acres in Werlulley, which Simon, complainant's father, demised to one Richard Togy for 20 years; which term has now elapsed. Complainant is to recover the land; fine, 3ᵈ

An inquisition finds that Nigel de Hadirshelf, executor of Thomas de Heitfeld, is wrongfully withholding from Alice d. of Thomas del Bothe, 12ˢ worth of goods bequeathed her by Julian formerly wife of Richard de Heitfeld. He is to make good the 12ˢ Fine, 3ᵈ. Surety—Richard Faber of Werlulley.

Roger de Grenewode & Roger Forester to be summoned to answer Cecilia del Bothe for debt. Cecilia appoints Hugh del Hylilee her attorney.

Elias, s. of Elias de Waddesworth, gives 2ˢ for a stray colt sold to him.

An inquisition finds that Robert s. of John, junior, is wrongfully withholding from Thomas s. of William de Werlulley, 4ˢ assigned to him by Adam s. of Roger. Fine, 4ᵈ

Robert de Bentleyrode, Robert s. of John, junior, William del Lonc, Henry del Lone, Thomas Preest, Adam Nelleson, John s. of Thomas de Skircoate & Hugh del Hilylee, mainpernors of Adam s. of Roger, give 8ˢ to have a respite of the mainprise of the said Adam for good & peaceable behaviour, until the Earl comes.

Henry de Luddingdene, living near Sourby, John del Hirst & Hugh Fampil, living at Soland, to be distrained for not carrying out what they gave security for, to wit, the good & peaceable behaviour of Adam, s. of Roger.

An inquisition finds that Henry de Ourum is wrongfully withholding from Adam s. of Magota, 5ˢ that he owes him for 3 quarters of oats, for which he was surety to the said Adam on behalf of John s. of Roger.   He is to pay the 5ˢ fine forgiven by the steward.

Sureties for Thomas de Luddingdene, for keeping the peace with the lord's tenants, to wit, Henry de Luddingdene & William del Lone; under penalty of losing a mare worth 6ˢ 8ᵈ

William de Roupighille surrenders 3½ acres in Werlulley; demised to John s. of Roger del Tounend; according &c.   Entry, 2ˢ

Thomas del Bothe & Agnes his wife, surrender a messuage & 1½ bovate of land in Sourby; demised to Adam Nelleson; according, &c.   Entry, 5ˢ

Adam s. of Adam Migge, surrenders an acre & 3 perches in Werlulleywode; demised to William le Turnur; according &c. Entry, 12ᵈ

William le Turnur gives 4ᵈ for license to take 1½ acre of unoccupied land in Werlulley at le Moregatehirst; according &c. Rent, 6ᵈ an acre.

John de Langley 6ᵈ for the escape of sheep.   Surety—Roger de Grenwod.   And 6ᵈ for the escape of pigs.   Surety—Thomas Culpoun.

Adam s. of Matilda 3ᵈ for the escape of a mare.   Surety— Goderobyn.

Thomas le Prest 3ᵈ for escape of pigs.

Adam Culpoun 3ᵈ for three cows.

John del Wyndibank 2ᵈ for escape of horses.   Surety— William de Coppley.

William the Weaver's son-in-law; William del Leghrode; Richard Mist; Roger del Hertleyrode; Hugh Cappe; Adam Migge; 2ᵈ each; John Shepherd; John del Erode & Adam de Southcliff, 4ᵈ each; John le Dishbinder, 10ᵈ; William de Roupighille, 1ᵈ; Sir Robert de Werlulley, 7ᵈ; Alan del Hey; William Thrift; Richard s. of Thomas de Saltonstal; Thomas Preest & Thomas de Holgate, 6ᵈ each, for vert, escapes, &c.

John s. of Elias de Waddesworth, 3ᵈ for an escape.

Total of this Halmote—41ˢ.   And new rent, 9ᵈ
All from Sourby.

TOURN held there the same day.

Sourby.   Stephen s. of Jordan de Waddesworth, 4ᵈ for brewing twice contrary to assize.

Alexander Sutor of Waddesworth & John s. of Henry del Shaghe, 3ᵈ each for not coming.

Cecilia wife of Michael del Ewode 4ᵈ for brewing twice, &c.

Johanna del Milnhous 12ᵈ for the hue justly raised on her.

Julian, wife of Alexander del Hingandrode, & Adam Megotson's wife, 3ᵈ each, for brewing commonly, &c.

Matilda de Kypask, 4ᵈ for the same three times.

William de Coppley & Margery wife of William del Estwode,
12ᵈ each for bloodshed.

John del Holrode, 3ᵈ for not coming.

William le Turnur of Werlulley, for the hue justly raised
on him, 12ᵈ

Hugh s. of John de Langley, 12ᵈ for blood.

Alice del Lone of Sourbi, 2ᵈ for brewing &c.

Total—8ˢ 5ᵈ. All from Sourby.

HALMOTE held at Brighouse on Wednesday after St. Barnabas'
day (June 11) 5 Edw. III [1331].

Hiperum. Matthew s. of Simon, complainant, & John Miller
of Hasilhirst compromise for debt.

An inquisition finds that John de Holway owes Roger de
Clifton 3ˢ for the leirwite of a certain daughter of his, deceased,
for whom he was surety . . . He is to satisfy the said Roger.
His fine forgiven by the Steward.

An inquisition taken by the oath of Roger de Clifton, Richard
del Hole, William del Rode, Peter de Southcliff, Simon del
Dene find that Ivo le Webster, accused of cutting down & removing 100 oaks without warrant, is not guilty. He is therefore
acquitted.

. . . John del Wyndybank, 12ᵈ for false claim against John
le Pinder of Hiperum for debt, as decided by an inquisition; 12ᵈ

. . . Sabina de Helay, 2ᵈ for false claim for dower against
John del Cliff.

. . . William s. of Robert, sues Robert Baret for 18ᵈ which
he states he owes him; damages, 12ᵈ. Robert comes & does not
defend in the words of the Court; he is therefore to pay the debt
& damages. Fine, 4ᵈ

Rastrik. William s. of Robert, sues Adam, s. of Beatrice de
Lynley, for a debt of 3ˢ; damages, 2ˢ. Adam comes, as above; is
to satisfy William for debt & damages. Fine, 4ᵈ

Hiperum. John de Holway surrenders a messuage & 8 acres
in Northourum; demised to John de Holway, junior; according
&c. Entry, 5ˢ

Henry del Welde surrenders a messuage & 12 acres in Northourum; demised to John de Holway for 8 years. Entry, 2ˢ

John s. of Henry Faber, surrenders a messuage & 7 acres in
Northourum; demised to Hugh s. of ? Ivo Kyng of Hortoun,
for 11 years. Entry, 4ˢ

Thomas le Waynwriht surrenders a rood in Hyperum;
demised to John s. of Adam de Hiperum; according, &c. Entry, 6ᵈ

John s. of Richard de Ourum, gives 5ˢ as a heriot on a
messuage & 12 acres in Northourum, on the death of his father
whose heir he is; to hold, according, &c

Matthew s. of Henry Faber of Ovindene, surrenders a messuage, ¼ bovate & 5 acres of Rodeland in Northourum; demised to Matthew s. of Simon, for 20 years from Michaelmas. Entry, 3ˢ 4ᵈ

William de Ourum surrenders a messuage & ½ bovate in Northourum; demised to Adam le Hird & his heirs, for 8 years from Michaelmas. Entry, 2ˢ

John de Birstalle surrenders ½ acre in Northourum; demised to Margery d. of Sabina, for 20 years from Michaelmas. Entry, 6ᵈ

Rastrik. Thomas Faber of Skammandene gives 8ˢ for license to inclose 5 acres in Skammandene close, previously rented to him. The 5 acres lie between le Ordhille & Coldcotes.

Total of the Halmote—31ˢ 6ᵈ   Rastrik, 8ˢ 4ᵈ
Hiperum, 24ˢ 2ᵈ

TOURN held there the same day.

Rastrik. Henry s. of Adam, 6ᵈ, & Alan de Bothomley, 12ᵈ, for bloodshed.

Agnes Dyedoghter, 6ᵈ, & Ellen wife of Robert, 3ᵈ, for brewing &c.

Henry de Stainland, 2ᵈ for not coming.

Hiperum. William Miller's wife, 4ᵈ; the wives of Thomas Baude & John de Helles, 2ᵈ each; the wife of John del Brighous, junior, 12ᵈ; & Agnes wife of Roger del Brighous, 6ᵈ, for brewing, &c.

John de Helles and Magota, d. of Richard le Tailur, 6ᵈ each for bloodshed.

Total of this tourn—5ˢ 7ᵈ   Rastrik, 2ˢ 5ᵈ
Hiperum, 3ˢ 2ᵈ

HALMOTE held at Wakefeld on Friday after St. Barnabas' day, (June 11) 5 Edw. III [1331].

Bailiff. An inquisition finds that Thomas del Belhous is wrongfully detaining from Hugh del Wro 6ᵈ, received as damages from the township of Horbiry, as awarded against them. Fine, 3ᵈ

Horbiry. An inquisition to come to the next court to try whether Thomas del Belhous felled a fence & trees growing near Hugh del Wro's house.

Bailiff. Matilda Swerd gives 2ˢ because she involved the lord's tenants in a plea in the Court Christian.

Ralph de Shefeld, Richard Short, Henry Tote, William Roscelin, Henry de Galeway, William Short & Robert Yonge, smiths at the forge, give 13ˢ 4ᵈ as a fine for a trespass in the Earl's wood, which they acknowledge.

Osset. Julian d. of Matilda, surrenders 3 roods in Osset, lying in Eley & Southill; afterwards demised to Thomas Hog, for 20 years from Michaelmas. Entry, 6ᵈ

Sourby. Richard Spiltimbir surrenders 3 acres in Werlulley in the graveship of Sourby; demised to Richard s. of Nigel s. of Ivo; according &c. Entry, 2ˢ

Stanneley. Henry s. of Richard Skaif, gives 5ˢ as a heriot on a messuage & 18 acres in Stanneley, after the death of his father, whose heir he is. He has till the 1st of August to pay the 5ˢ. Sureties—Robert Ricard & Adam le Nouthird.

Osset. Robert Passemer is convicted by an inquisition of receiving back from the Grave a horse of his, acknowledged a stray, without making a "haymald" thereon as is customary. Fine, 6ᵈ

It is found by an inquisition sworn *ex officio* that there has been no change of the impression with which oaks, that have been sold, are marked according to custom.

William s. of Richard, is convicted of unlawfully denying multure due to the lord from ½ bovate of land which he holds of the Graffard fee. He is to satisfy the farmers for the multure; fine, 6ᵈ

Hiperum. An inquisition finds that Mariota formerly wife of Richard Skaif, owes Robert s. of Ralph, 6½ bushels of oats, to be paid next Michaelmas. No fine recorded.

The inquisition between the farmers of the vill of Wakefeld & Richard Passemer, on the charge against him for toll, is respited till the Earl comes.

Horbiry. An inquisition finds that Thomas Gyge allowed his cattle to graze on Hugh del Wro's corn; damages, 6ᵈ. Fine, 4ᵈ

Also that Hugh del Wro beat Thomas Gyge's wife; damages, 6ᵈ. Fine, 3ᵈ

Total of this halmote—31ˢ 9ᵈ And new rent, 6ᵈ
    Osset, 21ᵈ
    Hiperum, 3ˢ 4ᵈ   And new rent, 6ᵈ
    Horbiry, 4ˢ 1ᵈ
    Sourby, 2ˢ
    Stanneley, 5ˢ
    Bailiff, 15ˢ 7ᵈ

TOURN held there the same day.

Bailiff. Margery Carter of Dewesbiry, 6ᵈ for brewing &c. Robert le Milner, 6ᵈ for the same commonly. Beatrice, d. of Robert Clerk, 2ᵈ for the same twice.

Tenants of the Hospital. Adam Gilmin of Normantoun, John le Baker, Adam le Carter, Silvester de Wodehous, Richard le Riche, Jordan del Mere & Thomas Cobard, presented for not coming; not fined.

Sandale. Beatrice d. of John Pikard, for brewing twice, 4^d

William s. of Robert Chaumbre, 12^d for blood.

The wife of John s. of Erkin, 6^d for brewing.

William Dawson's wife & Agnes d. of Matilda, 12^d each for blood.

Bailiff. Matilda Broun of Emmeley, 6^d for brewing.

Johanna de Birtoun of Emmeley, 6^d for bread contrary to assize.

Sandale. Beatrice w. of Adam de Wodehous, 6^d for brewing.

Thomas de Milnthorp's wife, & Nicholas Pecy, 12^d each for blood.

Adam Leulyn's wife, 6^d for brewing at $\frac{3}{4}^d$

Magota de Heghrode, 6^d for brewing at 1^d

Thomas Leulyn, John Brand, senior, & Thomas de Moseley of Crigleston, 12^d each for blood.

Alice Breuster of Erdeslowe, 6^d for brewing at $\frac{3}{4}^d$

Thomas Bonny's wife, 12^d for brewing at 1^d

Robert de Mora presented for encroachment; respited.

Thornes. Richard Carpenter, 4^d for not coming.

William Spending's wife, 6^d for the hue rightly raised on her.

Osset. William Webster & Matilda Wyse, 12^d each for blood.

John le Cartwriht's wife for brewing contrary to assize, 6^d

Stanneley. Robert Shirwod of Stanneley & William, s. of Jonot, 4^d each for not coming.

The wives of Richard Pesci, Robert le Leper & Philip le Sagher, 3^d each for brewing.

John del Bothom's wife, 2^d for selling ale contrary to assize.

Bailiff. The wife of Richard, s. of Robert & Alice & Beatrice her daughters, 12^d for raising the hue wrongfully.

Alvirthorp. William Roscelin, junior, 12^d for blood.

Bailiff. Robert de Tatirsale, 12^d; William, s. of John le Leche, & Sir John s. of Robert de Horbiry, chaplain, 12^d, for blood.

Thomas le Taverner presented for the hue rightly raised on him; respited.

Amice de Swilingtoun, 6^d for the hue rightly raised on her.

William Swerd's wife, 12^d for blood; & 6^d for the hue justly raised on her.

Thomas le Taverner's hand-maid, 2^d for constant trespasses in the lord's park.

Richard de Mora's daughter & Hugh Alware's handmaid, 4^d for the same.

Adam le Walker, smith, 12^d for wandering about at night against the peace.

Henry Bul, 6^d for blocking up he King's highway.

William s. of William Roscelin, 12^d for maintenance of malefactors.

Margery d. of Jordan, 3^d for constant trespasses in the park, &c.

John Harilul, senior, 6ᵈ because he enjoys the office of shoemaker & tanner.

John Harilul, junior; John Tup & Robert Nelot, 6ᵈ each; William Jose & Thomas Seele, 3ᵈ each, for the same.

William Filche's fine forgiven for the same.

The township of Wakefeld, 14ˢ 10ᵈ for not coming; the following excepted—John de Geirgrave, William de Locwod, Robert Goldsmith, William & John Goldsmith, Robert Carpenter, John Harilul, junior, Thomas Bate, William de Mora, William Milleson, William Gardiner, William Attelme, Thomas Filcok, Thomas, s. of Henry, Robert, s. of Ralph, & John Tasshe.

Total of this Tourn—59ˢ 4ᵈ	Bailiff, 32ˢ 5ᵈ
	Sandale, 15ˢ 6ᵈ
	Thornes, 22ᵈ
	Osset, 5ˢ
	Stanneley, 3ˢ 7ᵈ
	Alvirthorp, 12ᵈ

COURT held at Wakefeld on Friday after the Feast of the Nativity of St. John the Baptist, (June 24) 5 Edw. III [1331].

Essoins. Thomas de Thorntoun, by John de Thorntoun. Surety—William Templer.

William de Birtoun, by Henry Tasshe. Surety—Robert de Mora.

Sourby. Elias le Walker, complainant essoins against Jordan le Pynder & Amabilla his wife, for trespass, by Henry Tasshe. Surety—Robert de Mora. Defendants appoint Ivo le Webster their attorney.

Bailiff. Adam Leulyn & Alice his wife [essoin] against Thomas s. of Peter, by Robert de Mora. Surety—William Templer.

Stanneley. William Albray, surety for appearance of Edusa Preste, to answer Robert Ricard & Elizabet, his wife, 2ᵈ because Edusa does not come. She is to be distrained for next court.

Bailiff. Alice formerly wife of John de Hetoun, essoins against Agnes, formerly wife of Robert de Beaumont by Robert de Mora. Surety; —Robert de Stodeley.

Stanneley. Robert s. of Ralph, complainant, essoins against William Attetounend, by Henry Tasshe. Surety—Henry Faber.

Hiperum. Robert Faber of Bairstouwe, 4ᵈ for not prosecuting his suit against Gilbert de Mora for trespass.

Stanneley. Robert s. of Walter, grave of Stanneley, complainant, essoins against Henry de Stanneley, by Robert de Mora. Surety—William Templer.

Bailiff. Robert de Mora, complainant, offers himself against Thomas s. of German Filcok, & complains that when William de Migeley, on the first Thursday in August, 19 Edw. II, had distrained

German Filcok in the town of Stanneley, by a horse worth 7ˢ, for his rent then in arrears, the said German came & delivered the horse by pledge & security, & at the prayer of Thomas s. of the said German, complainant was surety for the return of the horse or made himself answerable for the value thereof, if it was adjudged to be returned. And afterwards Thomas removed the horse, so that William de Migeley had recovered the 7ˢ against complainant; damages, 20ˢ. Thomas denies the charge & wages his law. Surety— John de Castilford.

Bailiff. John Tyting to be distrained to answer William de Sandale, & Johanna his wife, for debt.

Alvirthorp. An inquisition to come to next court, to try whether John Gerbod, Matilda his wife, & Cecilia & Alice daughters of John Torald, on the Wednesday before Whitsuntide this 5th year, wrongfully mowed & carried off the vesture of a meadow belonging to Thomas le Roller in the vill of Alvirthorp, at Grisbiglee, to the value of 6ˢ 8ᵈ; damages, 20ˢ

Also to try whether Henry le Brounsmith wrongfully depastured his cattle on Robert de Mora's grass in Alvirthorp, in a place called Inetrode; damages, 6ˢ 8ᵈ

Sourby. John Pyper to be attached to answer Roger le Forster for debt.

Thornes. Hugh Snawe to be attached to answer Matilda, formerly wife of William Malyn, for trespass.

Stanneley. Willim s. of John de Stanneley, to be summoned to answer Thomas Gardiner for debt. Thomas appoints William Templer his attorney.

Alvirthorp. Robert Eliot surrenders ½ rood in Alvirthorp, in a place called Moldyerd; demised to John Gerbod; according &c. Entry, 6ᵈ

Osset. John Sonman surrenders a rood in Goukthorp; demised to Hugh Sonman; according &c. Entry, 6ᵈ

Alvirthorp. John de Welles in full Court surrenders a rood in Alvirthorp, bought by him from John Swerd of Wakefeld; demised to Henry de Swilingtoun, clerk; according &c. Entry, 6ᵈ

Holne. William Benet surrenders 3 messuages & 51½ acres of land & meadow in Thwong, in the graveship of Holne; demised to Thomas de la Bothe; according &c. Entry, 2ˢ

Robert de la Bothe, Adam Kenward & Adam de Holne, come into Court & acknowledge that they have in their custody 60ˢ worth of goods belonging to Thomas s. of Alice, & Agnes his wife, for safe keeping to the use of the said Thomas & Agnes, until the said Agnes shall be willing to be duly reconciled to her said husband.

Thornes. Robert de Lupsete surrenders 2 acres in Thornes; demised to Henry Nelot; according &c. Entry, 18ᵈ

Robert Malyn surrenders ½ acre in Thornes; demised to Henry Nelot; according &c. Entry, 6ᵈ

Sourby. William del Lone surrenders a messuage & 11½ acres in Hudplattes; demised to William s. of John de Lihthasles; according, &c. Entry, 4ˢ

An inquisition taken by the oath of Robert de Bentleyrode, Hugh del Hylilee, Hugh Wade, Robert sons of John, senior & junior, Adam Culpoun, Adam de Coventre, Richard de Ovendene, Henry de Luddingdene, John s. of Robert, William del Smallee, Ivo Sourmilk, Peter del Grene, & Adam s. of Hugh de Lihthasles, finds that £4: 6ˢ 8ᵈ of the money that William del Lone owed Adam s. of Roger, was arrested by the Receiver in the hands of the said William, for arrears on the account of said Adam; & also that William received divers goods & chattels belonging to Adam to the value of 4 marks of the liberty of the whole graveship of Sourby, to be paid to the Earl's Receiver in satisfaction of part of the arrears on Adam's account. Being called upon to state the amount of Adam's goods in William's hands on the day of Adam's indictment for the felony he committed, they say that the said £4: 6ˢ 8ᵈ remained in William's hands; moreover they say Adam de Horbiry & Alice del Lone had 30ˢ worth of oats belonging to Adam, arrested in their hands by William del Lone, Grave there; also that the said William was seised of 2 cows & 2 young oxen, worth 23ˢ 4ᵈ, which cattle William impounded in the lord's fold at Wakefeld; but how they had been delivered therefrom they do not know. They say further that 13ˢ 4ᵈ out of the said goods was paid to the Earl for the mainprise of said Adam; & thus there remains in the keeping of the said William, Adam & Alice, £6: 6: 8ᵈ

Total of this Court—28ˢ

Sourby, 4ˢ
Alvirthorp, 12ᵈ
Holne, 20ˢ
Thornes, 2ˢ
Stanneley, 2ᵈ
Osset, 6ᵈ
Hiperum, 4ᵈ

COURT held at Wakefeud on Friday before the Feast of St. Margaret the Virgin (July 13), 5 Edw. III [1331].

Thornes. John Bulneis, in mercy for not prosecuting suit for trespass against John de Geirgrave. Fine forgiven by the Steward.

Sourby. Elias le Walker, complainant, essoins against Jordan le Pinder & Amabilla his wife, by Robert de Grottoun. Surety— Robert de Mora.

Bailiff. William de Hacford, complainant, offers himself against John de Wyk, complaining that he is withholding 38ˢ 6ᵈ from him; he states that on Easter Sunday, 1330, in the town of Criglestoun he sold Richard Modisoule 12 sheep at 3ˢ 3ᵈ each, to be paid next Midsummer day, for which payment John de

Wyk was surety. And at the said Easter complainant asked them for the 38ˢ 6ᵈ, which they would not pay; damages, 20ˢ. John de Wyk defends, & wages his law. Surety—Adam Sprigonelle.

Thornes. Avelina d. of Beatrice Orre, gives 12ᵈ to have favour. Surety—Robert Clerk of Metheley. Fine forgiven by the Stewards.

Sandale. John s. of Geoffrey, Thomas Monk, William de Donecaster & Adam del Grene, 2ᵈ each, for not coming.

Bailiff. Thomas s. of German Filcok, defendant, essoins against Robert de Mora, by John de Castilford. Surety—William Cussing.

Alvirthorp. Robert Malin 4ᵈ, for false claim against William de Birkinshagh, with a charge regarding the custody of 22 sheep, on which William makes his law.

Bailiff. William Tirsy, complainant, essoins against Robert de Grottoun, by Adam Scot. Surety—German Kay.

An inquisition finds that Henry de Stanneley struck Robert, grave of Stanneley; damages, 12ᵈ. Fine, 3ᵈ

Horbiry. John s. of Hugh de Horbiry, & Richard his son, to be distrained to answer Cecilia d. of German Hodelyn, for debt.

Sourby. Henry del Bonk, 4ᵈ for not prosecuting his suit for debt against William s. of John de Migeley.

Roger le Forster sues John le Pyper for 20ˢ, stating that whereas William de Skargille, who had attached, with the said Roger & John, divers pieces of the paling of Ayrikdene park, to be put up & repaired, for £19, which William paid to John in full discharge of the agreement—out of this John paid Roger £8: 10ˢ, retaining 20ˢ which rightly belonged to him; damages, 10ˢ. John denies the debt, & wages his law. Roger le Forster appoints Adam de Covingtree his attorney.

An inquisition to come to the next court to try whether the said John received the £19 as above stated, half for himself & half for Roger le Forster, his fellow-workman on the palings.

Bailiff. Thomas s. of Robert Monk, tenant of the moiety of two pieces of meadow land in Criglestoun, to wit, the western part of the said meadows, comes in full court & does fealty to the lord thereon, & has a day to acknowledge before the Steward by what services he holds the tenements aforesaid.

Alvirthorp. An inquisition finds that John Gerbod & Matilda his wife, & Cecilia & Alice daughters of John Torald, did reap the vesture of a meadow belonging to Thomas le Roller, as previously charged against them; damages, 2ˢ. Fine, 3ᵈ

Stanneley. Walter Gunne, complainant, offers himself against Henry Bul & Agnes his wife, complaining that on Thursday after Sept. 8, 1330, in the vill of Ouchethorp, they reaped complainant's corn there without right; damages, 20ˢ Defendants say they are not guilty; both parties demand an inquisition.

Thornes. Matilda formerly wife of William Malyn, complainant, & Hugh Snawe (2^d) compromise for trespass.

Alvirthorp. An inquisition finds that Henry le Brounsmith did no damage to Robert le Mora in his rood of land at Inetrode, as Robert stated. Robert's fine for fase claim forgiven.

Bailiff. John s. of Thomas de Shepeley, to be distrained to answer Elias de la Graunge for debt.

Alvirthorp. Roger Dunning in full court surrenders a cottage and one acre in Alvirthorp; afterwards demised to Elias de Shitlingtoun; according, &c. Entry, 12^d

Hiperum. John del Cliff surrenders 4 acres in Hiperum; demised to Adam s. of Hugh de Ovendene; according &c. Entry, 2^s

Thornes. Robert de Lupsete surrenders 1½ acre in Thornes, demised to Cecilia d. of German Hudelyn; according, &c. after the terms of years that sundry tenants have therein. Entry, 6^d

Wakefeld. Robert le Taillur & Johanna his wife, surrender ½ acre in Wakefeld; demised to Richard Man: according &c. Entry, 6^d

Sourby. Robert s. of John de Sourby, to be summoned to answer Alice formerly wife of Henry de Migeley, for dower. Surety for the prosecution—German Kay. The vesture, &c. to be seised into the lord's hand.

Roger de Grenwod & Roger Forester to be summoned to answer Cecilia de la Bothe for debt.

Alvirthorp. Thomas Spink, complainant, offers himself against Robert s. of Adecok & Henry de Swilingtoun in a plea of land. It is found by inspection of the Court Rolls of the 4th year, that the said Thomas referred to a record of John de Donecaster's rolls, whereby he intended to recover certain land against the said Robert; but that he failed to bring the same; whereupon it was adjudged that Robert should keep the said land. It is now adjudged again that Thomas shall recover nothing by his complaint; fine, 4^d for false claim.

Holne. William s. of Adam del Mere, surrenders a messuage & 11 acres in Foulestoun; demised to Adam de Botreley; according, &c. Entry, 4^s

Thomas Hebson surrenders 2½ acres in Foulestoun; demised to Thomas s. of William de Bottreley; according, &c. Entry, 12^d

Sandale. John Tubbing surrenders 3 acres in Criglestoun; demised to John, s. of William; for 16 years, according, &c. Entry, 12^d

Total of this Court—12^s 10^d Alvirthorp, 2^s 3^d
Thornes, 10^d
Sandale, 20^d
Bailiff, 3^d
Wakefeld, 6^d
Holne, 5^s
Sourby, 4^d
Hiperum 2^s

COURT held at Wakefeld on Friday, the Vigil of St. Laurence (Aug. 10) 5 Edw. III [1331].

Essoins. Thomas de Thorntoun, by John de Thorntoun. Surety—Robert de Mora.

Hugh de Stanneley, by Henry Tasshe.

Bailiff. John de Wyk comes into Court & makes the law he waged against William de Hacforth, who is fined 3ᵈ for false claim.

Elias le Walker, complainant, offers himself against Jordan le Pinder & Amabilla his wife, & complains that on Sunday after the Feast of the Assumption (August 15), 1330, Amabilla came to Elias's house in the vill of Halifax, & took away a web of cloth, 14 ells long, worth 20ˢ; damages 20ˢ. Jordan & Amabilla defend tort & force, & deny the fact, waging their law. Surety—Ivo le Webster.

Alice formerly wife of Henry de Migeley, demands against Robert Hodde of Sourby the third part of a messuage, of 10 acres of land & 1 acre of meadow in Sourby, by right of dower after the death of Henry, her late husband, of which the said Henry died seised, & in which Alice has nothing, she says. Robert says that one John de Migeley, father of the said Henry, died seised of the said tenements, & that Ellen, his wife, was dowered therein & survived the said Henry; wherefore Alice has no right to bring an action for a third of the same. And, as regards the remaining two thirds of the tenements, after the vesture thereof had been carried, he granted Alice her dower therein as was right. Alice says her husband was seised of the tenements at his death, & demands an inquisition. The inquisition finds he was never seised thereof, & therefore she cannot recover her dower on the whole. Her fine of 6ᵈ for false claim is forgiven by the Steward, & she is to recover her dower in ⅔ of the said tenements from Robert.

At the request of the parties a loveday is given to William Tirsy, complainant, & Robert de Grottoun, until next court.

Sourby. Richard de Mankanhuls & John del Croft, in mercy for not coming, when summoned, to this court.

Richard del Brig, William del Estwode, & Adam s. of Peter de Crosseleghe, 2ᵈ each for the same.

Cecilia de la Bothe demands against Roger le Forster 3ˢ that he granted & undertook to pay her of the debt of Roger de Grenewod, if the latter refused to pay. Roger le Forster says he was not surety for Roger de Grenewod, nor did he undertake to pay the 3ˢ on his behalf as stated. Both parties demand an inquisition.

Sandale. Roger Bithebroke gives 40ᵈ to have an inquisition. Surety—Thomas Pelleson.

Essoin. Thomas s. of German Filcok, defendant, essoins against Robert de Mora by John de Castilforth. Surety—William Cussing.

Sourby. William del Holrode, who held the tenements formerly belonging to Peter Swerd in the graveship of Sourby, for 8ˢ a year for a term of 6 years, of which 2 years have elapsed, came here into court & freely granted that he holds the said tenements of the lord for 10ˢ a year for the remaining four years.

Stanneley. Thomas le Gardiner, complainant, & William s. of John de Stanneley 2ᵈ compromise for debt.

Bailiff. Robert de Tiengetinsel, complainant, offers himself against Hugh del Wro, complaining he is withholding 6ˢ silver that he owes complainant, wrongfully because on Friday in Whitweek, 3 Edw. III, in the vill of Wakefeld, complainant sold Hugh a mare for 6ˢ, to be paid the following September; and nothing has been paid; damages, 2ˢ Hugh acknowledges the debt & is in the mercy for wrongful detention. Fine not recorded.

Horbiry. Johanna del Stok to be summoned to answer Robert s. of William de Horbiry, for demising a messuage & bovate of land in Horbiry beyond the term of twelve years demised to her by Hugh del Wro, who now holds.

Bailiff. An inquisition taken by the oath of Adam de Wodosom of Waltoun, John Clerk of Waltoun, Richard le Litster of Waltoun, John le Wright of Waltoun, Robert Isand of Criglestoun, Thomas de Ketilthorp, Thomas Pelle, William s. of Robert, John de Wyk, Thomas s. of Robert, Adam de la Grene & John de Holgate, all of Ketilthorp, states, with regard to the two pieces of meadow that Thomas de Chivet & Julian his wife, held of the feoffment of Margery la Normaunt, (which Julian survived the said Thomas, dying about last Easter) that they never knew or heard that the said Margery made any status in the said land, other than to the said Thomas & Margery, & their heirs; of any other feoffments, if there were such, they know nothing.

Bailiff. An inquisition sworn *ex officio* finds that William Goldsmith of Wakefeld came by night with force of arms, with sundry persons unknown, to Sandale Field, & reaped & carried off the vesture of a rood of oats belonging to Thomas de Ketilthorp, worth 2ˢ. He is to be attached for next court to answer Thomas for this trespass.

Hyperum. John le Milner of Hasilhirst surrenders a messuage & 13½ acres in Shipdenheved in the graveship of Hiperum; demised to Matthew s. of Adam de Illingworth; according &c. Entry, 6ˢ 8ᵈ

Sandale. Elias de Donecaster surrenders 3 acres in Criglestoun; demised to John Daude; according &c. Entry, 18ᵈ

The lands & tenements formerly held by Peter Swerd in the vill of Langfeld, which William del Holrode holds for 4 years, demised to William s. of the said Peter, & Alice & Johanna daughters of said Peter, to hold for the term of the life of Henry s. of Peter Swerd, after the expiry of William de Holrode's term, at a rent of 13ˢ 4ᵈ yearly from the time they receive the said tenements.

An inquisition, taken by the oath of Adam de Wodosom of Waltoun, John Clerk of Waltoun, & their fellows, finds that Robert Monk, Roger Bithebroke, William Grindenoc, John de la More of Wolveley & Adam Whitbelt are severally tenants of a messuage, 11 acres of land & one acre of meadow in the vill of Criglestoun, which Thomas de Chivet & Julian his wife, had & held of the feoffment of Margery la Normaunt; and the Steward demands a fee of them, to wit, an ox from each of them, for seisin.

Bailiff. Thomas, s. of Laurence, in mercy for withdrawing his cart, so that the carriage of the lord's goods was delayed. Surety—John de Geirgrave.

Adam de Castilford to be distrained to satisfy the lord for the same.

Philip Damisel, for the same. Fine, 3ˢ 4ᵈ respited. Surety—John de Fery.

Henry Nelot, for the same, 2ˢ respited. Surety—Thomas Bate.

William Cussing, accused of the same, comes & says that he was in the lord's service selling wood at the time the Earl removed, & that he instructed his carter to do the lord's carriage with his cart, so that he holds he should not be charged with any default, & demands an inquisition. An inquisition afterwards comes & acquits him of withdrawing his cart by fealty.

Total of this court—12ˢ 5ᵈ. And increased rent, 2ˢ

i.e.,　Sta[nneley], 2ᵈ
　　　Hiperum, 6ˢ 8ᵈ
　　　Bailiff, 3ᵈ
　　　Sandale, 4ˢ 10ᵈ
　　　Sourby, 6ᵈ And increased rent, 2ˢ

COURT held at Wakefeld on Friday the Morrow of the Decollation of St. John the Baptist (Aug. 29), 5 Edw. III [1331]

Essoins. Richard de Birstalle, by Geoffrey de Normantoun. Surety—Robert de Wyronthorp.

Thomas de Thorntoun, by William Cussing. Surety—Robert de Mora.

William de Birtoun, by Robert de Stodeley. Surety—William Cussing.

Bailiff. Elias le Walker essoins against John le Pinder & his wife, by John de Northland. Surety—Robert de Mora.

Sourbi. Hugh del Hililee, attorney of Cecilia de la Bothe, essoins against Roger le Forster by John de Northland. Surety—Geoffrey de Normantoun.

Bailiff. Agnes formerly wife of Robert de Beaumont, 6ᵈ for not prosecuting her suit for debt against Alice formerly wife of John de Hetoun.

Thomas s. of German Filcok, & Robert de Mora, complainant, (3^d) compromise for trespass.

Wakefeld.   John Lorimer, complainant, essoins against **Alice**, d. of John le Walker, by Henry Tasshe. Surety—Henry Clerk.

Sandale.   Thomas de Ketilthorp, complainant, offers himself against William Goldsmith, complaining that on the night of the Vigil of St. James last past (July 25) he came & forcibly carried off the vesture of a rood of oats belonging to complainant in Sandale field; damages, 39^s.   William says he is not guilty & wages his law. Surety—John Dade.

Bailiff.   Elias de la Graunge, complainant, by Henry de Swilingtoun, his attorney, offers himself against John s. of Thomas de Shepeley.   The said John, distrained by a horse worth 5^s in the custody of William Templer, bailiff, does not come.   He is to be distrained by all his goods.

Bailiff.   The Bailiff of Nicholas de Meteham comes & demands his lord's court, &c.

John Withir, complainant, essoins against Adam s. of John de Leegther, by William le Birtoun. Surety—Henry Tasshe.

John Withir essoins in two other matters against the said Adam by Henry de Daltoun, chaplain. Surety—Adam de Holne, And by Robert de Mora. Surety—William de Birtoun.

Adam, s. of John de Leegther arraigned for having driven the cattle of John Withir, the lord's tenant, out of the lordship, into the lordship of Pontefract, in contempt of the lord, comes & says that one neighbour, living in another fee, can distrain his neighbour, & drive the cattle he has taken into the other fee; & demands an inquisition. He finds a surety to abide the inquisition, to wit, Robert de Stodeley.

Adam de Castilforth, 12^d for withdrawing his cart from the lord's service for carriage.

Agnes formerly wife of Robert de Beaumont, complains of Richard Gates, chaplain, for debt. Surety—Robert de Mora.

Holne.   Thomas s. of Simon, surrenders 1¾ acres in Hepworth, in the graveship of Holne; demised to Thomas Shepehird; according, &c. Entry, 2^s

Horbiry.   Hugh Gyge surrenders a messuage & 3 acres in Horbiry; demised to Agnes d. of Thomas Gyge; according, &c Entry, 40^d

Thornes.   Philip del Hille, by Robert de Mora, his attorney, surrenders 1¼ acre in a place called Evepighill; demised to John, s. of Robert de Mora; according, &c. Entry, 6^d

Bailiff.   Adam Leulyn, grave of Sandale, sues James del Okis for trespass.

Adam Rotel fines 13^s 4^d for mainprise till the next delivery of York Gaol.

Henry le Hird, 10^s for the same.

Henry s. of Hugh Fampil, 10ˢ for the same.

Total of this Court—40ˢ 11ᵈ   Bailiff, 35ˢ 1ᵈ
                                 Horbiry, 3ˢ 4ᵈ
                                 Thornes, 6ᵈ
                                 Holne, 2ˢ

COURT held at Wakefeud on Friday, the Vigil of St. Matthew the Apostle (Sept. 21), 5 Edw. III [1331].

Essoins. Peter Hood, by Robert de Mora. Surety—William Templer.

Thomas de Southwode, by William Templer. Surety—Robert de Mora.

Essoin. John Lorimer essoins against Alice, d. of John le Walker, by Henry Clerk. Surety—Henry Tasshe.

A piece of pasture land, by Wakefeld new park, called le Heys, is demised to farm to . . . for 6 years, at a rent of 10ˢ

At the request of the parties, a love-day is granted to John Withir & Adam, s. of John de Leegther.

An inquisition to come with regard to the custom of distraint & driving the distraint made into another fee.

An inquisition to come to next court, between Robert s. of William de Horbiry, and . . .

Thomas Spink, in the mercy for not prosecuting his suit against Robert del Hill . . . His fine forgiven.

Alvirthorp. Elizabeth de Bateley, 3ᵈ for contempt in full court.

Thomas Spink gives the lord 12ᵈ to have an inquisition . . .

. . . Walter Gunne, complainant, offers himself against Henry Bul & Agnes his wife, complaining that they are ousting him from ½ rood of land in Stanneley, of which he was seised; damages, 13ˢ 4ᵈ. Defendants deny the charge; both parties demand an inquisition.

Sandale. An inquisition to come to the next court to try if James del Okis reaped & carried off the vesture of half a rood of land in Sandale, which the Earl formerly granted to Henry de Waltoun, chaplain, as part of his salary for his chantry at Sandale.

An inquisition of 12 jurors finds, with regard to the petition of Robert de Wyronthorp, respecting his land inclosed by the Earl in the new park, that the Earl inclosed 15 acres of his land in the new park, which have not yet been restored to him. They say also that 4 bovates of land belonging to Sir Hugh de Herci have been inclosed by the Earl in the said park, & that the said Hugh received restitution both for the said 4 bovates, and for the 15 acres belonging to Robert, & for 1½ acre besides.

William del Holrode surrenders all the lands & tenements that formerly belonged to Peter Swerd in the township of Langfeld, which the said William had by demise of the lord for 4 years; afterwards demised to William s. of the said Peter, & Alice his sister, for the said term of 4 years at 10ˢ rent, & afterwards for the whole of the life of Henry s. & heir of the said Peter Swerd, at 13ˢ 4ᵈ rent.

At the presentment of Thomas Alayn, John de Geirgrave, Robert Goldsmith, German Kay, William Wyles, Thomas le Roller, William Cussing, John de Fery, John Harilul, William Carpenter, Richard de Finchedene & John de Castilforth, guardians of the peace, sworn with the consent of the community of the whole vill of Wakefeld, it is found that on Thursday after the feast of the Exaltation of the Cross (Sept. 14), 1331 Richard Withoundes came with a sword & stick, as though armed with force, to the vill of Wakefeld; they say also that the said Richard & Ralph de Fery first fell out with words, & afterwards fought together against the peace, & they say that by default of the said Richard & Ralph the underwritten damages & outrages were occasioned. They say also that John Haget & William, s. of William, s. of Hugh, assaulted Henry Petche, felling him to the ground with a blow from a stick on his head, & wounding him in the head with a sword when he lay on the ground; that Adam Grenhod & Thomas, s. of German Hudelyn, wounded said Henry in the legs whilst he was on the ground; & that William le Parmenter & Thomas Petche wounded one another, & that Henry Grenehod struck the said Thomas. They say further that William, s. of William, s. of Hugh, William de Houden, Thomas, s. of German Hudelyn, Ralph de Fery, Robert, s. of Elias, William Wayte, Henry Grenehod, John, s. of Robert de Mora & Adam Moloc constantly wander about at night in the said vill of Wakefeld, & that Margaret Hoore set on a certain stranger to beat Thomas de Louthe.

It is found, by an inquisition taken by jurors *ex officio*, that Richard, s. of Adam, father of Robert del Hille, sold to Adam Spink 4 acres of land in Spinkrode in the graveship of Alvirthorp, to him & his heirs in fee.

Thornes. Robert Malin surrenders ½ acre in Thornes; demised to William Nondy; according &c. Entry, 12ᵈ

Holne. Thomas Hancok surrenders 2½ acres in Holne, in Shagheley; demised to Alice d. of Nelle; according &c. Entry, 12ᵈ

Henry de Milleshaghe surrenders a messuage & 11¼ acres in Holne, in Hepworth; demised to Thomas Hancok; according &c. Entry, 5ˢ

Richard le Shepehird surrenders a rood in Apiltreker in Hepworth; demised to Richard de Hepworth; according &c. Entry, 6ᵈ

Hiperum. Adam s. of Hugh, gives 2ˢ for license to take ½ acre of unoccupied land in Blacker in the graveship of Hiperum; according, &c. Rent, 3ᵈ

Sandale. Walter Belle surrenders ½ acre in Raurode in Sandale; demised to Matthew de Shipdene; according &c. Entry, 6ᵈ

Holne. Richard s. of Thomas s. of Simon, gives 4ˢ for license to heriot on a messuage & 8¾ acres in Hepworth, after the death of his father, whose heir he is; to hold, according, &c.

Total of this Court—18ˢ 9ᵈ And new rent, 10ˢ 3ᵈ

    Holne, 10ˢ 6ᵈ
    Sourby, 3ᵈ
    Bailiff, 12ᵈ And new rent, 10ˢ
    Alvirthorp, 18ᵈ
    Horbiry, 2ˢ
    Hiperum, 2ˢ And new rent, 3ᵈ
    Sandale, 6ᵈ
    Thornes, 12ᵈ

INDEX OF PERSONS.

Daldeson, Peter, 16
Dale, John del, 113
Dalton, Elias de, 41, 58, 65, 72, 135, 143; Henry de, 196; John, 65; Thomas, 129
Dammeson, William, 140
Damysell, Damisele, Damisel, Philip, 28, 48, 55, 75, 90, 101, 113, 127, 134, 137, 138, 141, 148, 152, 154, 155, 195; William, 32, 138, 147, 154
Danays, Robert, 64
Dande, Daude, John, 146, 194
Dane, John del, 43
Daneys, Danays, Agnes, 64; Robert, 64
Dauber, John le, 40
Dantrine, John, 32, 36
Daweson, Dawson, Thomas, 95, 122; William, 187
Day, Adam, 78; Gilbert, 28
Dene, Den, Adam del, 98, 125, 149; Henry, 99, 132, 146; John del, 3, 4, 11, 13, 18, 26, 54, 57, 77, 89, 92, 103, 106, 108, 114, 128, 149; Margery, 106; Matilda, 11; Richard, del, 18, 80, 81, 85, 91, 130; Robert, 99; Simon del, 2, 9, 17, 23, 26, 30, 50, 54, 67, 68, 169, 184; Thomas del, 50, 63, 67, 126; William, 130
Deneby, John de, 41
Denias, Adam, 54
Dernelove, Henry, 106, 138, 148
Dewesbiry, Deusbiry, Elizabet, 146; Richard de, 14, 17, 70, 88, 89, 91, 105; Robert de, 145; William de, 89, 145
Dey, Adam, 132
Deyvill, Thomas, 38
Dicar, Henry, 90
Dighton, Dyghton, Dichton, John de, 10, 14, 20, 26, 28
Dikeman, Richard, 82
Dineton, Denieton, Dynyngton, John de, 28, 29, 30
Dipsy, Dypsi, Robert, 12, 41
Dishbinder, John le, 183
Disteford, Dissceford, Disceforth, Dissheforth, Hugh de, 32, 35, 36, 39, 48, 61, 62, 76, 78, 82, 88, 89, 104, 106, 108, 133, 135, 146, 149, 154, 180
Dobbeson, Dobson, John, 50, 85; William, 41
Dobyn, Hugh, 57
Dolfyn, Margery, 98; William, 14, 23, 51, 63, 96, 98, 141, 143, 144, 150, 175
Donecastre, Elias de, 3, 4, 15, 26, 113, 146, 176, 194; John de, 1, 3, 4, 16, 37, 44, 162, 166; Nelle, 132; Nigel de, 20, 70, 72, 143; Roger, 99, 123;

Thomas, 113; William, 99, 123, 142, 191
Doune, Robert, 13
Drabil, Drabel, Drebyl, John, 11, 57, 142, 160, 181; Margery, 159, 176, 181; Matthew, 88, 91, 111, 124, 130, 131, 181; Michael, 160; Thomas, 112, 124, 130, 131, 159, 160, 176, 181
Drak, Drake, Henry, 82, 139, 147, 152; John, 2, 10, 85; Thomas, 85; Walter, 128, 134, 147, 153; William, 139
Draper, Eva, 5; Hugh, 5; Robert le, 1, 5
Dronsfeld, Edmund de, 112; John de, 97, 102, 154, 155, 157, 165, 176
Dubber, Thomas, 99
Dunning, Roger, 90, 142, 192; Symon, 134, 154
Dyedoghter, Agnes, 185
Dyer, Bate, 83
Dyghton, John de, 3, 18
Dyker, Diker, Isoldde, 56, 60; Henry le, 55, 56, 60, 129, 131, 172
Dyneley, John de, 18, 93

Eccleshill, Richard de, 41
Edmund, Robert, 32
Eland, Adam de, 110, 121; James de, 21, 29; John de, 41, 47, 61, 94; Sir John, 47; Julian, 61; William de, 61
Elfletburgh, John de, 83, 109, 119, 126
Eliot, John, 145; Jordan, 57, 106, 120, 171; Robert, 189; William, 146
Elwardhuls, Elwardhulles, John, 116; Richard de, 32, 33, 88, 116; Thomas, 116
Elyas, John, 88, 89; Matilda, 7; William, 89
Elyotsone, Elyotson, John, 2, 5
Emmelay, Emmeley, Emeley, John, bailiff of, 135; Nalle de, 135; Paulinus de, 41, 55, 65, 89, 107, 118
Erkyn, Erkin, John, 146, 154; Margery, 154; Stephen, 146, 171, 172; Thomas, 154
Erkynson, Erkinson, John, 136; Margery, 66; Thomas, 66
Erl, Erle, Johanna, 129, 148; John, 28, 56, 62, 64, 77, 97, 105, 116, 117, 123, 139, 153; William, 33, 34, 42, 57, 72, 77, 82, 127, 129
Erneschagh, Richard de, 17
Erode, John del, 183
Erthe, Thomas del, 112
Eschefeld, Thomas, 7

INDEX OF PLACES.

Scamandene, Scamedene, Scamen-
dene, Skamandene, Skambandene,
27, 29, 31, 42, 63, 68, 74, 77, 121,
124, 168, 185
Shaghley, 159
Schepeley, 10
Schelf, 84
Schipedene, Schepedene, Shipedene,
9, 10, 53
Scolemere, 112
Scoles, le, 111
Shelley, 111
Sherrefforth, 113
Shittington, 167
Skircote, 66
Skoles, le, 21
Snaypethorp, Snaypthorp, 16, 26,
64, 105, 107, 140, 143, 167
Soland, 7, 163, 182
Soureby, Sourby, Sourbi, 7, 8, 14,
17, 18, 20, 22-24, 27-38, 43, 46, 47,
50-53, 56-63, 67, 72-75, 80-84,
92-105, 107-110, 114, 116-119,
122, 126, 130, 141, 142, 144, 145,
155-157, 159, 164, 165-167, 170,
172-174, 180, 182-184, 188-195,
199; Sourbishire, 139
Southwode, 19
Stanbrigsyk, 158
Stanley, Stanneley, 1-4, 6, 13-15,
17-28, 31, 32, 35-37, 41, 43-51,
56-66, 71, 73, 74, 76, 78, 80-82,
87-108 112-122, 124, 126-129, 131,
132, 134, 136, 139, 144-148, 151,
152, 155, 157-159, 161-163, 166-
168, 172, 174-177, 179, 180, 186,
188, 189, 190, 194, 195, 197;
Hospitaller's fee at, 88; Lunsdlade,
178
Stansfeld, 164
Stanydene, Stanyngdene, 83, 116
Stainland, 168
Stocklay, 48
Swannildene, 152

Tankerisley, 12
Thornehill, 75
Thornes, Thorns, 5, 13, 15, 17, 20,
23, 24, 28, 29, 31-34, 43-47, 51,
56, 58-65, 74-76, 78, 81, 82, 88-
99, 101, 103, 104, 106-108, 113-
118, 121, 122, 127, 128, 130-132,
134, 136, 139, 140-145, 149, 150,
161, 163, 166-168, 171-173, 175-
177, 179, 180, 189, 190-196, 198,
199; Euerode, 166; Evepighill, 196;
Wolmerrode, 177
Thornesryding, 72

Threpcroft, 165
Thurstanhaghe, 123
Thwong, 40, 189
Turmleemosse, pasture of, 163

Ustordrodes, 119

Waddesworth, 183
Wakefield, Wakefeld, Wakfeld, 1,
3-5, 12-14, 16-20, 22-24, 26, 27,
30, 32, 34, 36, 37, 40, 42-52, 55-
57, 59-66, 69-76, 79, 82, 87, 89,
90, 93, 95-100, 101-108, 112, 114,
115, 117, 118, 120-125, 127-134,
135, 137, 139, 140, 144-148, 150,
152, 154, 155, 159-164, 170, 172-
175, 176, 178, 180, 185, 188, 190,
192-198; Bichehill, 125; Burgess
Court, 48, 50, 52, 72, 74, 77, 80,
84, 87, 174, 178; Codlingcroft, 175;
Court, Christian, 112, 113, 140;
Great Meadow, 121, 129; Great
Wood, 113; Kergate, Kirkegate,
137, 138, 153, 161; Market, 101;
Mill, 80, 126, 159; Millpond, 115,
117, 119, 152; Netherfield, 161;
New Park, 105, 106, 119, 124, 131,
197; Old Park, 80, 105, 113, 119,
124, 131, 133; Outwood, 178;
Westgate, 113, 161
Walleschaghes, 8
Walton, 3, 4, 5, 15, 23, 42, 145, 167
Warcokhill, 119
Warnefield, 81
Werlulley, Warwolfley, Warwlley,
Werlouleye, Waroulay, War-
louley, Warulley, 1, 7, 21, 23, 35,
67, 82, 83, 100, 101, 105, 109, 142,
163, 164, 182, 183, 186; Werlulley-
wode, 183; Moregatehirst, 183
Westfeld, 14
Wheterode, 140
Wilbight, Wilbright, 81, 92
Wircester, 140
Withinheued, 142
Withnes, pasture of, 50, 163
Wodehall, Wodhall, 13, 15, 64, 118,
121
Wodehous, Wodeshous, 16, 20
Wodesom, 25
Wolvedale, Wulvedale, Wlvedale,
Wolfdale, 2, 11, 21, 33, 54, 55, 69,
73, 77, 95, 122, 132, 159, 160, 176,
181
Wyrunthorp, Wyronthorp, 121, 151,
153; Wyrunthorplone, 150

York, Gaol, 33, 133, 196

INDEX OF SUBJECTS.

For EU product safety concerns, contact us at Calle de José Abascal, 56–1°,
28003 Madrid, Spain or eugpsr@cambridge.org.